Visual Basic Da
Programming

Karen Watterson

▲
▼▼
Addison-Wesley Publishing Company
Reading, Massachusetts   Menlo Park, California
New York   Don Mills, Ontario   Wokingham, England
Amsterdam   Bonn Sydney   Singapore   Tokyo   Madrid
San Juan   Paris   Seoul   Milan   Mexico City   Taipei

ISBN 0-201-62661-6

Managing Editor: Amorette Pedersen
Production Editor: Jennifer A. Noble
Set in 11-point Palatino by Benchmark Productions, Inc.

1 2 3 4 5 6 7 8 9-MA-9796959493
First printing, December 1993

Addison-Wesley books are available for bulk purchases by corporations, institutions, and other organizations. For more information please contact the Corporate, Government, and Special Sales Department at (617) 944-3700 x2915.

This book is for my father, an engineer who took the time to talk math and science with his daughter—long before women's lib, ERA, and any notions of what was "politically correct." Thanks, Dad.

Table of Contents

Preface

This book does not teach you Visual Basic—it assumes you know it. What this book *does* do is help you build database applications with VB3. It's a fast-paced, no-nonsense book. We assume you have the Professional Edition of Microsoft Visual Basic 3.0, and we strongly recommend you also have Microsoft Access.

Part One is designed to provide you with the concepts and jargon you'll need to communicate with corporate MIS. Think of it as a crash course in relational databases and SQL.

Part Two explores client/server and database-specific programming issues and illustrates techniques for accessing database data. In Part Two, you'll also learn how to make the most of the Crystal Report Writer and techniques for mail-enabling your VB applications.

Part Three probes specific issues related to OLE 2.0, accessing SQL Server via the SQL Server Programmer's Toolkit for optimal performance, writing help files, and distributing your applications.

The data disk includes a rich assortment of programs you can add to your own VB toolkit, and we've also included an invaluable appendix which compares Microsoft's four major dialects of Basic: VB, Access Basic, VBA, and Word Basic.

K.W.
San Diego, California
76064,51 or MCI KWatterson

Part I
Database Survival Guide

1

Relational Databases and How To Design One

As a Visual Basic programmer, chances are you've written your share of database applications. You may not have called them database apps, but if you've used statements like `Open`, `Get`, `Input$`, `Line Input #`, `Put`, and `Close`, you've been there. You may have even written your own database engine and experimented with different indexing, searching, and sorting algorithms. Today though, it's generally not cost-effective to write your own database engine; most of us use existing databases created by someone else's commercial DBMS. That's the way it is.

The purpose of this book is to get you up to speed quickly in writing database applications.

It's a Relational World

Visual Basic 3.0 includes a copy of the Microsoft Access 1.1 engine (also known as "Jet"). Access is a relational database, as opposed to flat file or ISAM (indexed sequential access method). Forget using OPENs, GETs, and PUTs.

Your Visual Basic programs aren't forced to store data in Access, but Access is VB's native database. The data-aware controls that come with VB3 use the Access engine and its routines. Visual Basic lets you store data in Access .MDB files or use VB as a "front end" to data stored in a SQL database server such as Oracle, SQL Server, or IBM's DB2. You can even use both Access and SQL database servers in a single application, periodically pulling down data from a remote SQL server and storing it locally in Access for easy access (see Figure 1-1).

Microsoft's Database Products

Visual Basic isn't the only approach to writing Windows database applications, nor is it Microsoft's only database product. Microsoft recommends Access for desktop database applications, FoxPro for Windows if you need to work with dBASE/XBase data, and SQL Server as the server DBMS for high-end client/server applications.

Visual Basic is ideally suited for workgroup applications that require more intricate programming than Access and Access Basic can easily provide or for developing client applications that access(s) data in remote databases. Microsoft probably hopes that data would be in a Microsoft SQL Server database, but the truth is, your VB application can get at just about anybody's data, anywhere. You want to access DB2? Lotus Notes? Oracle? No problem. You may even want to write VB programs that read and write Paradox or FoxPro data. No problem.

Figure 1-1: *Common architectures where VB programs access data in databases*

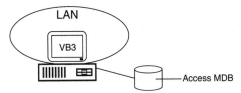

a. Single user or LAN application. Data is stored locally in Access MDB format

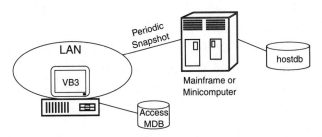

b. Decision Support architechure: All or portions of host database periodically exported
   as ASCII file and imported into an Access database for easy querying

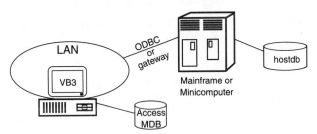

c. OLTP. Read/Write live data via ODBC or a gateway. Host data "attached" to local Access database

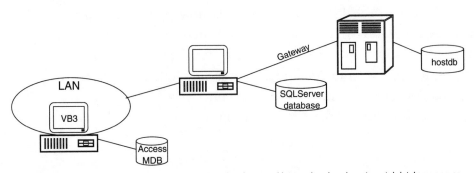

d. Replication server or warehouse architecture. Host data is staged into regional or departmental database server

Nevertheless, because of the pervasiveness of relational databases, it pays to understand how they work, and that's the goal of this chapter. Once you've got the relational model under your belt, we move on to SQL, the language that is used to manipulate most relational databases. You probably won't find these first chapters about the relational model and SQL exactly riveting reading, so we're going to start off with a taste of where we're going.

VB and Its Data Control

From both a programming and end-user's point of view, relational DBMSs are made up of spreadsheet-like tables. Each row is a record, and you can perform operations such as browsing through the records. Most relational databases don't have the concept of record number, though, so unlike dBASE, you won't be able to move to a particular record number.

VB3 ships with an Access database called BIBLIO.MDB. If you installed the samples, it should be in your \VB subdirectory. If you didn't install it or have made changes to it, you can copy it from the data disk that came with this book. We've also included a version of the BIBLIO database in dBASE III format. We'll assume that BIBLIO.MDB and the other data disk files are in a subdirectory called \VB\SAMPLES\VBDBBOOK.

Data Control

Start VB3. You'll probably want to create a new project, if your setup doesn't default to doing that. On your new Form1, locate the Data Control in the lower left corner of your form. The Data Control's Toolbox icon looks similar to the new outline control, except that Data Control has two buttons on it. The buttons have arrows that are supposed to represent movement through the records.

Press F4 or otherwise access the Data Control's properties. To link this control to the Access BIBLIO database, all you need to do is change two settings: DatabaseName and RecordSource. Make entries similar to the ones listed. Your DatabaseName may be different depending on where you've installed BIBLIO.MDB. Once you've entered the DatabaseName, you can double click on RecordSource to scroll through the database tables in order to select "titles." You can also simply type it in.

```
DatabaseName: \vb\samples\vbdbbook\biblio.mdb
RecordSource: Titles
```

If you try running the form, you shouldn't get any error messages, and you'll be able to click on the Data Control to scroll through the records, but you won't be able to see the data. To do that, you'll have to add some other controls. Add a text box, making it large enough to display a sometimes verbose title. Make these two entries the properties of Text1 (see Figure 1-2):

```
DataSource: Data1
DataField: Title
```

Now run the form again. This time, a title should appear in the text box, and you should be able to browse through the 50 titles. You may want to explore some more, adding individual text boxes or a control array for the other fields (Year Published, Au_ID, ISBN, and PubID). You may want to hide the Data Control and create your own command buttons to control scrolling through the records. You may want to add additional data controls and text boxes for BIBLIO's three other tables: Authors, Publishers, and Publisher Comments.

It won't take you long to discover some of the Data Control's limitations. Because the Data Control only has four buttons that let you move forward or backward one record at a time, or move to the top or bottom of a record set, you're out of luck if you want to move non-sequentially through the records. Well, not exactly out of luck, it's just that you'll have to do some coding.

Figure 1-2: *Setting properties with data-aware controls*

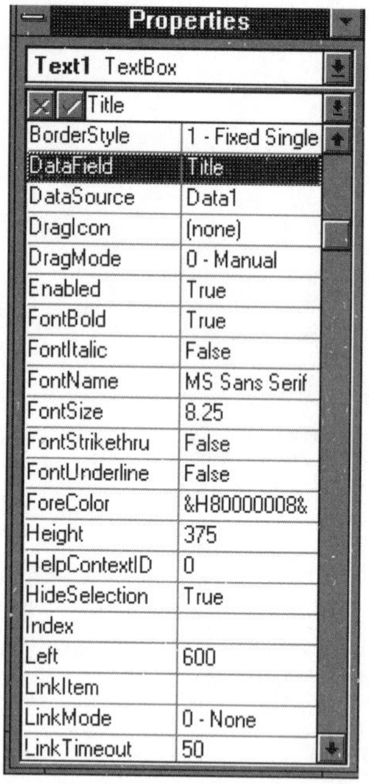

Another problem is that only *some* of the VB controls are "data aware." Data-aware controls can be "bound" to source data through the Data Control, saving you from having to set up links for each one. Although text boxes, standard and 3D check boxes, labels, images, picture boxes, the masked edit, and the 3D panel are data aware, VB doesn't provide data-bound combo boxes, list boxes, or an all-important data-aware grid control.

Don't waste time looking for data-aware combo boxes, list boxes, or a data-aware grid control. VB3 doesn't have them.

Nor does VB come with the ability to create an "instant" form based on fields in the source data or any kind of built-in query builder. Fortunately, though, a host of third-party vendors have jumped in with products to fill in the gaps. The VBPRODS database we've included on your data disk provides a list of many vendors of VB add-ins, along with their products.

Accessing dBASE Data

For now, though, we want you to see how easy it to access dBASE data. The data disk that came with your book, and whose files we recommend you install in the \VB\SAMPLES\VBDBBOOK subdirectory, has the dBASE III equivalent of BIBLIO.MDB. Since dBASE isn't really a relational database system, the data is stored in separate files for each of the tables. Because of DOS's 8-character filename rules, some of the tables' names have been truncated, but TITLES.DBF is intact.

To access non-Access databases, you need to specify a Connect property for your data control. For DatabaseName you also need to provide the subdirectory where the TITLES.DBF file is located. For example, you can make these changes to Data1 on Form1:

```
Connect: dbase iii
DatabaseName: \vb\samples\vbdbbook
RecordSource: titles
```

Running the form should work the same as it did before. The only difference is that VB is using data from the dBASE file. Pretty slick, eh?

Okay, recess is over. Time to hunker down into sponge mode and soak in some database concepts.

Relational Databases for All You History Buffs

Dr. E. F. Codd (see sidebar), the original "R-Man," first proposed the relational model in his frequently-cited, but rarely read, 1969 IBM research report, "Derivability, Redundancy, and Consistency of Relations Stored in Large Data Banks." He proposed the relational model as an alternative to the then-popular hierarchical and network (or CODASYL) database models. The main difference is that the relational model distinguishes between a database's physical file structure and its logical design. This means application programs don't need to "know" details about physical file storage and pointers.

Database pundits like to point out that the relational model is the only one with rigorous mathematical foundations. Part of the reason for this is that Dr. E. F. Codd is a mathematician. In fact, one of the reasons the relational model took so long to catch on may have been the mathematical language in which it was cast. Let's face it, most data processing professionals don't read formal mathematical proofs in their spare time or converse about notions like the "existential quantifier" over lunch. Dr. Codd's original paper, like today's relational model, was firmly steeped in predicate logic and couched in alien jargon.

Predicate logic differs from the more familiar two-valued propositional logic that is used as the basis for many computer operations. In two-valued Boolean logic, statements like "A = B" or "A > B" are evaluated as true or false. Period. Predicate logic, however, treats values as the *subjects* of its statements so more complex expressions can be constructed. "Is a number between," for example, is a predicate that requires three subject values in a statement like "A is a number between B and C." Predicate logic lets you do more interesting things than simple two-valued logic does.

"Ted" Codd

E. F. Codd invented the relational model in 1969. Later, in a well-known two-part *Computerworld* article (October 14, 1985 and October 25, 1985), he published 12 "basic rules" for "fully relational" databases. That list has subsequently grown to include 300 features organized into 18 classes. You can read all about it in *The Relational Model for Database Management Version 2* (Addison-Wesley, 1990). Dr. Codd and his partner, Chris Date, are generally considered the authorities on matters relational.

Ted Codd isn't an ivory tower mathematician. After obtaining his M.A. in mathematics from Oxford University, he served as a Royal Air Force pilot in WWII. He came to the United States in 1948 and found work with IBM as a programming mathematician. His first project involved the Selective Sequence Electronic Calculator, a sort of proto-computer that used 12,500 vacuum tubes and filled two floors of a Manhattan office building.

Codd briefly left IBM in 1953 for Canada, where he started a computing center for the Canadian guided missile program. Why Canada? "Because of Senator McCarthy." IBM coaxed him back in 1957 to head up the development of an operating system for Stretch, another early IBM computer. In the 1960s IBM sent Codd to the University of Michigan, where he earned a PhD and wrote a book about Cellular Automata.

By 1968, Codd had begun to study databases in earnest. He sensed they were at the confluence of document retrieval and inferential systems. He left IBM again in 1984 and is a co-founder of Codd and Date, a consulting firm based in San Jose, California.

Relational Database: The Table Model

The main difference between coding your own database and using relational databases is that with relational DBMSs, you don't worry about physical details that occur at the file level. Forget using pointers. Forget writing hash routines or sorting algorithms. You have to think at a more abstract level and focus on the data itself.

Relational guru Chris Date has said that the relational databases are ones that are perceived by the end user as being nothing more than a collection of tables. That may make life easy for the end user, but it means we have to force all of our data into two-dimensional tables. Unfortunately, not all data is two-dimensional. A classic example is a single invoice with multiple detail lines. Worse examples involve recursive data like parts that are used in subassemblies that are used in other parts, and so on—the infamous exploding parts or bill-of-materials problem.

To help you start thinking in terms of tables, let's look at some examples.

The Local Video Rental Store

The owner of the neighborhood video rental store needs to keep track of his inventory, to know what tapes are available for rental at any given instant, and to know where the rest of his tapes are—who has them and when they're due back. He needs to know how to track down his customers if they don't return tapes, and he needs to keep track of employee data, such as hours worked, benefits, and pay records. He also needs to keep certain accounting data like rental invoices and records of expenses. He might also like to make some of this data available to his customers so they can browse through the tape inventory searching for videos by title, star, director, or story line.

What tables will his database contain? He's likely to have tables for customers, tapes, rentals, employees, employee hours, and business expenses. He may actually set up two tables for his video tapes: one with basic video information (title, stars, film category, rating, director, year released, and a brief synopsis of the plot) and another with specific data about a physical copy (title, copy number, availability, total number of times it's been checked out). Otherwise, there would be a lot of duplication of basic information for each of the copies.

The idea is that each table contains data about a single entity, and that basic data about entities is only entered once. This minimizes both redundancy and the associated problem of inconsistent data. Let's look at another example.

Temporary Employment Agency

What kind of data does an employment agency need to track? Employment agencies typically have two kinds of customers: potential employers and candidate employees.

An employment agency needs to keep track of employers and the contracts and placements the agency has with those employers or potential employers. It also needs to keep track of the pool of candidates, including their abilities and performance ratings. The agency may want to maintain a document database with scanned résumés, performance evaluations, and various contracts. Like the video store, the temporary agency will also have to keep data on its own employees, revenues, and expenses.

What tables would be needed for the operational database? You'd probably want tables for employers, job openings, contractual terms with employers, referrals, candidates, candidates' work histories, and so on. The employment agency would also need tables for its internal human resources and accounting functions; tables with information about its own employees, revenues, and expenses.

Customer Service Department

Many organizations have customer service departments, and somewhere along the line, you may have worked in technical support. What kinds of data do customer service people care about? Customers, products, complaints, known problems. If you've worked in technical support, you may have had to log phone calls, including the time you spent on problem resolution. Management typically wants summary reports on performance by individual techs, on recurring problems, and on overall response times.

You've probably figured out that the things in the work environment map pretty well to relational tables. Customer service departments usually have a database with tables for customers, techs, registered products, bugs and workarounds, customer calls, and resultant actions.

Relational Databases: Not a Perfect Model

Despite the popularity of relational databases and the relational model in general, you'll discover they're not always perfect tool for modeling the real world.

One feature of well-designed relational databases is that they tend to consist of lots of "little" tables that have to be reassembled to correspond to useful information. For example, invoices are typically modeled with basic invoice data in one table, customer data in another table, and details about invoice items and quantities in another table. An end user who looks at the invoice table is likely to see only invoice numbers, customer numbers, invoice dates and totals, and probably information about how the payment was made. The information our video store owner would need to use to print out an invoice would probably come from the customer, transaction, transaction detail, video, and video copy tables.

Unfortunately, storing data from a single event into multiple tables and being able to get it back the way we need it only works if the database was well designed. That's where you come in. Your VB applications reconstruct the tabular data into whatever form the end user needs. But your application won't be able to get the right answers if the tables weren't designed right.

That's why you need to learn about designing relational databases. Even though you may not have to create new databases, chances are you'll have to work with existing databases, so you need to recognize a good design and be aware of the results of design flaws.

The Components

To review, relational databases consist of tables that are sometimes called *entities* or *entity classes*. Tables generally represent "things" like employees or products or invoices. Tables, like spreadsheets, have rows and columns. Individual rows in the database tables are sometimes called *records*, *tuples*, or *entity occurrences* and represent the facts related to an individual employee, product, or invoice.

Relational databases are sometimes defined as "self-describing collections of tables," since some of the tables in a relational database contain *metadata*—data about the database. Metadata is typically stored in one or more system or systems catalog tables. Access has system tables, but Visual Basic also packages metadata as collections of TableDefs and Indexes and Fields. To see Microsoft Access system tables, you need to run Access itself (as opposed to the Access engine that comes with VB), open a database, and select View|Options|Show System Objects. Once you've done that, you'll see a variety of system tables with the "MS" prefix (see Figure 1-3 below).

Figure 1-3: *Some of the Microsoft Access "system" tables*

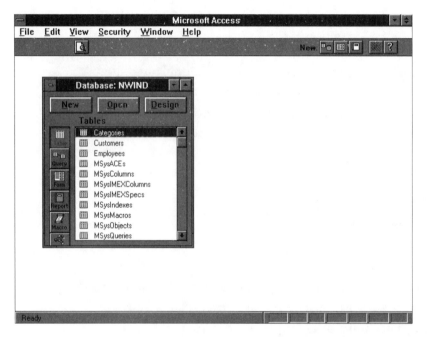

Columns in a table are sometimes referred to as *fields* or *attributes*. Attributes represent the most granular level of data—the smallest meaningful units of information. Typical fields might contain employee first names, product part numbers, or invoice dates. Columns have to be assigned names and data types, and some columns will serve as keys and/or indexes.

Relationships are the final major component of relational databases. As the term implies, they reflect the nature of relationships between tables. Tables are often related to others in a one-to-many relationship, such as one department with many employees, one invoice with many invoice items, one publisher with many titles, or one supplier with many products. Related tables are logically linked by a common column.

Pointers Are Passé, Long Live Keys

Earlier we said that part of your job is to combine data from related tables. Indirectly, you'll be using "relational algebra," which is based on set theory and consists of operators like union, intersection, select, project, difference, and division. Multi-table selects are often called *joins*. Unfortunately, join is a multi-valued concept. In the next chapter we'll plunge into the differences among inner joins, outer joins, natural joins, and so on.

The important idea for now, though, is that we're not talking navigational, record-at-a-time processing associated with sequential files, but set processing. For the algebra to work so that ad hoc queries return the correct results, relational databases need to be *normalized*. In normalized databases, all tables have *keys*—fields that uniquely identify a given row. The extra, link columns are called *foreign keys*.

One-to-many relationships aren't the only game in town. Some tables have many-to-many relationships. And, of course, some tables simply aren't related at all.

Unfortunately, relational databases can't handle many-to-many relationships directly. For example, if a restaurant buys wine from several distributors and if some of the wines on the restaurant's wine list are carried by several of the distributors, we have a many-to-many relationship. Perhaps the house wine is a Paul Masson Burgundy. Sometimes our restaurateur buys Paul Masson Burgundy from Wine Merchants, Ltd. and sometimes from Fine Wines 'R Us. One wine has many possible distributors. But each of the distributors also sells many wines, so we've got a many-to-many relationship between wines and distributors. What we have to do is decompose the complex relationship into two one-to-many relationships by creating an intermediate wine/distributor table (see Figure 1-4).

Figure 1-4: *Many-to-many relationships are "decomposed" into two or more one-to-many relationships*

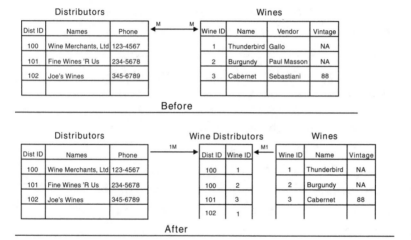

Not Perfect, But . . .

We've pointed out some of the limitations of relational databases, but it's important to remember that the relational model is popular because it offers a more palatable solution that most of the alternatives. Think about a simple address book database application. You could write an address book application using Visual Basic's OPEN "path\filename" command, but you'd probably be forced into awkward design decisions that lead either to data redundancy or lots of empty fields. For example, do your contacts each have single address? Probably not. Chances are some of your business contacts will have separate mailing, shipping, and billing addresses. You may also want to keep track of personal addresses for some of those business contacts. If you want to keep all this in a single flat file manager, you run into the problem of trying to anticipate all the possible addresses and setting up fields for each of them. You might come up with a list of fields like this:

```
LastName
FirstName
BusinessAddressLine1
BusinessAddressLine2
City
State
Zip
ShipToAddressLine1
ShiptToAddressLine2
City
State
Zip
BillToAddressLine1
BillToAddressLine2
City
State
Zip
HomeAddress
City
State
Zip
```

Of course, each of the different addresses would probably have its own phone number and fax number. Most of your contacts, however, probably won't have multiple addresses, so if you design your list this way, there will be a lot of empty space.

There are other problems with this design. You may have multiple contacts at the same company, such as John in Marketing and Sally in Customer Service, with the same business, ShipTo, and BillTo addresses. Do you want to type in that information twice? Worse yet, do you want to have to remember to update it twice if something changes? You may also run into problems with this design when dealing with phone numbers: Some people have car phone numbers that aren't associated with locations.

Perhaps you want to keep a log of calls associated with your contacts, where you record the date of the conversation and a summary of the call. You might even want to assign some sort of action flag to the conversation like "Urgent Action Required" or "Follow up in 30 days." You wouldn't want to store this log information with the basic list of contacts, since some contacts would have lots of phone calls and others wouldn't have any. If you tried to use fields like PhoneCall1Date, PhoneCall1Summary, Phone-Call1Action, PhoneCall2Date, where would you stop?

The addresses, phone numbers, and phone call log really represent different tables; lists that are related to the contacts list. The relational model, you've probably surmised, was invented to avoid some of the problems associated with modeling complex, interrelated as a single sequential file.

The Quasi-Relational World of XBase

XBase-style systems, which are "quasi-relational," let you manage multiple lists of interrelated data, but in most cases they aren't quite as easy to use as today's more visual desktop relational products. With Windows products like Access, you create links between related tables by pointing and clicking. In older, quasi-relational XBase products like FoxPro, you assign related database files to separate work areas and write code that establishes links with "SET RELATION" statements.

Designing Relational Databases

As we said earlier, you may or may not ever have to design a relational database from scratch. In many cases, you'll inherit a ready-made relational database. But even if that's the case, don't skip this section. Understanding how relational databases are designed will help you navigate the data you inherit. It will also alert you to potential causes for sluggish data retrieval.

Step One: Think about the data and how it will be used. Talk to end users and find out what they like and don't like about their current system. Scrutinize existing data entry forms (paper or screen) to see what's included and how they're organized. Ask management and find out what kinds of reports they want and what kinds of ad hoc queries they're likely to perform. Find out if any anticipated legislation or industry changes are going to make new demands on information requirements. In other words, be curious, ask lots of questions, and take lots of notes.

Step Two: Get out a pencil and some paper and brainstorm. As you do, jot down words that describe the data. You'll probably end up with a combination of major data categories like "contacts" and smaller data units like "business phone." The major entities will map into database files or tables. At this point, you may want to start sketching tables as rectangles and start listing potential attributes inside the rectangles (see Figure 1-5).

Step Three: Look at your grouped data to see whether and where each group has a logical name and single theme. If you see "repeating groups" like business address, bill to address, ship to address, or realize that you will need to keep multiple items like phone numbers or conversation summaries, you probably need to split up your data. The process of subdividing large tables into smaller ones is sometimes called *normalization*.

Figure 1-5: *Sketching entities and attributes*

CONTACT	COMPANY	SHIP TO	BILL TO
LastName	CompanyName	CompanyID	CompanyID
FirstName	CompanyID	Address1	Address1
Title	Address1	Address2	Address2
CompanyID	Address2	City	City
Phone	City	State	State
Fax	State	Zip	Zip
Pager	Zip	Phone	Phone
Car Phone	CentralSwitch	Fax	Fax
E-Mail	800 line		
	Fax		

AT HOME

AT HOME
LastName
FirstName
Address
City
State
Zip
Phone
Fax

Normalization. The process of taking an initial database design and applying rules to transform it into first, second, third, fourth, or fifth normal forms (1NF, 2NF, 3NF, 4NF, 5NF).

Step Four: Think about the groupings (or tables) you have so far and about how they're related. In the previous example, you'd probably want to draw an arrow between Company and Contacts to show the one-to-many relationship (sometimes abbreviated 1-M and called parent-child or master-detail) between them. This would be true only if your data is such that you can have several contacts at a single company.

Step four means more than drawing arrows, however. The way you "relate" or "link" related tables is by putting some common field in both of them. This is where keys and referential integrity comes in. Every table needs to have its own *primary key* field. Primary keys are fields that contain unique identifying data for each record. Primary keys don't have to be single fields; most DBMSs support composite or compound keys. Our preliminary sketch in Figure 1-5 doesn't have any good primary key fields, since lots of people have the same last name. Similarly, it's not uncommon for two different companies to have the same name. You would probably want to create both Contact# and CompanyID fields above to serve as primary keys.

Primary Key. A column or group of columns in each table that provides a unique value for individual rows. Example primary keys are social security number, account number, and product ID.

Single-field primary keys are often somewhat artificial—numbers like a customer number. Driver's license numbers, social security numbers, and invoice numbers are the kinds of data used as primary key fields. They were probably invented to serve as primary keys in a database. Sequence numbers are another popular primary key. Most DBMSs help you enforce data integrity by requiring unique, non-null values in primary key fields. Once you've made sure each table has a primary key field, you can proceed with adding link columns.

Tables that are on the "many" side of the one-to-many relationship will need to have the primary key from the "master" side of the relationship. Since Company to Contacts is a 1:M relationship, you need to have the CompanyID field in the Contacts table to establish the link. This extra link field in the "many" table is called the *foreign key*. Detail tables—the "many" tables in 1:M relationships—need both primary keys of their own and foreign keys. This linkage, by the way, is one of the ingredients of referential integrity.

Foreign Key. An extra column added to a table on the "many" side of a one-to-many relationship that serves to link the related tables. The primary key in the "parent" table becomes a foreign key in the "child" table.

Step Five: Decide on names for the tables and fields, and or data types for the fields. The actual data type you select will depend on the tool you use. Visual Basic and Access Basic have seven data types: Integer, Long, Single, Double, Variant, Currency, and String (up to about 64K), but Access has different data types for data fields. Access field types are defined as Text (up to 255 characters), Memo (up to 32,000 characters), Number, Date/Time, Currency, Counter, Yes/No, and OLE Object.

And, if that isn't complicated enough, Access *SQL* supports Boolean, Byte, Integer, Currency, Single, Double, Date/Time, Text, Binary, and Memo fields. Where do user-defined Visual Basic types fit in? You won't be using them as data types in your database tables, only in your programs.

Once you've gone through these steps, defining the database is usually just a formality. (You can experiment with VB's DATAMGR.EXE to create new Access 1.0 or Access 1.1 databases, or to create dBase III, dBASE IV, FoxPro 2.0, FoxPro 2.5, Paradox 3.5, or Btrieve databases, but you won't be able to use DATAMGR to define indexes or establish rules.)

Most often, you use a DBMS' own SQL data definition language (DDL) to create the database, and DDL is one of the topics we'll cover in Chapter 2. In addition to setting up tables and primary key fields, you'll probably also want to define other *index fields* for columns that are likely to be used as selection criteria for queries and reports. For example, indexing the Last Name field in the Contacts table would probably result in faster retrieval of ad hoc queries. The Access engine, by the way, doesn't let you define index fields for Memo, Yes/No, or OLE Object field types. It only makes sense, right?

Index Field. A sort of lookup table that allows a DBMS to retrieve records faster than it could with a simple sequential search. DBMSs usually maintain indexes on primary key fields, but indexes should probably be set up for other fields that will be used frequently as the basis of sorting or ad hoc queries.

Design Pitfalls

The five-step method generally yields a good relational design. It's ironic, but despite its mathematical origins, database design is still considered as much an art as a science. It's also something you get better at with practice. Experienced designers seem to have an intuitive skill at coming up with and identifying a good design. One technique that helps you come up with a good database design is to recognize the symptoms of poor designs. Here are some common design pitfalls.

The Spreadsheet Design   You create a database table that reflects your spreadsheet. That means you put everything you need into a big table with lots of columns, some of which include computations. You might have aggregate sales data for different regions by salesperson, along with data from statistical and trend analyses.

There are two problems here. One is that the "spreadsheet" table tends to include data related to multiple entities. A well-designed relational database won't have basic data about customers, sales people, and orders in a single table. The second problem is that a well-designed database generally doesn't include derived data—data based on calculations—since that can be calculated on demand. Why *store* data that can be calculated when needed for ad hoc queries or reports? This is a subtle issue that ultimately affects performance. Sometimes it will pay to store derived data in the database in order to speed up queries or reports.

Megafields   You should avoid using fields that contain more than one discrete element of data. If you use a simple Name megafield for example, with entries like John Doe and Jane R. Smith, you'll run into trouble trying to alphabetize them. The same logic applies to lumping together state and zip code data, for example.

No Key Field   You can design databases that don't have any logical key fields, and, since the purpose of a key is to ensure unambiguous retrieval of data, this can be a major problem. For example, let's say you have a list of people with first names, last names, and phone numbers. Given a large enough list of names, neither first nor last names is a good choice as a key, since you're likely to have more than one John and more than one Smith. Even the combination of first and last names isn't a good choice for a key, since there's a good chance you'll have more than one person with the same name. What about phone number, then? Although phone numbers are better candidates, they're still not a good choice. Some people on your list may have the same phone number, such as family members or employees who work for the same company. Other people (far more rare) might not have any phone number, or at least not a phone number to which you are privy.

If not having a logical key field is one problem, not officially declaring it is another problem. Most of today's DBMSs encourage you to assign formal keys that will be "physically" maintained by the DBMS. Depending on the DBMS, this may mean (1) not allowing null entries in key fields, (2) not allowing duplicate entries in key fields, and/or (3) maintaining a physical index for the key field.

Bad Keys   The issue of what constitutes a "bad key" is more complex, since it ultimately depends on individual DBMS architecture and optimization routines. Setting up a long text field or memo field as a key is generally a bad idea, because of the overhead associated with maintaining and using a long text field as either a key or an index. Similarly, it may be possible to designate a multi-column composite key, but you may be better off, from a performance point of view, using a surrogate key. Surrogate keys are new artificial fields that don't correspond to any real data. They're set up solely to serve as keys.

Another kind of bad key is one that's likely to change. That's another good reason for not using phone numbers for keys.

Kitchen Sink Syndrome   Some people like to collect things, and it can be tempting to save data just because it's there. When you design a data-driven database, however, your goal is to make sure data is available for queries, reports, and analysis. Don't store data that probably won't ever be used, since that will require more work at data entry time and will result in larger physical database files than necessary.

No Links   Links are the basis for relating tables. If you carefully separate customer and invoice tables but don't include any customer information (the customer table's primary key) in the invoice table, you won't know whose invoice is whose. Customer-to-invoice is a one-to-many relationship, so you need to put the key from the Customer table into the Invoice table. If CustomerID is the Customer table's primary key, it becomes a foreign key in the Invoice table. The Invoice table will have its own primary key—probably the invoice number.

Wrong Links or Too Many Links   One of the most common mistakes beginners make is putting link fields in the wrong table. Using the Customer and Invoice tables as an example, it would be a mistake to put the invoice number field in the Customer table. A little thought will show you why. If you try to store all of a customer's invoices in the Customer table, how do you design it? Put 20 invoice fields in the Customer table? What about all those one-time customers? What about the customer who has more than 20 invoices? The other extreme would be to keep only the most current invoice number in the Customer table. In that case, you risk losing information about old invoices.

Another common problem with one-to-many relationships is the likelihood that links will be forcedin both directions. Even though you're only supposed to put the key from the "one" side into the "many" table. beginners sometimes get confused by this rule and overcompensate by putting the keys from both tables into the other table. Not only does this represent unnecessary data storage, it can yield erroneous query results.

Cryptic Table and Field Names   Avoid fieldnames like T1C1 (table one, column one, right?). We've all traveled that road with variable names. Enough said.

Duplicate Column Names   Just because employees and products both have IDs doesn't mean you should refer to both of them with the same column name, such as ID. Unless you differentiate Product

IDs from Employee IDs, you'll run into problems when you perform a query or print a report that combines the two fields.

International Issues   Databases that need to accommodate international currencies, phone numbers, and addresses need to be designed more flexibly than databases that will only contain U.S. data. Similarly, applications that will serve international customers may need to have different help files, color schemes, and data displays. Even if international issues don't appear to be relevant today, you may want to design for the future.

Business Rules   *Business rules* are the formal and informal SOPs (standard operating procedures) that emerge in all organizations. Examples of business rules might be having employee numbers set between 1000 and 2000 or requiring a supervisor's signature on POs over $500. Most DBMSs make it easy to set up constraints that are enforced by the database engine. If you define employee numbers as having to be between 1000 and 2000, your DBMS shouldn't accept data outside that range.

Here are some other examples of business rules:

- The programmer who updates the bug database must be identified.

- A canceled order cannot have been previously shipped or invoiced.

- State residency is defined as maintaining an in-state address continuously for a minimum of the previous six months.

- Delete customers who haven't placed an order in the last 24 months from the active mailing list.

- Regular part-time employees who have worked continuously for at least six months are eligible for education benefits.

- Descriptions of all incident reports from customers 1-20 must be e-mailed to the VP of customer service.

- Valid commissions are 1.5, 2.5, and 3 percent, based on gross invoice amount.

- A checking account becomes interest-bearing when the balance is $1000 or more.

- Refunds over $100 must be approved by a supervisor.

- An employee cannot have two job titles.

- Employee travel expense reports (except for the CEOs) must have a corresponding approved travel request.

Business Rule: A constraint on data dictated by business policy. Business rules can usually by incorporated into a database design, allowing the DBMS engine to play policeman.

Referential Integrity   *Referential integrity* is one of those terms that is sometimes referred to in hushed tones, almost reverentially. Although referential integrity *sounds* hard, it isn't really. All it means is that data in related tables has to be kept in sync. Based on the Customer-to-Invoice relation, you normally wouldn't want to delete a customer record when the customer has open invoices. That's what referential integrity means—maintaining the integrity of related tables or not allowing "orphan" rows. Until it became a common feature of DBMSs, referential integrity had to be maintained by individual application programs.

There are two standard methods for establishing referential integrity: *declarative*, in association with a SQL CREATE TABLE statement, and with *triggers*. Triggers are short programs, stored with the database itself, that automatically "fire" or run in conjunction with INSERTs, DELETEs, and/or UPDATEs. Referential integrity is often set up for DELETEs as a *cascading delete* so that related child records are automatically deleted when a parent record is deleted.

Referential Integrity. Making sure you don't end up with orphan records in parent/child relationships. Referential integrity comes in two flavors: declarative or in the form of short procedures called triggers.

Defaults and Edit Masks   One of the easiest techniques for maintaining general data integrity is the intelligent use of defaults. If most of your customers are in Michigan, set up data entry forms where MI is the default state. If your DBMS permits it, use hyphens and parentheses where it makes sense—for example, in phone numbers and social security numbers—to save keystrokes.

Database Security   Every DBMS has a variety of techniques for controlling access to data. You need to educate yourself about your DBMS's options for defining group rights and passwords, using SQL's GRANT and REVOKE commands, and defining virtual tables, called *views*.

Maybe we shouldn't have listed so many pitfalls; it looks like designing a relational database is a mine field. It certainly wasn't our intention to come up with an intimidating array of mistakes waiting to happen—we offer them simply as our rules of good design.

Constraints

Constraints refer to a broad class of rules and techniques that help maintain data integrity. Referential integrity is sometimes referred to as a constraint, as are business rules. Sometimes constraints are categorized as *domain constraints* and *column constraints*.

The set of legal values for a column is its domain. Some domains—such as city names or last names—are extremely long lists of potential values, and it probably doesn't make sense to try to explicitly define a domain with millions of items. Other domains, such as legal state abbreviations or employee job titles, are better candidates. Numeric and date domains are usually easier to define: for example, "integer values greater than x," "non-negative currency values between x and y," or "dates between today and today + 30."

Some DBMSs let you create, alter, and drop domains explicitly, just like tables and columns. More often, you create them implicitly as column constraints or business rules. Microsoft has integrated the process of setting constraints and defaults in Access's Design Mode (see Figure 1-6) but doesn't include that functionality in VB.

System Tables

Relational DBMSs store metadata, or information about individual databases, in *schemas* or *data dictionaries*. A SQL schema is the series of SQL statements required to define a single database. *System tables* or the DBMS *catalog tables* are metadata about the DBMS itself and all of its databases. The term "data dictionary" is sometimes used as a synonym for schema or data repository. *Data repository* is generally used to mean a central database containing metadata for several DBMSs and/or servers. Bear in mind that system tables are normal database tables that can be queried—even manipulated, by the intrepid—like any other database table.

Figure 1-6: *Constraints for Access in Design Mode*

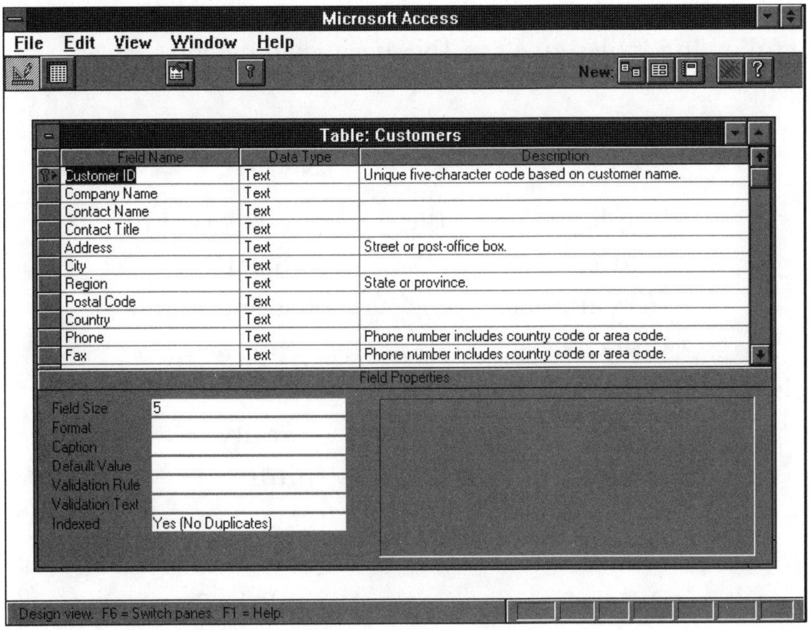

Normalization

Normalization is an analytic (as opposed to synthetic) process that produces a stable set of data items and results in semantic integrity. Dr. E. F. Codd refers to normalization as "a very simple elimination procedure;" others use the term "decomposition."

Earlier in the chapter, we alluded to five normal forms. Most professionals view third Normal Form (3NF) as "normal enough." Although additional normalization may yield a purer, more elegant design, it invariably does so at the price of performance.

First Normal Form (1NF)   A table is said to be in 1NF if it contains no repeating groups of data items. In other words, all occurrences of a record contain the same number of fields and does not have multiple occurrences of the "same" field within one record; records contain atomic values for all attributes. Additionally, one or more columns has been assigned primary key status in tables meeting the criteria for 1NF.

For example, the following tables *aren't* in 1NF because they contain repeating groups:

PATIENT	EMPLOYEE	INVOICE
Patient (key)	EmployeeName (key)	Invoice# (key)
Address	Address	InvoiceDate
HomePhone	HomePhone	CustomerName
1stVisitDate	WorkExt	Account#
1stVisitDiagnosis	School1	Item1
1stVisitCharge	Degree1	Quantity1
2ndVisitDate	School2	Unitprice1
2ndVisitDiagnosis	Degree2	Item2
2ndVisitCharge	School3	Quantity2
. . .	Degree3	UnitPrice2
	. . .	. . .

The problems with these tables is fairly obvious. What is the maximum number of patient visits—or degrees, or invoice items—should we plan for? If we overestimate, we'll end up with a lot of space-consuming blank fields filled with nulls. Nulls, by the way, are a problem in themselves, since not all DBMSs treat nulls quite the same way. On the other hand, if we underestimate, we'll run into problems when we need more fields than we've provided.

The solution is to create a new table for the repeating fields, where each group of repeating fields will have its own row. This second table becomes the *detail* or *child* table and is related to its *master* or *parent* table in a many-to-one relationship. The detail tables in our examples might be called PatientVisits, EmployeeDegrees, and InvoiceItems.

Second Normal Form (2NF)   A table is in 2NF if, in addition to meeting the criteria of 1NF, all non-key attributes are *functionally dependent* on the entire key. Primary keys are fields or combinations of fields that provide unambiguous references to individual records. 2NF only pertains to tables with *composite keys*—keys consisting of more than one attribute. If your table doesn't have any composite keys and is in 1NF, it's automatically in 2NF as well.

In a functional dependency, for any relation R, attribute A is functionally dependent on attribute B if, for every valid instance, the value of B determines the value of A.

One way of thinking of second normal form is that it precludes multi-thematic tables. The following examples of tables *aren't* in 2NF because of partial key functional dependencies. In the first table, invoice and product data have been combined. In the second table, product and supplier data are stored together. Both cases are almost guaranteed to result in data redundancy and all of its associated headaches, such as modification and deletion anomalies. Look at the second table and assume you order a dozen products from the same supplier. What if the supplier moves? You'll have to update the supplier's address data in the product table for all the supplier's products. If you don't, you've lost your data integrity, since the supplier's address will no longer be an unambiguous value.

INVOICE

Invoice# (key)

InvoiceDate

ProductCode (key)

ProductName

ProductDescription

ProductSize

ProductWeight

InvoiceQuantity

InvoicePrice

PRODUCT

ProductCode (key)

ProductName

ProductDescription

SupplierName (key)

SupplierAddress

SupplierPhone

SupplierContact

QOH

Cost

UnitPrice

Third Normal Form (3NF)   A table that, in addition to meeting the criteria for 2NF, contains no transitive dependencies, is said to be in 3NF. A data item or attribute is *transitively dependent* on another data item (the key) if the attribute data item is functionally dependent on a second attribute data item, which in turn is functionally dependent on the key data item.

Does that definition leave your head spinning? Try this: Transitive dependencies occur when a data item in a record is not a key, but identifies other data items as though it were a key. Don't be surprised if normalizing to 2NF also achieves 3NF. Real-world examples with multi-thematic tables, like INVOICE and PRODUCT, generally have transitive dependencies, and those transitive dependencies tend to disappear when you split the tables to gain 2NF.

It's important to recognize when a table is in third normal form, since 3NF has become the *de facto* standard in the industry. Here's an easy way to remember 3NF: nonkey fields that are "determined by the key, the whole key, and nothing but the key."

Fourth and Fifth Normal Forms (4NF and 5NF)   Most tables meeting the requirements for 3NF also satisfy the criteria for 4NF and 5NF. Fourth and fifth normal forms both deal with rarely-encountered multi-valued dependencies. Somewhere between 3NF and 4NF, however, is another widely-recognized normal form, *Boyce-Codd Normal Form*, BCNF. You may want to know the subtle distinction.

BCNF differs from 3NF only for tables that have more than one candidate composite key. *Candidate keys* aren't simply megakeys that contain all the attributes in a table, for example. Candidate keys are those that contain the same number of attributes as the chosen key which itself is usually referred to as the primary key or superkey. Clear as mud, right? Consider an employee table that contains both social security numbers and employee IDs, with social security number as the primary key. The employee ID field represents a candidate key.

Since BCNF only affects tables with composite keys, it's really just another manifestation of the multi-theme table problem, so often you'll intuitively achieve BCNF when you are decomposing tables to attain 2NF. Consider, for example, a project management database where employees can be either project team members or advisors. Assume further that employees can be assigned to several projects concurrently, and that projects will be assigned one or more project advisors, but that any individual advises no more than one project. A ProjectEmployee table (ProjectNumber, ProjectMember, Project-Advisor) might be established with ProjectNumber and Project-Member as the primary key. The combination of these two data items uniquely identifies the ProjectAdvisor. But ProjectMember and ProjectAdvisor also uniquely identify the ProjectNumber. This table is not in BCNF. To satisfy BCNF, the table must be split into two two-column tables. Perhaps you begin to see the problems of going beyond 3NF. To achieve BCNF in this example, you would have to decompose the ProjectEmployee table into two two-column tables, and this entails the overhead of an extra column. What do you gain? Elimination of the redundancies associated with repeating ProjectAdvisor names and ProjectMember. If a project advisor quits, the change has to be made to all records for which the advisor was associated.

Fourth and fifth normal forms are often dismissed as being "beyond the scope of this discussion" largely because they deal with independently-valued attributes that make up a composite primary key. Like BCNF, 4NF and 5NF address design problems that you have probably solved intuitively by the time you achieve 3NF.

Another employee table example illustrates problems associated with having a table that isn't in 4NF. Visualize records in a table that consists of EmployeeName, EmployeeJobSkill, and ForeignLanguage, where knowledge of foreign language is not associated with EmployeeJobSkill. For talented employees who know several languages, we have a real problem that is based on having independently multi-valued attributes as our primary key. The solution? You guessed it—break up the table into two two-column tables: EmployeeSkills (EmployeeName, EmployeeJobSkill) and EmployeeLanguages (EmployeeName, ForeignLanguage).

Fifth normal form only applies to tables that contain cyclic dependencies and results in a single table being decomposed into three or more tables. A table that does not meet 5NF consists of a composite key and probably nothing but a composite key. I think of 5NF as an extension of 4NF, one that requires simultaneous, rather than iterative, decomposition of the initial table. See Figure 1-7 for an overview of the different normal forms.

Figure 1-7: *Approaching normalization nirvana*

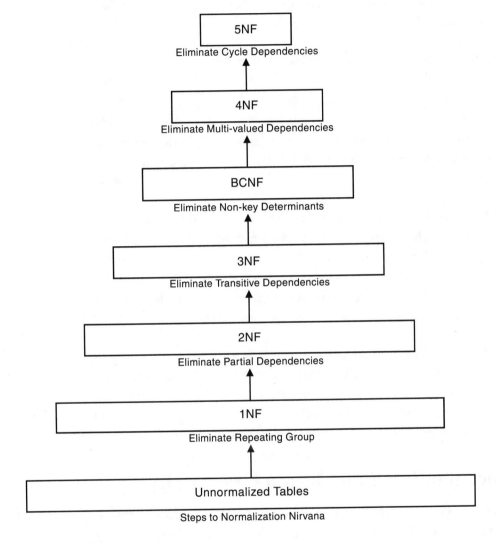

Denormalization

You're probably wondering about the performance hit associated with fully normalized designs that consist mainly of three- or four-column tables. If one of the columns is the primary key, and another one is the foreign key, that's a lot of overhead. Furthermore, in order to recombine the data in response to user queries, the DBMS has to perform time-consuming joins. End-users could care less about normal forms—they want accurate answers fast.

As you've seen, any database design can be fully normalized. The question is whether it should. Sometimes we need to compromise our "correct" database design to achieve better performance. We recombine tables, and that's called *denormalization*. Unfortunately, there aren't any easy rules of thumb to guide you in denormalization decisions. Here's a tactical checklist to help you approach the problem:

- Narrow down the situations that correspond to poor performance. Measure actual response times for different situations on different terminals at different times of day. Does the situation occur often or is it a rare, but time-killing occurrence? Does the situation involve adding new records, changing existing data, during queries, or some combination of those?

- Consider potential alternatives to denormalization. Can you minimize the problem with a faster CPU or a larger, faster hard disk? What about an alternate architecture where the queries are made on replicated data that has been staged locally? Unfortunately, that means trial and measurement.

Documenting Your Design Graphically

Once you've gone to the trouble of coming up with a good normalized database design, it's important to document it. That can be as easy as printing out the schema or data dictionary. You may also want to purchase a CASE tool that gives you a graphical representation of how your tables are related. There are a variety of CASE tools that use more or less standard methods for representing entities, keys, relationships, and so on. Some of them even analyze your design for normalization.

Most CASE tools offer the additional advantage of actually creating database tables and related structures—or at least generating schemas that contain code to perform the database creation. Furthermore, most will generate schemas for more than one kind of DBMS. In other words, once you've set up your database definition with a CASE tool, not only do you have a data dictionary from which you can print a variety of charts, chances are you can also crank out code that physically creates the database for several popular back ends.

Summary

We called this chapter "Relational Databases and How to Design One," but the best way to understand how relational databases are designed is to create one yourself. We've included some textbook style "Design Exercises" in this chapter only to spur you on.

In the next chapters, we'll probe SQL, the "structured query language" that has become the lingua franca of the relational database world.

Design Exercises

1. Here's part of an unnormalized PARTS table. Make intelligent assumptions and come up with a normalized design.

    ```
    PARTS (PartNumber, PartDescription, Warehouse,
    SupplierName1, Price1, SupplierName2, Price2,
    SupplierName3, Price3, SupplierName4, Price4,
    QuantityOnHand, MinimumReorderQuantity)
    ```

2. Here's part of an unnormalized EMPLOYEE table. Make intelligent assumptions and come up with a normalized design.

    ```
    EMPLOYEE (EmployeeSSN, EmployeeName, HireDate,
    DateOfBirth, Age, Department, Supervisor, Salary,
    MedicalPlan, MedicalOption1, MedicalOption2,
    MedicalOption3, DentalPlan, RetirementPlan,
    SpouseName, SpouseDateOfBirth, SpouseMedicalPlan,
    SpouseMedicalOption1, (etc.), Dependent2Name,
    Dependent2 DateOfBirth, Dependent2MedicalPlan,
    (etc.) EvaluationReport, OfficePhone, OfficeFax,
    HomePhone, HomeFax, Beeper, CarPhone)
    ```

3. Imagine that you've been asked to design a database for a child care center. What tables would you need?

References

Codd, E. F. "A Relational Model of Data for Large Shared Data Banks," *Communications of the Association for Computing Machinery (ACM)*, June 1970, pp. 377-387.

Codd, E. F. *The Relational Model for Database Management, Version 2.* Reading, MA: Addison-Wesley Publishing Co., 1990.

Date, C. J. *An Introduction to Database Systems, Volume 1, Fifth Edition.* Reading, MA: Addison-Wesley Publishing Co., 1990.

Dutka, Alan F. and Howard H. Hanson. *Fundamentals of Data Normalization.* Reading, MA: Addison-Wesley Publishing Co., 1989.

Fagin, R. "The Decomposition vs. the synthetic approach to relational database design," *Proceedings of VLDB (Very Large Data Bases) III*, 1977 (Tokyo, Japan), pp. 441-446.

Finkelstein, Richard. "Breaking the Rules has a Price," *Database Programming and Design*, June 1988, pp. 11-14.

Fleming, Candace and Barbara von Halle. *Handbook of Relational Database Design*. Reading, MA: Addison-Wesley Publishing Co., 1989.

Kent, William. "A Simple Guide to Five Normal Forms in Relational Database Theory," *Communications of the Association for Computing Machinery (ACM)*, February 1983.

Rodgers, Ulka. "Denormalization: Why, What, and How?" *Database Programming and Design*, December 1989, pp. 46-53.

Disk Files

BIBLIO.ZIP	A "fresh" copy of BIBLIO.MDB plus a dBASE version
DATAMGR.ZIP	Microsoft's VB source code for DATAMGR.EXE
VBPRODS.ZIP	The VB add-ins database and related files

2

SQL Fundamentals

If you're a programmer, you probably rate database programming in the same league as Cobol programming—certainly not nearly as much fun as writing your own compiler or animation routine. But database programming is where the action is today.

Chances are you've been avoiding SQL like the plague. But SQL is *the way* to communicate with most databases, and knowing SQL will let you leverage your Visual Basic programming skills. Oh, in case you're wondering, SQL is simple, relative to Visual Basic.

So what exactly *is* SQL? It's a non-procedural, relational, data access language that lets you to create, manipulate, and control relational databases. It's important because it's a common denominator—a sort of *lingua franca*— for communication both between applications and DBMSs and between DBMSs themselves.

If that isn't enough to motivate you, consider this: Microsoft's OBDC is based on SQL, and Open DataBase Connectivity (OBDC) is part of VB3. ODBC is a published API, and it's one of the components of Microsoft's Windows Open Systems Architecture (WOSA). The other main reason to learn SQL is that VB's native Access engine includes its own dialect of SQL, called Access SQL.

SQL (pronounced either "es-cue-ell" or "sequel") isn't a complete programming language. It's only a database access language and doesn't have constructs for looping or branching.

The History of SQL

SQL has been evolving since 1974, when it was first implemented as Structured English QUEry Language (SEQUEL) on a prototype relational DBMS called System R at the IBM San Jose Research Laboratory, by it was an IBM team led by Donald Chamberlin. System R eventually evolved into IBM SQL/DS and IBM DB2, and SEQUEL became SQL. The terms "SQL" and "relational" are related, but they're not synonymous.

SQL is a non-procedural, English-like query language based on relational calculus. Relational calculus itself is a non-procedural, mathematical formalization, based on first-order predicate logic, of the relational algebra operations. Theoretically, SQL queries should always return the right answer, since SQL is based on math and logic.

Unfortunately, there is not a single SQL. A host of standards organizations, notably the American National Standards Institute (ANSI), the International Standards Organization (ISO), and X/Open, are constantly updating their versions of formal, *de jure* SQL standards. Other organizations that influence or monitor SQL standards include the SQL Access Group (SAG) and the U.S. Department of Commerce's National Institute of Standards and Technology (NIST, based in Gaithersburg, Maryland) and its Federal Information Processing Standard (FIPS).

SAG was founded in 1989 at least partially in response to the lethargic pace of formal standards efforts. SAG is a consortium of approximately 50 hardware and software companies and interested users who are "committed to advancing the goal of universal database access." SAG considers itself a group of pragmatists and shuns the description "standards organization." SAG has an arrangement with X/Open, an independent standard-setting organization based in the U.K., to publish SAG specifications. One of the first SAG specifications was the call-level interface CLI, but it has also defined its own superset of SQL-92 and a specification for Remote Data Access (RDA). For more information about SAG or to order X/Open publications, contact SQL Access Group, POB 5559, Manchester, NH 03108. Phone: 603-434-0802.

NIST FIPS PUB 127-1 (2/90) specifies conformance to SQL-89, and FIPS PUB 127-2 (10/93) outlines basic conformance to SQL-92, both of which include comprehensive test suites. NIST publishes a quarterly, *Validated Processor List*, and ratings are valid for one year. You can find out more about FIPS PUB 127 from NIST, Computer Systems Laboratory, Software Standards Validation Group, Gaithersburg, MD 20899. Phone: (301) 975-3258.

SQL-92

SQL2 or SQL-92 is the most recent SQL standard. It was developed concurrently by the ANSI's X3H2 Database Committee and the ISO as a major update of the original SQL-86 standard. SQL-86 defined two levels of compliance, Level One and Level Two, but was still appallingly incomplete. Because so many features were either simply missing or explicitly left to vendor implementation, all DBMS vendors added their own non-standard extensions.

Some of the holes were plugged with two new 1989 documents: the Integrity Enhancement Feature and Database Language Embedded SQL. Together, these are often referred to as SQL-89.

SQL-92, like SQL-86, defines multiple levels of compliance, notably Entry SQL, Intermediate SQL, and Full SQL. Entry SQL, by the way, is essentially the same as SQL-89. As of late 1993, SQL-92 is an unattained target for most DBMS vendors. Only Sybase System10 had officially received SQL-92 Entry SQL compliance Several other major vendors hadn't even achieved SQL-86 Level Two compliance.

Nevertheless, work is already proceeding on SQL3, which borrows popular features from object-oriented models. Meanwhile, vendors have also defined database access APIs based on SQL (see Figure 2-1). The Microsoft-led camp supports ODBC, and IBM has defined Distributed Relational Database Access (DRDA) for its architecture. Finally, Borland and others are promoting another database API called IDAPI (Integrated Distributed API).

Using SQL

Not only are there a variety of SQL standards and a host of DBMS-specific extensions, there are also different ways of using SQL.

- *Interactive SQL.* Often abbreviated isql or I-SQL. Microsoft's SQL Server and other database servers typically ship with a primitive isql program that database administrators (DBAs) can use to define databases and perform ad hoc queries. Sometimes also called direct or immediate SQL.

Figure 2-1: *Evolution of SQL*

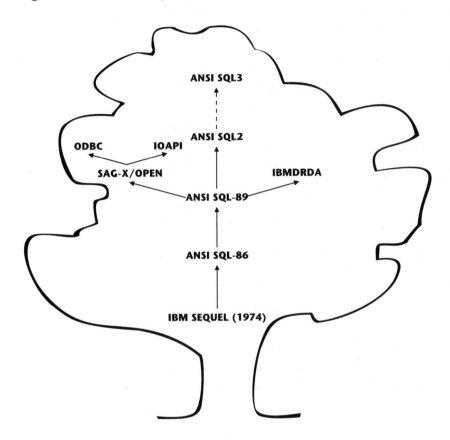

- *Static SQL.* In an application, "normal" SQL that is limited to SQL statements whose contents are known at compile time.

- *Dynamic SQL.* SQL that uses either host language data structures or a DBMS-maintained SQL descriptor area to accommodate data, such as column or table names, whose contents are not known at compile time. Interactive SQL (isql) and end-user query tools are examples of programs that use dynamic SQL. Prior to SQL-92, most implementations of dynamic SQL used the SQLDA structure approach, in which dynamic information was stored in host language data structures. Actual data was stored in a buffer and accessed by a pointer if the language supported pointers.

- **Embedded SQL.** SQL statements that are interspersed in a 3GL such as C, Ada, Fortran, or COBOL (Basic isn't included in the SQL standard!). Embedded SQL uses a pre-processor that verifies the SQL syntax and semantics, stores the statements in an optimized form in the database, and then generates function calls to retrieve and execute the statements at runtime. Preprocessors basically translate the SQL into equivalent 3GL code so that SQL statements become an extension of the 3GL.

SQL's Data Definition Language (DDL)

Broadly speaking, you can classify SQL statements into four or five functional categories: those used for data definition (DDL), those used for data manipulation (DML), various data control language (DCL) statements associated with connections, transaction processing, and error messages, and statements associated with dynamic SQL. In this chapter, we focus on the data definition and data manipulation languages. `CREATE` and `SELECT` are the biggies.

Logically enough, `CREATE` is the main SQL verb for creating various database components. SQL-92 defines the following `CREATE` statements:

```
CREATE ASSERTION
CREATE CHARACTER SET
CREATE COLLATION
CREATE DOMAIN
CREATE SCHEMA
CREATE TABLE
CREATE TEMPORARY TABLE
```

```
CREATE TRANSLATION
CREATE VIEW
```

A lot of these CREATE statements are new to SQL-92 and are likely to be introduced gradually into commercial DBMSs. *Assertions* are basically complex constraints that may involve several columns and tables. *Character sets*, *collations*, and *translations* are primarily for international SQL support defining alternate sort orders, and mapping a given character like a delimiter to another character. *Domains*, as discussed in Chapter 1, are sets or ranges of values that represent legal (logical) field contents. Domains aren't quite the same as user-defined types, since they're built from primitive SQL data types. *Schemas* are more or less comprehensive database definitions, including definitions for tables, views, domains, and so on.

Tables, sometimes called *base table* are the primary logical repository of your data, and *views* are *virtual tables*. Views can be subsets of tables or predefined joins which can include selection criteria, such as a WHERE clause. Views are not physically stored except as definitions; they are recreated dynamically when accessed. In Visual Basic/Access, however, views aren't called views; they're called *dynasets*.

Dynasets are one kind of recordset objects, the others being table objects and snapshots. Snapshots are just what they sound like: a picture of a dynaset frozen in time.

A *view* in a relational database is a pseudo-table or virtual table. It isn't physically stored in the database except as a view definition. A single view definition will dynamically return different data today and tomorrow if the underlying data is changed between the two queries.

Interestingly, the SQL standard doesn't define a `CREATE INDEX` or a `CREATE DATABASE`. All DBMSs support indexes, but because of vast differences in types of indexes and syntax, it's something you have to double-check for each DBMS. Similarly, all DBMSs let you create databases, but the implementation varies.

You might wonder about other things that have to be created. Why aren't there any `CREATE AUTHORIZATION` or `CREATE` statements, for example? Both of those concepts exist, but they're handled with different SQL verbs. You don't create authorizations; you `GRANT` (privileges). Similarly, you don't create cursors; you use the `DECLARE CURSOR` statement.

Some DBMSs include additional `CREATE statements`. DB2, for example, allows you to `CREATE TABLESPACE` and `CREATE ALIAS`. Some DBMSs also have an explicit `CREATE SYNONYM` statement. SQL Server 4.x lets you `CREATE DEFAULT`, `CREATE PROCEDURE`, `CREATE RULE`, and `CREATE TRIGGER`.

Indexes are so important that X/Open and SAG have defined SQL statements for creating and dropping indexes as extensions to the SQL standard. Perhaps `CREATE INDEX` will become part of SQL3, especially since many vendors use the following X/Open syntax:

```
CREATE [UNIQUE] INDEX index-name
        ON base-table-name (column-identifier [ASC|DESC]
        [, column-identifier [ASC|DESC]]...)

DROP INDEX  index-name
```

Throughout the book, we'll do our best to use standard notation appropriate to the topic. Most often that will mean standard VB notation, but at this point it means standard SQL notation.

In standard SQL, upper-case words and parentheses are literal syntactic elements of SQL. Words in lower case, including the hyphens, are generally user-provided elements like specific table names that relate to a particular database. Square brackets ([]) enclose optional syntax items, and vertical bars (| |) indicate mutually exclusive options. Braces ({}) delimit a range. An ellipsis (...) means that the syntax enclosed by the immediately preceding pair of braces or brackets may be repeated.

Creating Tables

The important things you need to know how to create are tables and views. Tables are quite a bit more complicated than indexes because of the options that can be associated with column definitions. The basic CREATE TABLE syntax is as follows:

```
CREATE TABLE base-table-name
(column-definition [,column-definition]...)
```

where *column-definition* is defined as

```
column-identifier data-type [NOT NULL]
```

The SQL standard defines data types as

```
CHARACTER(n)
CHARACTER VARYING(n)
BIT(n)
BIT VARYING (n)
NUMERIC(p,q)
DECIMAL(p,q)
INTEGER
SMALLINT
FLOAT(p)
```

```
DATE
TIME
TIMESTAMP
INTERVAL
```

where the string length specification (n), precision specification (p,m), and scale specifications (q) are unsigned decimal integers. The standard supports various abbreviations like CHAR, INT, and DEC, as well as alternates like REAL and DOUBLE PRECISION for FLOAT. Dates and intervals are new in SQL-92 and will continue to present conversion problems as they have in every programming language.

Here's an example of a simple table definition:

```
CREATE TABLE Employee
   (EmpID              INTEGER,
   EmpLastName    CHARACTER 40,
   EmpFirstName   CHARACTER 30)
```

In practice, though, virtually no DBMSs use the basic CREATE TABLE syntax, since they provide varying degrees of support for integrity features. Here's the X/Open CREATE TABLE syntax:

```
CREATE TABLE base-table-name-1
(column-element [,column-element]...)
```

where *column-element* is

```
column-definition|table-constraint-definition
```

column-definition is

```
column-identifier data-type [DEFAULT default-value]
[column-constraint-definition [,column-constraint-
...definition]...)
```

and *column-constraint-definition* is

```
NOT NULL [UNIQUE|PRIMARY KEY]
|REFERENCES base-table-name-2[(column-identifier)]
|CHECK (search-condition)
```

Default-value is

```
literal|NULL|USER
```

and *table-constraint-definition* is defined as

```
UNIQUE (column-identifier [,column-identifier]...)
|PRIMARY KEY (column-identifier [,column-identifier]...)
|CHECK (search-condition)
|FOREIGN KEY referencing-columns REFERENCES base-
...table-name-2 [referenced-columns]
```

where both *referencing-columns* and *referenced-columns* are

```
(column-identifier [,column-identifier]...)
```

Including the integrity constraints in a CREATE TABLE definition is referred to as *declarative referential integrity*. Sybase and Microsoft SQL Server and some other DBMSs use a trigger method to enforce referential integrity.

A CREATE TABLE statement that includes options referring to foreign keys is said to use *declarative* referential integrity. Some DBMSs, such as SQL Server 4.x, don't use declarative referential integrity; they accomplish the same thing with triggers or stored procedures.

The following are a few more complex table definitions:

```
CREATE TABLE Employee
   (EmpID         INTEGER NOT NULL PRIMARY KEY,
   EmpLastName    CHARACTER 40,
   EmpFirstName   CHARACTER 30,
   HireDate       TIMESTAMP)

CREATE TABLE Sale
   (InvoiceNo     INTEGER NOT NULL PRIMARY KEY,
   EmpID          INTEGER FOREIGN KEY EmpID REFERENCES Employee,
   InvoiceDate    TIMESTAMP,
   InvoiceAmount CURRENCY,
   Terms          CHARACTER 20,
   Status         CHARACTER 10)

CREATE TABLE LineItem
   (Order#        CHARACTER 5 NOT NULL,
   Part#          CHARACTER 10 NOT NULL,
   Qty            INTEGER
   PRIMARY KEY (Order#, Part#)
   FOREIGN KEY (Order#)
      REFERENCES Invoices ON DELETE CASCADE
   FOREIGN KEY (Part#)
      REFERENCES Products) ON DELETE RESTRICT
```

Creating Views

The other important CREATE command is CREATE VIEW. Views are virtual tables that act almost exactly like tables for queries and reports. You can define single-table views that are row and/or column subsets of the parent table, or multi-table views, such as the equivalent of a JOIN or UNION, that are constructed as needed. The basic syntax is as follows:

```
CREATE VIEW view-name [(column-identifier [,column-
...identifier...])
AS table-expression
[WITH[CASCADED|LOCAL] CHECK OPTION]
```

Views can be a bit dicey. For example, consider the question of whether or not users should be able to update views. Views, after all, are virtual tables, and aren't subject to the transaction and concurrency controls that real tables must have. Although most DBMSs support single-table views that can be updated, many of them do not allow users to update multi-table views. Views also inherit certain characteristics from their parent tables, such as column names and the CHECK OPTION. You'd think column names would be innocuous enough. However, when you're dealing with multi-table views, as when two tables share a common column-name and you want to include that column in your view, the SQL standard says you have to create new, unique column names for the view. The CHECK OPTION is only relevant to updatable views and refers to performing referential integrity checking. For example:

```
CREATE VIEW NewEmps
    AS SELECT  *
    FROM Employee
    WHERE HireDate > '1/1/93'

CREATE VIEW BigSale (EmpID, EmpLastName, InvoiceAmount)
    AS SELECT Sale.EmpID, Employee.EmpLastName,
    ...Sale.InvoiceAmount
    FROM Sale, Employee
    WHERE Sale.InvoiceAmount > 50000
```

These CREATE VIEW examples both contain SELECT statements. SELECT is the most complex SQL statement and is your major tool for data retrieval when you have to use SQL. The asterisk (*) means the same as "all columns."

Deleting and Altering

SQL-92 CREATE statements all have DROP counterparts, and most of them also have ALTER statements. There is no ALTER VIEW command, however. The syntax for dropping a table is:

```
DROP TABLE base-table {RESTRICT|CASCADE}
```

If RESTRICT is specified and the base-table is part of a view definition, the DROP will fail. CASCADE will propagate the deletion and eliminate any views that reference the table being dropped.

Granting and Revoking

In addition to CREATE, DROP, and ALTER, the SQL GRANT and REVOKE statements are usually also lumped into the DDL category. GRANT and REVOKE are used to fine-tune user access to SQL data, and GRANTing privileges is one of the first tasks that has to be done after creating a new database, table, or view.

The prescribed syntax for GRANT is

```
GRANT {ALL [PRIVILEGES|grant-privilege [,grant-
...privilege]...}
ON table-name
TO {PUBLIC|user-name [,user-name]...}
[WITH GRANT OPTION]
```

where the privilege can be DELETE, INSERT, SELECT, and/or UPDATE. In the case of UPDATE privileges, a list of updateable columns should be specified. Most DBMSs also let you grant privileges on views, and vendors with declarative referential integrity may allow a grant-privilege of REFERENCES, which grants the right to reference column-identifiers from a foreign key.

Most SQL DBMSs take the conservative approach and deny users access to data, except the user who actually created the table. In other words, anyone who creates a table has the responsibility for setting up read or read/write access to the data, typically by using the GRANT command.

If you create tables and you want others to be able to see and/or update their contents, you'll need to be familiar with the GRANT command. That's because almost all SQL DBMSs force the table creator to explicitly grant others access to his table. No grant, no see.

REVOKE is the flip side of GRANT and has the following basic syntax:

```
REVOKE {ALL [PRIVILEGES]|revoke-privilege [,revoke-
...privilege]...}
ON table-name
FROM {PUBLIC|user-name [,user-name]...}
[CASCADE|RESTRICT]
```

DDL with Visual Basic

Visual Basic doesn't have a good equivalent of SQL DDL. Microsoft has made it easy to create new Access databases both programmatically and with the DATAMGR program, but not nearly as easy to create either new databases or tables for other DBMSs. Because of the complexity of the topic, we cover the options in Chapter 5.

SQL's Data Manipulation Language (DML)

Data definition is fine, but, let's face it, you don't define databases as often as you use them. As programmers, you're more likely to be concerned with accessing and using *existing* databases than with creating new ones, so you need to know the syntax for INSERT, UPDATE, DELETE, and, of course, SELECT. The SELECT statement is the workhorse of the database world, and it's the one to learn.

Getting Information About a Database Structure

Relational databases are supposed to be *self-defining* collections of tables, meaning the database definition should reside within the database itself. As mentioned earlier, vendors use terms like *schema, metadata, system catalog*, and *data dictionary* to refer to this internal data about the database structure. Unfortunately, implementation of these system tables is non-standard, so you'll have to— no, not that!—refer to the DBMS documentation to learn the details. Sometimes, a SELECT * FROM SYSTABLES will do the trick.

There are also a variety of ways of getting database structure information about an open database from VB. For example, the ListTables method—Set snapshot = database.ListTables( )—creates a snapshot containing one record for each Table or QueryDef in a specified database. However, it's much easier and more efficient to use the TableDefs collection, which, logically enough, is a collection of TableDef objects. A database's default collection is the TableDefs collection, and the default collection of a TableDef is the Fields collection.

If you're only going to learn one SQL statement, learn how to use the SELECT statement.

SQL's Powerful SELECT

OK, let's tackle the SELECT statement. It's by far the most complex SQL statement, but if you tackle its syntax one chunk at a time, you'll discover SELECTs are not that tough, they're just multifaceted.

You can use a single SELECT to retrieve information from one or more tables or views. SELECTs also let you

- retrieve columns in any order

- impose conditions on your query with complex WHERE clauses

- have data returned in sorted order

- use aggregate functions like COUNT, AVG, MAX, MIN, and SUM

- use arithmetic, Boolean, and relational operators

- use predicates such as BETWEEN, IN, LIKE, NULL, and EXISTS

- perform nested SELECTs (subselects)

In Visual Basic, you can also use a SELECT statement for a data control's RecordSource property, with a "passthrough SQL" statement that bypasses the Access engine, or even when creating a DynaSet, Snapshot, or QueryDef. The basic SELECT command has the structure

```
SELECT [ALL|DISTINCT] selectlist
FROM table-reference [,table-reference]...
[WHERE search-condition]
[GROUP BY column-name [,column-name]...]
[HAVING search-condition]
[ORDER BY sort-specification [,sort-specification]...]
```

where *selectlist* is

```
*| select-sublist [,select-sublist]...
```

a *select-sublist* is

```
scalar-expression [AS column-identifier] | {table-name|
...correlation name}.*
```

and a *sort-specification* is

```
{column-identifier|unsigned-integer} [ASC|DESC]
```

In SQL, the "*" symbol is a synonym for `ALL`, as in `SELECT * FROM` Employees. `DISTINCT` allows you to prevent duplicates from being returned, but not just for complete rows. After all, in a well-designed database, where you have defined a unique primary key, you won't have any duplicates of entire rows! However, you can use `SELECT DISTINCT` state `FROM CLIENTS`, for example, to get a list of all the states in which you have clients. Even if you have 100 clients from Missouri, you'll find that Missouri will only be listed once. Most vendors' `SELECT DISTINCT`s automatically sort the data returned.

If you include more than one field in the selectlist, separate the field names with commas and list the fields in the order in which you want them to be retrieved. If a field name appears in more than one table listed in the `FROM` clause, precede the field name with the table name and the dot (.) operator. In the following example, the Dept field is in both the Employees table and the Supervisors table. The SQL statement selects the Dept field from the Employees table and the SupvName field from the Supervisors table.

```
SELECT Employees.Dept, Supervisors.SupvName
FROM Supervisors, Employees
WHERE Employees.Dept = Supervisors.Dept
```

You're bound to run into *aliases*—also known as correlation names—frequently in SQL, because they save typing. The preceding example could be rewritten with aliases S and E for the Supervisors and Employees tables respectively:

```
SELECT E.Dept, S.SupvName
FROM Supervisors S, Employees E
WHERE E.Dept = S.Dept
```

These SQL correlation-name aliases are good for the duration of a query only and shouldn't be confused with the formal aliases that some DBMSs and front-end programs create for end-user convenience. These product-specific aliases allow end users to see table and column names such as Products and ProductNumber instead of T1_Pro and PN, for example.

SQL prescribes a handful of basic aggregate functions, but most DBMSs include more than the minimum. The Access engine, for example, also supports domain aggregate functions such as DAvg, DCount, DFirst, DLast DLookup, DMin, DMax, DStDev, DStDevP, DSum, DVar, and DVarP. However, you can count on SUM, COUNT, MIN, MAX, and AVG. Aggregate functions can't be intermixed with non-aggregate columns in a single SELECT unless combined with a GROUP BY.

The optional ORDER BY clause lets you sort output on the fly. Some DBMSs support an integer number in lieu of a column name for the sort column. You could ORDER BY 3 to sort by the table's third column.

Using AS lets you create simple report-like output with custom column headings. The alternative column headings that follow AS are sometimes called aliases. In the SQL world, the term *alias* sometimes refers to a formal data dictionary entry, sometimes to a table abbreviation, and sometimes (as used here) to a column heading.

A GROUP BY clause lets you specify grouping columns and performs the function sometimes referred to as a control break. You could use GROUP BY to return all sales for a given salesperson or region. A field in the GROUP BY field list can refer to any field in the FROM clause even if the field isn't included in the selectlist, provided the SELECT statement includes at least one aggregate function. HAVING applies conditions for grouping and can include another SELECT statement. When it does, the second SELECT is called a nested SELECT or subquery and is enclosed by parentheses.

More complex SELECTs include the following:

```
SELECT Supplier.SerialNum AS ProductID, Product.Pro-
...ductName
FROM Supplier, Product
WHERE Supplier.SerialNum = Product.SerialNum
GROUP BY Supplier
HAVING Supplier.OrdersToDate > 1000


SELECT DeptNo, MAX(Salary) FROM Employee GROUP BY DeptNo
...HAVING COUNT(*) >3
```

The WHERE Clause

The WHERE clause lets you define one or more predicates (conditional expressions) and combine them with logical operators AND, OR, or NOT. As well as having three logical operators, SQL is based on three-valued logic: TRUE, FALSE, and UNKNOWN. Three-valued logic, unlike two-valued (T/F) Boolean logic, accommodates UNKNOWN.

Here's a summary of how the three logical operators work. For example, ANDing a false condition with a true condition yields a false, whereas ORing then yields an overall true.

AND	T	F	U
T	T	F	U
F	F	F	F
U	U	F	U

OR	T	F	U
T	T	T	T
F	T	F	U
U	T	U	U

NOT	
T	F
F	T
U	U

Complicating the issue of comparisons are NULLs. A NULL is a data value equivalent to the empty set. Programmers learn early on that NULLs are different from both zeros and the space symbol. Math operations involving NULLs usually result in a NULL, but logical operations are more complex, as the charts indicate. One counterintuitive aspect of NULLs is that two NULLs aren't considered equal. You can use the IS [NOT]NULL predicate in WHERE clauses such as "SELECT * FROM Customer WHERE TotToDate IS NULL" to obtain a list of customers who apparently haven't placed any orders recently.

Searches can contain comparisons that use any of the standard comparison (theta) operators (=, <>, >, >=, <, or <=) and involve expressions or subqueries.

SQL also supports BETWEEN, IN, and LIKE predicates, such as the following:

```
SELECT * FROM Suppliers
WHERE State IN ('CA', 'NY', 'OH') AND OrdersToDate > 1000
```

```
SELECT * FROM Employee
 WHERE BirthDate BETWEEN '1/1/60' AND '12/31/65'

SELECT * FROM Employee
WHERE LastName LIKE 'SM%'
```

The LIKE predicate works like DOS wildcards, except the characters are different. In SQL, the underscore (_) stands for a single character and the percent symbol (%) for zero or more characters.

Nulls and Missing Data

The SQL standard specifies usage both for NULL and EXISTS. The NULL predicate "column-name IS [NOT] NULL" returns True or False, depending on the value of the column referenced by column-name. EXISTS is used in conjunction with a subquery and tests for the existence of a row satisfying some condition, as shown in the following examples:

```
SELECT ItemName, SupplierName
FROM Inventory I, Supplier
WHERE EXISTS
(SELECT * FROM Inventory I2
WHERE I.ItemNo = I2.ItemNo
AND (I2.Qty * I2.Cost) > 1000)
SELECT * FROM Invoices I
WHERE NOT EXISTS
(SELECT * FROM Clients C
WHERE I.ClientID = C.ClientID)

SELECT Dept#, DeptName, Manager
FROM Dept
WHERE EXISTS
(SELECT DISTINCT Dept# FROM SalariedEmployee)
```

Even XBASE Has SELECT

Just in case your eyes are glazing over, here are some examples of
why it pays to know SQL and especially the SELECT statement.
Even FoxPro has a SELECT statement:

```
SELECT [ALL|DISTINCT]
[<alias>,]<select_item>[AS <column_name>]
[,<alias>,]<select_item>[AS <column_name>]...]
FROM <table> [<local_alias>] [,<table> [<local_alias>]...]
[[INTO <destination>]
|TO FILE <file> [ADDITIVE]
|TO PRINTER [PROMPT]
|TO SCREEN]]
[PREFERENCE <name>]
[NOCONSOLE]
[PLAIN]
[NOWAIT]
[WHERE <joincondition> [AND <joincondition>...]
[AND|OR <filtercondition> [AND|OR<filtercondition>...]]]
[GROUP BY <groupcolumn> [,<groupcolumn>...]]
HAVING <filtercondition>]
[UNION [ALL] <SELECT command>]
[ORDER BY <order_item> [ASC|DESC]
[,<order_item>[ASC|DESC]...]]
```

Despite its XBase quirks, it is clearly a SQL SELECT statement.

But No Two Vendors Do It Exactly the Same

Now look at the syntax for an IBM DB2 Version 2.3 SELECT:

```
SELECT {ALL|DISTINCT}
[[*|expression|table-name.*|view-name.*|correlation.*,]]
INTO [host-variable,|host-structure]
```

```
FROM [[table-name|view-name]{correlation},]
{{WHERE search-condition
GROUP BY column-name,
HAVING search-condition
ORDER BY [column-name|column-number] {ASC|DESC},
FOR UPDATE OF column-name,}}
```

or for the SQL Server 4.x SELECT:

```
SELECT [ALL|DISTINCT} select_list
INTO [[database.]owner.]table_name]
FROM [[database.]owner.]{table-name|view-name}
[HOLDLOCK]
[,[[database.]owner.]{table_name|view_name}
[HOLDLOCK]]...]
[WHERE search_conditions]
GROUP BY [ALL] aggregate_free_expression
[,aggregate_free_expression]...]
HAVING search_conditions]
ORDER BY
{[[[database.]owner.]{table_name|view_name}]
column_name|select_list_number|expression}
[ASC|DESC]
[,{[[[database.]owner.]{table_name|view_name.}]
column_name|select_list_number|expression}
[ASC|DESC]]...]
[COMPUTE row_aggregate(column_name)
[,row_aggregate(column_name)]...
[BY column_name [,column_name]...]]
[FOR BROWSE]
```

The idea isn't to memorize every vendor's exact syntax. What you can do, however, is master a generic SELECT statement:

```
SELECT * FROM table-name(s)
```

```
WHERE condition(s)
ORDER BY column-name(s)
```

Adding and Editing Data

Adding data to a table with SQL is straightforward, if tedious:

```
INSERT INTO table-name [column-identifier [,column-
...identifier]...]
{query-specification|VALUES (insert-value[, insert-
...value]...)}
```

Note that the word VALUES must be followed by the data in parentheses. As you might expect, you have to be careful to provide as many data items as there are column identifiers. INSERTs won't succeed unless the user attempting to add data has INSERT privileges. And, finally, using a query specification is an easy way to move data from one table to another domain-compatible table.

In dynamic SQL, insert values can refer to host variables or other dynamic parameters. Here, as with other SQL statements, you're responsible for error handling. This is especially important when there are errors that reflect integrity problems, such as attempts to add records with a key that already exists or other attempts to add data in violation of business rules. For example:

```
INSERT INTO Customer
VALUES (132, 'Bodwald', 'Jeremy', 'Sunshine Travel', '123
...Main', 'Dallas', 'TX')
```

and

```
INSERT INTO NYCust
SELECT * FROM Cust WHERE State = 'NY'
```

Deleting and Updating Rows

DELETE is one of those statements you learn to use with care, since an unqualified DELETE FROM table-name typically empties all rows from a table, without the "Are you sure?" prompt DOS users often expect. (The difference between DELETE FROM table-name and DROP table-name is that the latter also deletes the table definition. Most DBMSs have a REORG or PACK utility you need to run to reclaim physical disk space left by DELETEs.)

Bear in mind that the DELETE statement checks DBMS integrity constraints and DELETE privileges before removing data. Here's the syntax:

```
DELETE FROM table-name
[WHERE search-condition]
```

The UPDATE statement is fairly straightforward:

```
UPDATE table-name
SET column-identifier = {expression|NULL}
 [column-identifier = expression|NULL}]...
[WHERE search-condition]
```

For example

```
UPDATE Part
SET UnitPrice = UnitPrice * 1.1
WHERE UnitPrice < 15
```

Cursors and Embedded SQL

Cursors are like record pointers; they're a way for a host program (typically C/C++ or Cobol) to access a table, one row at a time. Because SQL is a set-oriented language, it needs a concept such as cursors to support row-oriented activities like positioned updates and both backwards and forward scrolling. In general, you'll use cursors like this:

```
EXEC SQL DECLARE A CURSOR FOR table-name;
EXEC SQL OPEN A;
EXEC SQL FETCH A INTO :varname1, :varname2, :varname3;
EXEC SQL DELETE FROM table-name WHERE CURRENT OF A;
EXEC SQL CLOSE A;
```

Cursor Pointer to a record. Since SQL is set-oriented rather than record-oriented, the concept of a cursor has been invented to mimic the more intuitive record orientation.

Declaring a Cursor

Cursors are defined with a DECLARE CURSOR statement and need to be explicitly opened or closed. The basic syntax for defining a cursor is:

```
DECLARE cursor-name CURSOR FOR cursor-specification
```

where *cursor-specification* is defined as

```
query-expression
[FOR [READ ONLY
|UPDATE [OF column-identifier [,column-identifier]...]}]
[ORDER BY sort-specification[,sort-specification]...]
```

query specification is defined as

```
query-expression UNION [ALL] query-expression
|(query-expression)
|query-specification
```

and *sort-specification* is the familiar

```
{column-identifier|unsigned-integer} [ASC|DESC]
```

UNIONs—think about those Venn diagrams—are a combination of everything in two logical tables. If you specify ALL, the system returns all rows in both tables; if you don't use ALL, you don't get any duplicates that might exist. Here are some examples of defining cursors:

```
DECLARE SunshineOwe CURSOR FOR
SELECT PayeeName, Address, AmtOwed, CheckNum
FROM AcctPayable
WHERE PayeeName = 'Sunshine Travel'
FOR UPDATE OF AmtOwed, CheckNum
```

Embedded SQL needs to be preceded by EXEC SQL statements. To declare a zip_code variable in C, you might use the following code:

```
EXEC SQL
BEGIN DECLARE SECTION;
char *zip_code;
EXEC SQL
END DECLARE SECTION;
```

Notice that both the BEGIN DECLARE SECTION and END DECLARE SECTION are prefixed by EXEC SQL. You'll also run into an alternative SQL declarative construct, INCLUDE SQLDA, which was the *de facto* standard until SQL-92.

Dynamic cursors are defined much like cursors used in static SQL, except that they need to be preceded by a PREPARE statement for the statement-identifier in the host language. We cover dynamic SQL in more depth in Chapter 3. The syntax for defining a cursor is as follows:

```
DECLARE cursor-name CURSOR FOR statement-identifier
```

Using Cursors and Embedded SQL

Once you've declared a cursor, you can open or close it, do positioned updates and deletes, insert rows, and use the FETCH statement to advance the cursor. The syntax for opening and closing a cursor is simple: OPEN cursor-name or CLOSE cursor-name.

To move the cursor to the next row, all SQL provides the FETCH statement:

```
FETCH cursor-name
INTO host-variable-reference [, host-variable-reference]...
```

Host-variable-references are identified by a leading colon:

```
EXEC SQL
DECLARE NYCust CURSOR FOR
SELECT CustName, Phone
FROM Customer
FOR UPDATE OF Phone;
/* your code */
EXEC SQL
OPEN CURSOR NYCust;
/* your code */
EXEC SQL
FETCH CURSOR NYCust INTO :CName, :NewPhone;
NewPhone = "212-456-7890"
EXEC SQL
UPDATE Customer
SET Phone = :NewPhone;
WHERE CURRENT OF NYCust;
```

As you can see, you use the WHERE CURRENT OF clause to perform positioned updates or deletes:

```
DELETE FROM table-name WHERE CURRENT OF cursor-name
```

```
UPDATE table-name
SET column-identifier = {expression|NULL}
 [column-identifier = expression|NULL}]...
WHERE CURRENT OF cursor-name
```

Unless you're a C programmer, you probably won't use embedded SQL. However, Visual Basic provides several constructs for embedding SQL within VB. For example, you can use the `Execute` statement with SQL statements or queries as follows:

```
dbobject.Execute {queryname|sqlstatement }[,options ]
querydef.Execute [ options ]
```

You can also issue an `ExecuteSQL` statement to SQL ODBC databases, provided the SQL statement doesn't return any recordsets. You use `ExecuteSQL` only to find out the number of rows affected:

```
rows = database.ExecuteSQL(sqlstatement)
```

Miscellaneous SQL Statements

SQL supports transaction processing with `COMMIT` and `ROLLBACK`. These commands let you treat a series of SQL statements as an all-or-nothing unit of action. If hardware problems or a software lock prohibits a transaction's completion, the entire transaction can be rolled back. Both `COMMIT WORK` and `ROLLBACK WORK` also close all open cursors.

Connection Statements

SQL-92 introduces three new statements, `CONNECT TO`, `DIS-CONNECT`, and `SET CONNECTION`, which theoretically support multiple connections to multiple servers. The syntax is as follows:

```
CONNECT TO {server [AS connection-name]
[USER user-identification [USING authentication]]|DEFAULT}

DISCONNECT {connection-name|ALL|CURRENT|DEFAULT}

SET CONNECTION {connection-name|DEFAULT}
```

The DBMS is supposed to maintain a state table with connection status information, such as which connection is the current one.

Diagnostics

We all know the importance of error handling. Historically, this has been one of the least standard parts of SQL, although many vendors implemented an integer SQLCODE. SQL-92 finally specifies a GET DIAGNOSTICS statement along with standard error codes. SQLCODEs are still supported, but five-character SQLSTATEs are preferred.

SQLSTATE values consist of a two-character class value followed by a three-character subclass value. The basic two-character values are defined in Table 2-1, and obviously vary depending on vendor implementation:

Table 2-1:   *Two-character SQLSTATE values*

Class	Condition
00	successful completion
01	warning
02	data not found
07	dynamic SQL error
08	connection error
0A	feature not supported
21	cardinality violation
22	data exception

Table 2-1: *(Continued)*

Class	Condition
23	constraint violation
24	invalid cursor state
25	invalid transaction state
27	triggered data change violation
28	invalid authID specification
2A	direct SQL syntax or access error
2B	dependent privileges exist
2C	invalid character set name
2D	invalid transaction termination
33	invalid SQLDA name
34	invalid cursor name
35	invalid condition number
37	dynamic SQL syntax or access error
3C	ambiguous cursor name
3D	invalid catalog name
3F	invalid schema name
40	rollback
42	syntax or access error
44	check option violation
HZ	Remote Database Access Condition

Some of the error codes will become old friends.

Summary

Whew! In our humble opinion, it's time for a breather. After all, one can only take so much SQL at a time. In this chapter, you've learned the basics of standard SQL, including the crucial CREATE, SELECT, INSERT, and UPDATE statements and the omnipresent WHERE clause. In the next chapter, we tackle two additional topics—joins and dynamic SQL—and explore the Access SQL used in Visual Basic.

References

Date, C. J. with Hugh Darwen. *A Guide to the SQL Standard*. Third Edition. Addison-Wesley Publishing Co., 1993. 414 pages. ISBN 0-201-55822-X.

McGoveran, D. and C. J. Date. *A Guide to SYBASE and SQL Server*, Addison- Wesley Publishing Co., 1992. 548 pages. ISBN 0-201-55710-X.

Melton, Jim and Alan Simon. *Understanding the New SQL: A Complete Guide*, Morgan Kauffman Publishers, 1992. 536 pages. ISBN 1-55860-245-3.

X/Open Company Limited. *Structured Query Language (SQL) CAE Specification*, 1992. 156 pages. ISBN 1-872630-58-8.

3

SQL: The Rest of the Story

In Chapter 2 you cut your teeth on the core of the SQL language. You should now recognize and be reasonably comfortable with the SELECT, CREATE, INSERT, UPDATE, and DELETE statements, as well as the WHERE clause.

In this chapter, we focus on three topics: multi-table operations such as JOINs and UNIONs, dynamic SQL, Access SQL, and ODBC SQL. We'll refer to sample data from Tables 3-1 and 3-2 in some of our examples.

Table 3-1: *Sample Contact*

Contact's Name	FirmID	Title	Phone
Bill Gates	1	CEO	206-882-8080
Philippe Kahn	2	CEO	408-438-8400

Table 3-1:   *(Continued)*

Contact's Name	FirmID	Title	Phone
Terry Cunningham	3	CEO	604-681-3435
VBGuru	1	Tech Support	206-646-5105
FaxBack	1	FaxBack	800-936-4300
Mom		Mom	111-222-3333

Table 3-2:   *Sample Firms*

FirmID	FirmName
1	Microsoft
2	Borland
3	Crystal Services
4	Q+E Software

Multi-Table SQL

In the last chapter, you probably figured out how important the SELECT statement is in the SQL world. You probably also figured out that, because of the nature of the relational model, multi-table SELECTs are a way of life. What you may not realize, though, is that there are often several ways to get the same answer. Some are single-statement solutions, some might require constructing intermediate temporary tables. The point is, if performance isn't a big issue, don't get hung up on elegance. It's more important to get the right answer at a snail's pace than to get the wrong answer fast. You can delay optimizing until later. Before we plunge into JOINs and UNIONs, let's review subqueries.

Subqueries

In Chapter 2, you saw some examples of simple subselects—also known as subqueries, nested SELECTs, or nested queries. A *subquery* is a SELECT within another SELECT. Subqueries take some practice getting used to and are governed by a few basic rules.

The first rule of subqueries is that the inner SELECT must be enclosed in parentheses. Subqueries must always appear on the right side of a comparison operator, an quantified predicate, an IN, or an EXISTS. Except for the latter, you can use the subquery to return multiple rows, but only one column. Remember also that subqueries used on the right side of a comparison operator need to return a single value (for comparison purposes).

A *subquery* is a SELECT within a SELECT. The inner SELECT—and you can have more than one—is enclosed in parentheses. Access SQL doesn't support subqueries. To perform the same thing, you nest a query within another query.

Using Table 3-2 to find out all the CEOs whose firms are California-based, you'd use a nested query:

```
SELECT Name, Phone
FROM Contacts, Firms
WHERE FirmID = (SELECT FirmID FROM Firms WHERE State =
...'CA')
AND Contacts.Title = 'CEO'
```

Correlated Subqueries

Correlated subqueries are subqueries as a subquery that can't be executed on their own. With normal nested queries, the innermost query is evaluated first and the results are passed to the outer query. In a correlated subquery, however, the evaluation of the inner query is dependent on the outer query, and the inner query is evaluated over and over with values from each row in the outer table.

Correlated subqueries are constructed with an EXISTS or NOT EXISTS. You need a correlated subquery when the subquery depends on the value of a column in a row of an outer query. Imagine you had another table, called Branches. You could use a correlated subquery to find firms with both headquarters and branches in a given city.

```
SELECT FirmID FROM Firms
WHERE EXISTS
(SELECT * FROM Branches
WHERE Branches.City = Firms.City)
```

Self-joins, which are covered in the next section, are a special case of a correlated subquery.

A *correlated subquery* is a subquery with an EXISTS or NOT EXISTS.

Join Operations

You've already seen some joins in the last chapter. In its most general terms, a *join* is simply a multi-table operation. Unfortunately, vendors use the terms JOIN, UNION, and INTERSECT to mean different things. We'll follow the usage prescribed by SQL-92.

Cartesian Products: MegaJoins

*Cartesian product*s are the biggest joins you can have, since they result in a set of rows that is a concatenation of every row from one table with every row from another (or the same) table. In other words, if one table has 50 rows, and the other one has 1000 rows, the Cartesian product will result in 50*1000 rows—and, generally, not much meaningful information. In SQL-92, Cartesian products are called *cross joins* and can be created with a syntax such as

```
SELECT * FROM Table1 CROSS JOIN Table2
```

For example, the Bill Gates row in Table 3-1 would combine with all four rows from Table 3-2, producing four rows. So would each of the other rows in Table 3-1 producing Table 3-3.

Table 3-3:

<------------------from table 1------------------>				<------from table 1------>	
Bill Gates	1	CEO	206-882-8080	1	Microsoft
Bill Gates	1	CEO	206-882-8080	2	Borland
Bill Gates	1	CEO	206-882-8080	3	Crystal Services
Bill Gates	1	CEO	206-882-8080	4	Q+E Software
Philippe Kahn	2	CEO	408-438-8400	1	Microsoft
etc.					

Cartesian joins, as you can see, generate useless result sets and are to be avoided. In GUI query builders, you can get a Cartesian product result set by joining two tables that don't have a common column.

Natural Joins

Natural joins, unlike Cartesian products, tend to be quite useful and are also fairly intuitive. Natural joins basically combine two tables on a common column and don't include a double copy of the common column in the result set. In most DBMSs, the common column doesn't have to have the same name, but it must have the same data type.

An *equijoin* is a natural join with duplicate copies of the common column. The term *equijoin*, by the way, comes from the implicit comparison operator of equality. When other comparison operators are used, you have *theta joins*.

A natural join might yield the results in Table 3-4, from Tables 3-1 and 3-2.

Table 3-4:

Name	FirmID	Title	Phone	FirmName
Bill Gates	1	CEO	206-882-8080	Microsoft
Philippe Kahn	2	CEO	408-438-8400	Borland
Terry Cunningham	3	CEO	604-681-3435	Crystal Services
VBGuru	1	Tech Support	206-646-5105	Microsoft
FaxBack	1	FaxBack	800-936-4300	Microsoft

Natural joins combine records from two tables whenever there are matching values in a field common to both tables. In this example, an equijoin would have resulted in two identical columns with FirmID.

The default natural join is an *inner*, as opposed to *outer* join. The syntax for *join-table-expression* is

```
table-reference CROSS JOIN table-reference
|table-reference [NATURAL] [join type] JOIN table-
...reference
[ON conditional-expression|USING (column-list)]
|(join-table-expression)
```

where *join-type* can be

```
[INNER]
|LEFT [OUTER]
|RIGHT [OUTER]
```

|FULL [OUTER]
|UNION

Outer joins differ from inner joins by including rows that *don't*
match the join condition. For example, to select all Contacts (even
those that don't have corresponding Firms) from Table 3-1, you'd
do a LEFT JOIN of Contacts and Firms, resulting in Table 3-5.

Table 3-5:

Name	FirmID	Title	Phone	FirmName
Bill Gates	1	CEO	206-882-8080	Microsoft
Philippe Kahn	2	CEO	408-438-8400	Borland
Terry Cunningham	3	CEO	604-681-3435	Crystal Services
VBGuru	1	Tech Support	206-646-5105	Microsoft
FaxBack	1	FaxBack	800-936-4300	Microsoft
Mom		Mom	111-222-3333	

To select all Firms (even if some don't have corresponding
Contacts) from Table 3-2, you'd perform a RIGHT JOIN, resulting
in Table 3-6.

Table 3-6:

Name	FirmID	Title	Phone	FirmName
Bill Gates	1	CEO	206-882-8080	Microsoft
Philippe Kahn	2	CEO	408-438-8400	Borland
Terry Cunningham	3	CEO	604-681-3435	Crystal Services
VBGuru	1	Tech Support	206-646-5105	Microsoft
FaxBack	1	FaxBack	800-936-4300	Microsoft
	4			Q+E Software

LEFT JOINs include all of the records from the first (left-hand) columns of two tables, even if there aren't any matching values for records in the second (right-hand) table. RIGHT JOINs are the opposite. Bet you can guess what you'd get with a FULL OUTER JOIN, eh?

Joins can be qualified pretty much like SELECTs, by specifying columns to include in the output, search conditions, WHERE clauses, and so on.

Self-Joins

Many DBMSs support self-joins, which are useful for certain kinds of queries. A *self-join* is logically equivalent to joining two separate tables with identical structures and data. For example, you might have a table with employees and committees they're assigned to, and you want to know exactly which employees were assigned to both committee1 and committee2. You can't construct a single-table SELECT that returns the right answer, since single-table SELECTs are limited to looking at one record at a time. A self-join emulates two related queries so that the engine can look at two records at a time.

Another way to look at a self-join is when the values of your WHERE need to be derived from values in the table containing the WHERE. If you have an invoice table, you might want to find all the invoices that are higher valued than Acme Manufacturing's. Or you might want to find a list of all the suppliers that are in the same city as Acme Manufacturing.

Joins with the Access Engine

When you connect to an SQL database using VB's ODBC connection, you can use the Access engine's INNER and OUTER JOINs. The syntax for a natural join is as follows:

```
table1 INNER JOIN table2
ON table1.field1 = table2.field2
```

Following are two examples that use Access SQL. Note that field names with spaces must have brackets around them. In the first example, PubID won't appear in the result set, since it isn't included in the SELECT column-list. The second example creates two equijoins: one between the Order Details and Orders tables, and another between the Orders and Employees tables. This kind of complex JOIN syntax is part of the overhead of using the relational model and is necessary to accommodate the fact that the Employees table doesn't contain sales data and the Order Details table doesn't contain employee data. The result would be a list of employees and their total sales.

```
SELECT Title, [Name]
FROM Titles, Publishers,
Titles INNER JOIN Publishers
ON Titles.PubID = Publishers.PubID

SELECT DISTINCTROW
Sum([Unit Price] * [Quantity]) AS [Sales],
[First Name] & " " & [Last Name] AS [Name]
FROM [Order Details], Orders, Employees,
Orders INNER JOIN [Order Details]
ON Orders.[Order ID] = [Order Details].[Order ID],
Employees INNER JOIN Orders
ON Employees.[Employee ID] = Orders.[Employee ID]
GROUP BY [First Name] & " " & [Last Name]
```

In the following examples, Access' LEFT JOIN and RIGHT JOIN are part of a FROM clause:

```
table1 LEFT JOIN table2
ON table1.field1 = table2.field2
```

```
table1 RIGHT JOIN table2
ON table1.field1 = table2.field2
```

Finally, a LEFT JOIN could be used to select all departments, including those with no employees:

```
SELECT [Department Name], [First Name] & " " & [Last Name]
...AS Name
FROM Departments, Employees,
Departments LEFT JOIN Employees
ON Departments.[Department ID] = Employees.[Department ID]
ORDER BY [Department Name]
```

Union, Difference, and Intersection Operations

These three operations are based on the union, difference (subtraction), and intersection operations from set theory, and they all require that the tables being operated on have the same degree, that is, number of columns, with corresponding data types. (An OUTER UNION, which does permit a union of tables of different degrees, is referred to as a UNION JOIN.)

Let's start with the union by comparing it to a join. It may be useful to think of a JOIN as a method for combining tables horizontally— welding columns from one (or more) tables onto the end of the first one. A union, on the other hand, is more concerned with combining tables vertically. The basic syntax for the SQL-92 UNION statement is

```
table-expression {UNION|EXCEPT} [ALL]
[CORRESPONDING [BY (column-list)]] table-term
```

where ALL permits duplicate rows. The union operation is useful when you have two tables with the same structure. The union can happen when you deliberately partition a large table for performance reasons or during replication operations. UNION is also useful when you want to combine data you've split data by region or division, for example.

Access SQL does not support the UNION statement.

Intersection and *difference* are complementary operations and together should return the same rows as a UNION. An intersection is essentially a special case of a natural join, where the comparison is made on all columns, returning entire rows that are common to two tables. A difference operation (EXCEPT), returns rows that aren't the same. Syntax for an intersection is similar to that for a union.

```
table-term INTERSECT [ALL]
[CORRESPONDING [BY (column-list)]] table-primary
```

Access SQL currently does not support union, difference, or intersect operations.

Codd's Eight Relational Operations

E. F. Codd's eight relational operations (see Figure 3-1), sometimes referred to as single-set and binary relational operations, are just another way of talking about SELECTs, JOINs, and so on. For the record, Codd's eight operations are

- select

- project

- product

- join

- union

- intersection

- difference

- division

Figure 3-1: *The Eight Basic Relational Operations*

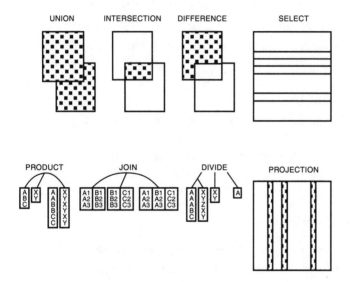

The first two, select and project, are single-set operations; the remaining operations are all binary operations. A *projection* is a subset of a table with only some of the columns. In contrast, *selection* is a row subset. The only one of Codd's relational operations not supported by SQL-92 is relational division. And that's okay with most folks, who are usually hard-pressed to come up with a situation when they'd need a division anyway. In relational division, a divisor and a dividend table results only in column values (quotient) in one table for which there are other matching column values corresponding to every row in the other table.

Dynamic SQL

Dynamic SQL, as mentioned in Chapter 2, is a special form of SQL that uses either host language data structures or a DBMS-maintained SQL descriptor area to accommodate data, such as column or table names, whose contents are not known at compile time. Think of dynamic SQL as a step beyond embedded SQL, where the SQL is precompiled.

Prior to SQL-92, most implementations of dynamic SQL used the SQLDA structure approach, where dynamic information was stored in host language data structures. Actual data was stored in a buffer and accessed by a pointer, if the language supported pointers. The following is pseudocode for SQL-89 style dynamic SQL:

```
DECLARE the SQL descriptor area structure
Use SQLCODE to return status information
PREPARE the dynamic SQL statement
If no cursor is needed, issue an EXECUTE IMMEDIATE
Otherwise, DECLARE a cursor
Allocate a descriptor (SQLDA) for the query
DESCRIBE host (bind) variables into the bind SQLDA
OPEN the cursor using the bind SQLDA
DESCRIBE the SELECT list into the select SQLDA instance
FETCH rows using the output descriptor until finished
CLOSE the cursor
```

The SQL descriptor area is a data structure that holds information regarding either the host variables for items in a SELECT list or bind variables. The SQLDA can be used for input and output, and for metadata or data. The problem with the SQLDA approach is that different vendors have come up with incompatible SQLDA structures. A typical SQLDA has both fixed and variable areas with internal information about how the SQLDA itself is organized, and external information about the data it will be storing. Such SQLDAs are sometimes referred to as application SQLDAs, since they are application-specific.

The SQL-92 standard replaces the application-oriented SQLDA approach with a *system* SQLDA, replaces SQLCODE with SQLSTATE, and adds a handful of descriptor statements. A typical flow of dynamic SQL based on SQL-92 is as follows:

```
Issue an ALLOCATE DESCRIPTOR
Use SQLSTATE to return status information
PREPARE the dynamic SQL statement
Use DESCRIBE INPUT to pass the SQL string based on a
...descriptor area
If no cursor is needed, issue an EXECUTE IMMEDIATE
Use DESCRIBE (or DESCRIBE OUTPUT) based on an output
...descriptor area
Otherwise, DECLARE a cursor
OPEN the cursor
FETCH rows using host variables or the output descriptor
...until finished
Use GET DESCRIPTOR and SET DESCRIPTOR as needed
CLOSE the cursor
DEALLOCATE the descriptor
```

> In SQL-92, SQLSTATE is in, SQLCODE is out as the status parameter.

Since the descriptor area is the key to using dynamic SQL, it bears describing. Depending on the situation, each item descriptor area may describe a selected column, an input value, or an output value. Except during a DESCRIBE, the item descriptor area contains a value as well as fields that describe the value's attributes, such as its data type, length, and whether it can contain a NULL. Following is the syntax for GET DESCRIPTOR:

```
GET DESCRIPTOR descriptor-name get-descriptor information
```

where *get-descriptor information* is defined as

```
embedded -variable-name-1 = COUNT
|VALUE item-number get-item-info [,get-item-info]...
```

get-item-info is

```
embedded-variable-name-2 = field-name
```

and field-name is

```
TYPE|LENGTH|PRECISION|SCALE|NULLABLE|INDICATOR|DATA
|NAME|UNNAMED|RETURNED_LENGTH
```

Other than descriptor areas, dynamic SQL is a lot like embedded SQL. You work with cursors and perform queries, deletes, and updates.

Normally, you won't have to get involved directly with either SQL-89 or SQL-92 dynamic SQL unless you need to write some C routines. You'll be able to embed your SQL into VB and let Access SQL talk to the ODBC drivers or pass through your SQL directly to the host DBMS. So it's time to focus more on Access SQL and how it differs from the SQL standard.

Access SQL

We've devoted a fair number of pages to SQL. At this point, you're like a non-native who may speak grammatically perfect English, but who needs to spice it with regional dialect, street English, or even rap. That means knowing Access SQL, SQL Server's Transact-SQL, and how ODBC handles SQL.

ANSI SQL and Access SQL

Access SQL seems to have aimed for SQL-89, not SQL-92, compliance, and it's not even SQL-89 compliant. There are some significant differences between ANSI SQL and Access SQL you should know about, such as differences in data types, shown in Table 3-7.

Table 3-7:   *Differences Between Access SQL and ANSI SQL Data Types*

Microsoft Access SQL	ANSI SQL
BINARY	none
BYTE	none
CURRENCY	none
DATETIME	TIMESTAMP
DOUBLE	FLOAT
LONG	INT, INTEGER
LONGBINARY	none
LONGTEXT	VARCHAR, CHARACTER VARYING
SHORT	SMALLINT
SINGLE	REAL
TEXT	CHAR, CHARACTER
none	DATE
none	TIME
none	INTERVAL
none	BIT
none	BIT VARYING
none	NUMERIC
none	DECIMAL
none	DOUBLE PRECISION

Then there's the entire area of DDL, SQL's Data Definition Language. Access SQL simply doesn't have a command-line DDL; it uses a graphical paradigm instead. In other words, don't waste any time trying to perform an SQL `CREATE TABLE` or `ALTER TABLE` from Access or Visual Basic. And, although Access supports referential integrity, domain and other constraint-setting, those capabilities aren't available from Visual Basic or through ODBC.

Access SQL also deviates significantly from the SQL standard in that it has no subqueries, no UNION command, and no `GRANT` or `REVOKE` command. That is, Access SQL doesn't support subqueries or `UNION`s. With Access SQL, you can nest multiple queries, but you can't do subselects directly. Access SQL uses its own security scheme in lieu of the standard SQL `GRANT` and `REVOKE` commands.

Another significant difference is that the syntax for `INSERT` in Access SQL doesn't use the `VALUES` keyword:

```
INSERT INTO table-name (column-name-list) [in-
...clause][select-statement]
```

where the *in-clause* is

```
IN database-name [connect-string]
```

Finally, Access SQL uses non-standard wildcards with LIKE. Instead of using the "_" (single character) and "%" (zero or more matching characters) borrowed from Unix, Access SQL uses the "?" and "*" symbols, which are more familiar to DOS denizens, and supports user-defined *charlist* symbols for custom pattern matching.

Crosstabs and Extra Functions

Access, like all other DBMSs, offers a wealth of non-SQL extensions. For example, Access SQL adds `DISTINCTROW` as an extra option in addition to the `SELECT` statement's `ALL` or `DISTINCT`. Access SQL also has a very useful `TRANSFORM` statement that makes it easy to output crosstabs. Its syntax is:

```
TRANSFORM function-reference select statement PIVOT
...column-name
```

The function-reference argument is an aggregate function that provides the data for pivot column. The mandatory SELECT statement specifies the fields used as row headings and a GROUP BY clause that specifies row grouping. It can also have other clauses, such as WHERE, that specify additional selection or sorting criteria.

The column-name associated with PIVOT refers to the field, column, or expression you want to pivot (rotate) to form the column headings. When you pivot a field, the unique values of pivot column become columns. For example, by pivoting the sales figures on the month of the sale you get a crosstab with twelve columns containing monthly data.

Access SQL also supports more than the bare minimum aggregate functions (SUM, AVG, COUNT, MIN, and MAX), notably adding StDev and VarP, and lets you define your own.

Some additional Access SQL reserved words include LEFT, LEVEL, OPTION, OWNERACCESS, PARAMETERS, PROCEDURE, RIGHT, TABLEID, and VALUE.

Sometimes you wonder why we have standards at all. But then, these kinds of deviations from standard SQL are what we get paid for, right?

There are two more dialects of SQL you'll probably want to know— SQL Server's Transact-SQL and the SQL you're going to run into with ODBC.

SQL Server

Chances are pretty good you'll run into SQL Server sooner or later, which is why we devote some ink explicitly to it, as opposed to all the other SQL DBMSs out there. There are several compelling reasons to be familiar with SQL Server. One, it's a Microsoft product that's available from Microsoft both under OS/2 and NT. Second, you can also get NetWare NLM, Unix, and VMS versions of it from Sybase. Third, Visual Basic ships with an ODBC driver for SQL Server. Finally, Microsoft also sells a Programmer's Toolkit for SQL Server, usually referred to as VBSQL, which gives Visual Basic programmers access to a hefty subset of SQL Server's DB-Library API. We cover VBSQL in more depth in Chapter 10.

Sybase and Microsoft's SQL Server ship with a version of SQL called Transact-SQL. There are several areas where SQL Server deviates from the SQL standard. One well-known area is referential integrity. SQL Server 4.x doesn't support *declarative* referential integrity, where referential integrity is built into CREATE and related statements. Instead, it maintains referential integrity through user-defined triggers. (Sybase's newest version of SQL Server, Sybase System 10, *does* support declarative referential integrity.)

Sybase also pioneered the notion of stored procedures, another extension to SQL that has been adopted by many other vendors, including Oracle. Stored procedures aren't part of Access SQL, at least not yet.

Transact-SQL

Transact-SQL, like most SQLs, includes flow-of-control statements. These looping and branching statements borrowed from the procedural heritage of 3GLs are the foundation of most stored procedures.

Transact-SQL includes over a hundred built-in functions, including a rich variety of string manipulation functions, functions for date/time processing, and other functions associated with data type conversion. Transact-SQL has added options for COMPUTE, FOR BROWSE, and HOLDLOCK clauses to its SELECT statement.

SQL Server also lets users define their own datatypes (as Access Basic does), as well as create rules and defaults.

Additional Transact-SQL commands you'll want to explore if you're accessing SQL Server data include SET, UPDATE STATISTICS, and RAISERROR. Finally, you'll want to get familiar with SQL Server's system tables and the built-in stored procedures with sp_help[objectname].

ODBC

ODBC, which stands for Open Database Connectivity, is a specification for database access that's based on SQL. However, ODBC isn't synonymous with SQL. Since ODBC is rapidly becoming a fact of Windows life, you're going to want to know something about ODBC drivers in general, as well as how they fit into the SQL picture.

There are two kinds of ODBC drivers: single-tier, where the driver processes both ODBC calls and SQL statements, and multiple-tier, where the driver processes ODB0C calls (see Figure 3-2) and passes SQL statements to the data source. The ODBC 1.0 specification defines conformance levels for drivers in two areas: the ODBC API and the ODBC SQL grammar.

API Conformance Levels   The ODBC API defines a set of core functions that correspond to the functions in the X/Open and SQL Access Group Call Level Interface specification. ODBC also defines two extended sets of functionality, Level 1 and Level 2. The following list summarizes the functionality included in each conformance level.

Figure 3-2: *How ODBC Works*

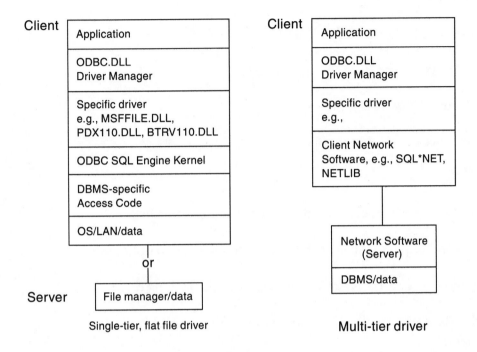

Core API

- Allocate and free environment, connection, and statement handles

- Connect to data sources

- Use multiple statements on a connection

- Prepare and execute SQL statements

- Execute SQL statements immediately

- Assign storage for parameters in an SQL statement and result columns

- Retrieve data from a result set

- Retrieve information about a result set

- Commit or roll back transactions

- Retrieve error information

Level 1 API

- Connect to data sources with driver-specific dialog boxes

- Set and inquire values of statement and connection options

- Send part or all of a parameter value (useful for long data)

- Retrieve part or all of a result column value (useful for long data)

- Retrieve catalog information (columns, special columns, statistics, and tables)

- Retrieve information about driver and data source capabilities, such as supported data types, scalar functions, and ODBC functions

Level 2 API

- Browse available connections and list available data sources

- Send arrays of parameter values. Retrieve arrays of result column values

- Retrieve the number of parameters and describe individual parameters

- Use a scrollable cursor

- Retrieve the native form of an SQL statement

- Retrieve catalog information (privileges, keys, and procedures)

- Call a translation DLL

So, although the ODBC API is inextricably related to SQL, the ODBC specification and ODBC drivers both have separate compliance levels that are more closely related to the SQL language we've been exploring the last two chapters.

SQL Conformance Levels   In addition to the ODBC API, the ODBC 1.0 spec defines a core grammar that corresponds to the X/Open and SQL Access Group CAE SQL draft specification (1991). ODBC also defines a minimum grammar, to meet a basic level of ODBC conformance, and an extended grammar, to provide for common DBMS extensions to SQL:

Minimum SQL Grammar
    CREATE TABLE and DROP TABLE
    Rudimentary SELECT
    INSERT
    UPDATE SEARCHED
    DELETE SEARCHED
    Expressions: simples ones like A B + C
    Data types: CHAR

Core SQL Grammar
  ALTER TABLE

  CREATE INDEX and DROP INDEX

  CREATE VIEW and DROP VIEW

  GRANT and REVOKE

  Full SELECT

  Positioned UPDATE and positioned DELETE

  Expressions: subquery, set functions such as SUM and MIN

  Data types: VARCHAR, DECIMAL, NUMERIC, SMALLINT, INTEGER, REAL, FLOAT, DOUBLE PRECISION.

Extended SQL Grammar
  OUTER JOIN

  Expressions: scalar functions such as SUBSTRING and ABS, date, time, and time stamp literals

  Data types: LONG VARCHAR, BIT, TINYINT, BIGINT, BINARY, VARBINARY, LONG VARBINARY, DATE, TIME, TIMESTAMP

  Batch SQL statements

  Procedure calls

Having an ODBC driver doesn't mean much unless you know what level SQL support you're getting. You don't have to worry about subselects and JOINs with ODBC drivers that only support the minimum SQL grammar.

The ODBC specification is being revised as an enhanced version 2.0. ODBC 2.0 defines both better single tier drivers and better scrollable cursor support. Single tier drivers under ODBC 1.0 have been plagued by disappointing performances.

Unless you're a C programmer or need to write your own ODBC driver to connect a VB application to some non-standard data source, you generally won't work directly with ODBC functions. That's the role of the ODBC driver that comes with ODBC clients like VB. They map SQL statements from your application program into the target DBMS's SQL. What your application will have to handle is—surprise—error messages from the server.

Summary

In this chapter, we've probed some of the more advanced multi-table SQL statements and described embedded and dynamic SQL. You've also seen how extensions are used to modify different vendors' SQLs and how different Access SQL is from standard SQL. Finally, you've seen a bit of the architectural underpinnings of ODBC.

Part II
Making the Connection

4

Client/Server Application Development

In this chapter, we describe some of the common programming issues you will face in developing database applications. Most of these issues aren't specific to Visual Basic—they're associated with any multiuser application, with client/server architecture, and with database access and transaction processing in general.

We start by looking at the basic architectural and design issues you'll face at the beginning of almost any client/server project. We focus on different approaches needed for OLTP and decision support applications and talk about locking and concurrency. Finally, we give you some hints you can use to help manage your project development from its inception.

Let's start by thinking about client/server applications and what they mean to a programmer.

Client/Server Architecture

Client/server is term that refers to a division of work, and it doesn't have to be database work. You've undoubtedly run into printer servers and Fax servers, not to speak of PC LAN file servers.

The client/server world divides players into clients, who request services, and servers, who provide them. It's essentially a master/slave relationship, since the client is really in control.

The terms *client* and *server* are sometimes used to refer to physical computer systems. Your PC would be a client, and the superserver, mini, or mainframe down the hall or across the country would be a server. Sometimes though, clients and servers refer to the operating system *processes* running on the client or server computer. Client and server processes typically run on separate physical computers, but they don't have to.

Your VB application will be a client, so one of your main tasks will be managing requests for services. Your other major task will be handling the user interface. As a VB programmer, you're already familiar with designing forms consistent with the Windows "look and feel," so you've probably got the UI stuff under your belt already. However, if you're at all interested in the Microsoft "party line" and haven't explored it yet, take a few minutes to check out the VB Pro Visual Design Guide. It's a sort of graphical style sheet.

The minimal client/server application using VB as the client would access a local .MDB database managed by the Access Engine. Some people might say that's stretching it, since VB and the Access Engine ship in the same box. Without stopping to pick nits, let's just say you can make an argument for VB applications that interact with Access data as being client/server, whether the Access database is local or shared.

Data Warehouse

A increasingly popular architecture is what is loosely called a *data warehouse*, a copy of operational data from the corporate database. If you give managers access to relatively recent data, they can browse through it, performing slice-and-dice operations and complex joins that might bring an operational database to its knees. But most decision-making doesn't have to be based on up-to-the minute data. New copies of the database can will have to be made periodically, typically during a night-time or weekend batch process. These warehouse copies are sometimes called *replicas*, *extracts*, or *snapshots* and may be copies of an entire operational database or merely a subset of it.

Depending on the quantity of data involved, data warehouses can be on individual PCs or on departmental database servers. In the latter case, you might have the corporate database on a mainframe and a data warehouse on a Unix workstation or PC superserver. The data warehouse DBMS might be SQL Server, Oracle, or Access (see Figure 4-1). Managers might use a custom decision support system—written in VB, of course—or access the warehouse data directly from within a spreadsheet or end-user query tool like Gupta's Quest, Microsoft's Query, or PowerViewer.

Data warehouses can store selected data from multiple operational databases, consolidated into a relatively accessible format. For example, data might be joined on-line from multiple tables in the operational database for storage as a single record in the warehouse. Or you might simply create a data warehouse that associates disparate data physically when it is accessed. Another possibility is to perform calculations with the operational data and physically

Figure 4-1: *Sample data warehouse architecture. Because it involves three levels (PC, data warehouse server, and corporate database) this client/server architecture is sometimes called a three-tier model*

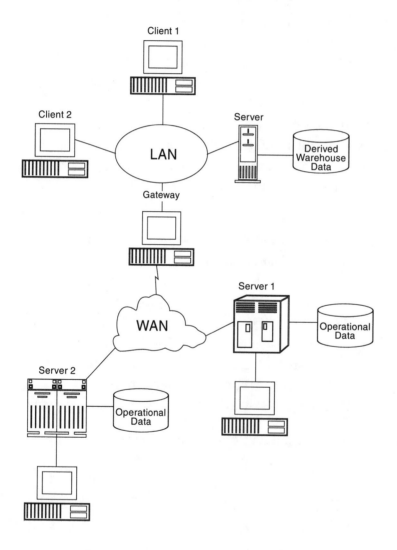

store the results in the data warehouse, so that decision-support queries asking for totals can be performed quickly. In other words, a data warehouse doesn't have to mirror the design of the operational databases. You can have tables that combine data from several sources. You can use different data types and create indexes that work for the new design. You can also create column names and/or aliases that are meaningful and easily recognized by the end users.

Another point to keep in mind is that with the data warehouse model, the data is generally being used in read-only mode, so you don't have to worry about transaction processing issues like commits and rollbacks, recovery logs, or locks. The data warehouse model is best suited for decision support and is especially useful for consolidating data from distributed systems, including heterogeneous databases.

Distributed Databases

Distributed database means different things to different people. For starters, you can distribute both data and processing. If you're talking distributed data, you might simply mean a database or a single database table that spans several physical disks or servers. You might have the data distributed—fragmented, if you will—either horizontally or vertically, but all under the control of a single vendor's DBMS. The way the data is distributed might reflect local processing needs, historical evolution, or political realities. Distributed data is not fun to work with because of synchronization problems and/or access costs. On the other hand, you might mean data distributed among *heterogeneous* database servers. It's not uncommon for organizations to have accounting data on the mainframe, manufacturing on a mini, and lots of tactical data on local PCs.

Your challenge will be to understand the status quo and then either work with it or build an easier, more centralized solution. Understanding the status quo means performing an inventory not only of existing data, but also of existing applications and their associated business rules.

Applications can also be distributed, and, again, there are several levels of spreading out the application logic and processing (see Figure 4-2). At one end are mainframe applications, where all processing is done on the mainframe and the terminal is simply a vehicle for data entry. At the other extreme are applications, like most of the ones you'll be building, where display and significant data manipulation are accomplished on local PCs (see Figure 4-3).

Figure 4-2: *Traditional processing models use terminals only for display. Client/server models harness processing power at the workstations.*

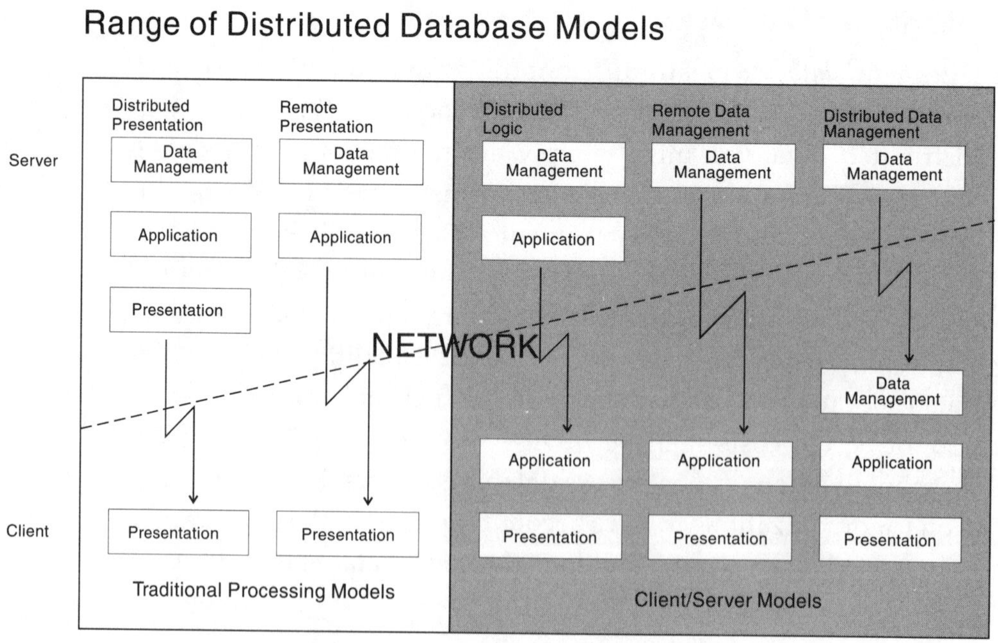

Range of Distributed Database Models

Source: The Gartner Group

Figure 4-3: *Distributed logic occurs when the logic of the application is split across the network. The design goal of distributed logic applications is to minimize messages between components. The "stacks" of network protocols represent the OSI 7-layer model.*

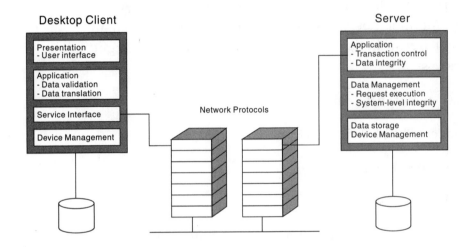

On-Line Transaction Processing and Decision Support

On-line transaction processing, or OLTP, systems are typically positioned on the opposite end of the spectrum as decision support systems. OLTP invokes images of heads-down data entry and hundreds—or even thousands—of transactions per second. In reality, there aren't many such systems worldwide. Airlines and large financial institutions have heavy OLTP needs, but many organizations have real-time transaction processing needs more on the order of a few dozen or hundred transactions per hour. Do you call those systems OLTP? Hard to say.

What differentiates OLTP from decision-support systems is the need for on-line data access. Most decision support is done off-line with "old" data. That's not the case with OLTP systems. OLTP systems need to be live and are considered mission critical, line-of-business applications.

A *transaction* is a series of operations that are treated as a single unit of work, so that if any part of the transaction fails, the entire transaction is aborted. Financial transactions using an ATM (Automatic Teller Machine, not Asynchronous Transfer Mode) are classic examples of transactions. A complete ATM transaction might involve these steps:

- User submits bank card

- Back card identified by ATM

- User types in code

- ATM validates code

- User selects type of transaction, e.g. cash withdrawal

- User types in amount

- ATM checks quantity against balance and/or authorized maximum

- ATM debits account

- ATM dispenses cash

Banks tend to view the entire procedure as a single unit of work. If you get the cash, they want to make sure your account is debited. On the other hand, you have a vested interest in the idea of a transaction, too. After all, you want to make sure that your account doesn't get debited if there aren't any more $20s in the cash hopper.

Transactions are supposed to be atomic, consistent, isolated, and durable. Hence the mnemonic acronym ACID.

Atomicity   *Atomicity* is the all-or-nothing characteristic of transactions. From a code point of view, transactions are usually wrapped within BEGIN TRANSACTION and END TRANSACTION statements. (In VB, it's BeginTrans and CommitTrans, and the Transactions property needs to be set to True or otherwise support transaction processing.) If the transaction succeeds, the changes are posted, or *committed*, to the database. If the transaction fails, changes to the database are rolled back. Transactions remain open until the application or user issues what amounts to a COMMIT or ROLLBACK.

Consistency   *Consistency* is the requirement that the application move the database from one state of consistency to another state of consistency. In other words, when a transaction is committed, the application must ensure that *all* the data affected is now in a consistent state. Consistency within a transaction is maintained by application-supplied validation routines. In long transactions, programmers may establish checkpoints that establish points of consistency to which the database can be rolled back if necessary.

Isolation   *Isolation* is the requirement that the behavior of a transaction not be affected by other transactions. Transactions should execute in isolation from other transactions such that once a transaction is initiated, its effects will be the same irrespective of other actions on the database. In other words, concurrent transactions behave as if they were executed serially.

Many database servers provide selectable levels of transaction isolation, ranging from *read uncommitted* or *dirty read*, which allows other transactions to read changes to the database as they're made, even before they're committed or rolled back, to *serializable*, the strictest isolation level, which gives the illusion that all transactions are executed in a serial fashion. The SQL-92 standard prescribes four levels of isolation: READ UNCOMMITTED, READ COMMITTED, REPEATABLE READ, and SERIALIZABLE.

Cursor stability is an intermediate isolation level, where in only the current row pointed at by the cursor is locked. The lock is released on non-updated rows as the cursor scrolls forward or backward. Locking, by the way, is something you need to learn about whether you're working with OLTP or decision-support applications. Most DBMSs support a range of locking granularity, such as field, record, page, file, and database, but vary in their support for programmer overrides. Locking is needed because of potential problems in situations such as these:

- You and I want to read the same record.

- You and I want to modify the same record.

- I am reading a record and you are modifying it.

- My application has read a group of records. Now I want to modify one of them. Has anyone changed it?

- I want to sum all the rows in a table, and you want to modify one.

Durability   *Durability* is the requirement that, once a transaction is committed, its effects are permanent and durable. This requires a thoughtful backup policy.

Transactions should pass the ACID test for atomicity, consistency, isolation, and durability. Transactions, or discrete units of work, should generally be as small as logically possible to avoid unnecessary locking.

VB supports transaction processing with the three statements:

```
BeginTrans
CommitTrans
Rollback
```

VB Development

So far, we've talked about broad-brush development issues you'll face at the beginning of a project—whether the application targets decision support or on-line transaction processing and whether the architecture will use a data warehouse-three-tier scheme or not. Now let's address client/server development issues at a more granular level. You're likely to encounter hard decisions that range from project management to performance and tuning. Let's tackle them in the order in which you're likely to run into them.

Naming Conventions

You've probably developed your own arsenal of standards and standard operating procedures (SOPs). We suggest you adopt naming conventions for your VB programs and that you use version control software for any team projects. Table 1 is based on the naming conventions used by Microsoft Consulting Services (MCS) for controls, but modified by Microsoft's VB and VBA teams.

Table 4-1: *Recommended control names*

Prefix	Control Type Description
ani	Animation button
bed	Pen Bedit
cbo	Combobox and dropdown Listbox
chk	Checkbox
clp	Picture Clip
cmd	Command Button

Table 4-1:   *(Continued)*

Prefix	Control Type Description
com	Communications
ctr	Control (used when the specific type is unknown)
dat	Data Control
db	ODBC Database
dir	Dir List Box
dlg	Visual Basic Pro Common Dialog
drv	Drive List Box
ds	ODBC Dynaset
fil	File List Box
frm	Form
fra	Frame
gau	Gauge
gpb	Group Push Button
gra	Graph
grd	Grid
hed	Pen Hedit
hsb	Horizontal Scroll Bar
img	Image
ink	Pen Ink
key	Keyboard key status
lbl	Label
lin	Line
lst	Listbox
mpm	MAPI Message
mps	MAPI Session
mci	MCI
mdi	MDI Child Form
mnu	Menu
opt	Option Button
ole	OLE
out	Outline
pic	Picture
pnl	3d Panel
rpt	Report

Table 4-1:   *(Continued)*

Prefix	Control Type Description
shp	Shape
spn	Spin Control
txt	Text/Edit Box
tmr	Timer
vsb	Vertical Scroll Bar

Menus provide a special challenge, since menu handlers can be so numerous. MCS recommends that menu prefixes extend beyond the initial Mnu label by adding an additional (upper case) character prefix for each level of nesting, with the final menu caption being spelled out at the end of the name string. When there is ambiguity caused by character duplications, such as a menu having both main Format and File menus, use an additional (lower-case) character to differentiate the items. Here are some examples:

Help.Contents	mnuHContents
File.Open	mnuFiOpen
Format.Character	mnuFoCharacter
File.Send.Fax	mnuFSFax
File.Send.Email	mnuFSEmail

Variables and Routines   Variable and function names have the structure

```
<prefix><body><qualifier><suffix>
```

where the prefix describes the use and the scope of the variable, as in iGetRecordNext and sGetNameFirst. The qualifier is used to denote standard derivatives of a base variable or function. The suffix is the optional Visual Basic type char, such as, $, %, or #.

MCS recommends that you use prefix naming consistent with variable/function naming conventions based on Hungarian C, but they tend to reflect a bias towards C/C++ programming. Prefixes that seem to be more common in the VB community are indicated in parentheses. These are listed in Table 4-2.

Table 4-2: *Recommended variable prefixes à la Hungarian C*

Prefix	Description
b (bln)	Boolean (vb type = %)
c (cur)	Currency - 64 bits (vb type = @)
d (dbl)	Double - 64 bit signed quantity (vb type = #)
db	Database
ds	Dynaset
dt (dat)	Date+Time (vb type = variant)
err	Error
f	Float/Single - 32 bit signed floating point (vb type = !)
h	Handle (vb type = %)
i	Index (vb type = %)
l (lng)	Long - 32 bit signed quantity (vb type = &)
n (int)	Integer (sizeless, counter) (vb type = %)
obj	Object
s (str)	String (vb type = $)
sng	Single
u	Unsigned - 16 bit unsigned quantity (must use &)
ul	Unsigned Long - 32 bit unsigned quantity (must use #)
udt	User defined type
vnt	Variant
w	Word - 16 bit signed quantity (vb type = %)
a	Array
	User defined type
g	Global
m	Local to module or form
st	Static variable
v	Variable passed by value (local to a routine)
r	Variable passed by reference (local to a routine)

The body of variable and routine names should use mixed case and should be as long as needed to describe their purpose. Function names should also begin with a verb, such as InitNameArray or CloseDialog, and should include qualifiers, as in sGetNameFirst, sGetNameLast, that make the logic and structure of the application easier to understand. Here are some common qualifiers:

First	First element of a set
Last	Last element of a set
Next	Next element in a set
Prev	Previous element in a set
Cur	Current element in a set
Min	Minimum value in a set
Max	Maximum value in a set
Save	Used to preserve another variable
Tmp	A scratch variable whose scope is highly localized within the code
Src	Source
Dst	Destination

Static Variables   Use static variables with care since it's very easy to create subtle bugs with them. Be *extremely* careful when using them inside branching and looping constructs, and when errors may cause a change in execution. It also makes sense to have a particular value assigned when errors occur, i.e. in your error handler. And make sure that any code which re-initializes the variable, or updates it in any non-linear way, is clearly documented, especially for counter variables. Static variables can be a handy counter when used in recursive procedures or in events that may be triggered multiple times. Use a static variable and count the calls.

Database Objects

Here are recommended standards for naming data objects:

Prefix	Data Object
db	Database
ds	Dynaset
fd	Field Object
ix	Index
qd	QueryDef object
Qry	Query (suffix)
ss	Snapshot
tb	Table object
td	TableDef object

Vendor Prefixes

As vendor controls become common, you may want to note the following also:

Vendor Prefix	Vendor
agi	Apex/Agility
cs	Cresecent
dw	Desaware
fp	FarPoint Technologies
mp	Microhelp
qe	Q+E Software (formerly Pioneer)
ss	Sheridan Software

Constants   The main thing to remember about constants is to use UPPER_CASE with underscores ("_") between words.

Variant Data Types

MCS strongly discourages the use of variants, even when a type conversion is needed. The only exception is when you use a generic service routine that doesn't need to know the type of in order to process or pass on data it receives. Database message, DDE, and OLE processing are examples of when variant data types can be tolerated. However, the variant data type is also useful for if you're writing code that may be use against multiple back ends. Variants can help paper over the differences in data types supported.

Option Explicit and Comments

You should always ("Yes, mother") use Option Explicit. You know that already. You also know you should preface your procedures and functions with a brief comment describing the functional characteristics of the routine including descriptions of any parameters, function return values, and global variables that are changed by the routine. Many VB programmers are adopting procedure header comment blocks that include sections with Purpose, Inputs, Assumes, Returns, Effects, Programmer, and Date.

More Advice

- Always define variables with the smallest scope possible. Global variables can create enormously complex state machines and make understanding the logic of an application extremely difficult. Likewise, try to put as much logic and as many user interface objects in Dialog Boxes as possible. This will help segment your application's complexity and minimize its run-time overhead.

- It's probably smart to indent your code the default four spaces, but as long as you're consistent, it really doesn't matter that much.

- Use lots of white space. Keep your procedures and functions short. Don't use single line IF/THENs—it's just too easy to overlook something at the end of the line. Block constructs help to make code structure a whole lot clearer.

- Use Call with subroutines. When calling subroutines, you can call them in either of two fashions:

  ```
  MySub Param1, Param2
  ```
  or

  ```
  Call MySub (Param1, Param2)
  ```
  The second method is much safer and cleaner.

- If you explicitly reference controls outside of their normal scope, i.e., the form on which they reside, then use the exclamation(!) operator between the form and control name instead of the dot(.) operator. It doesn't cost you anything and it helps distinguish controls from properties. It also protects you in case Microsoft ever decides to add a property to forms that has the same name as your control . . .

- Use "&" for concatenating strings and "+" when working with numerical values to avoid ambiguity. Finally, use standard tab-based block nesting indentations somewhere between two and four spaces.

- If you pass properties directly as parameters, enclose them in parenthesis to ensure they are evaluated properly. Also, your code will be even clearer if the property value is assigned to a temporary variable which is then used in the procedure call. This allows you to name the variable so that it more clearly documents its purpose or more closely matches the name of the parameter in the procedure.

- On a related note, if you have a procedure that's supposed to modify a parameter passed to it, be careful that the parameter isn't passed as a literal. If a literal, e.g., "MyString", is passed, instead of a variable, the calling procedure won't ever see a change.

- Although you don't *have* to put all your global declarations in a single module, lots of programmers do, and call it GLOBAL.BAS. We recommend doing this unless you have strong reasons not to.

- Avoid multivariable DIM statements. It's too easy to make mistakes.

- Use MsgBox as a debugging device to display information about unexpected—aren't they all?—errors. You might include module name, procedure name, and so on.

- Save ASCII versions as well as binary versions.

- When in doubt, use ByVal in the definition of a parameter in a Declare call to another DLL. And always predimension string variables targeted to hold the return value of a call to a DLL.

- Discover the WPS gem (\VB\CDK) to report on Windows processes, e.g., which DLLs are loaded. WPS has helped me find problems associated with multiple copies of a DLL.

- Read Microsoft's PERFORM.TXT file in your VB subdirectory.

- Create test suites with good end point and out-of-bounds data during development. Don't wait until the day before the project is due to start testing. Consider using a product like Microsoft Test for Windows ($495) to develop test scripts. You'll find test programs especially useful in testing multi-user applications.

Conventions take a little extra work and getting used to, but they're worth it in the end.

Version Control

Source code management is about as fun as managing your hard-disk files and backing up your hard disk. All is takes is one mistake and you'll wish you'd done a better job at it.

There are a handful of traditional version-control programs like Intersolv's PVCS (Figure 4-4) and Legent's Endevor that offer solid, multi-platform version-control support.

Figure 4-4: *The Windows version of Intersolv's PVCS 5.1 offers sophisti-cated version control*

Your disk includes a shareware VB program (Figure 4-5) written by Dan Rogers that offers a convenient VB interface to PVCS.

Some of the high-end version control packages tend to be complex, with a Windows interface that reflects their mainframe heritage and command-line bias. More recent packages like One Tree Software's SourceSafe and Microsoft's new Delta product were developed for Windows programmers and have obviously been built

Figure 4-5: *Dan Rogers' shareware VB front-end to PVCS is on your disk*

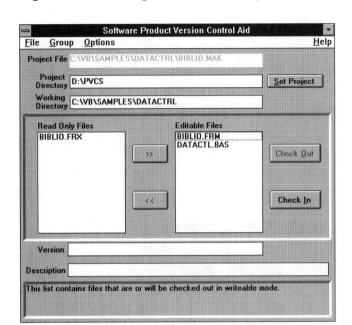

with Visual Basic programmers in mind. SourceSafe and Delta are both easy to use. In other words, you can probably get them up and running without reading the manual.

The idea with Delta and other version control packages is that a Project Administrator has overall responsibility for setting up initial project files and team members. The Master Project files are typically stored on a network drive, and individual programmers check them out as needed.

When files are checked back in, the version control program updates the Master Project file. In some programs, but not Delta, team members are notified by e-mail when a project file has been updated. In virtually all version control packages, a log or audit trail is kept with check-out/check-in records. This servers as a project history file. Similarly, a settable number of back versions of files are archived.

After Delta is installed on the programmers' workstations, the project administrator needs to define a project and set up the source files. This is typically done on a file server. The message in Figure 4-6 indicate that files have been added to the project called "Stealth1."

Figure 4-6: *Microsoft Delta version control software can help you manage client/server projects*

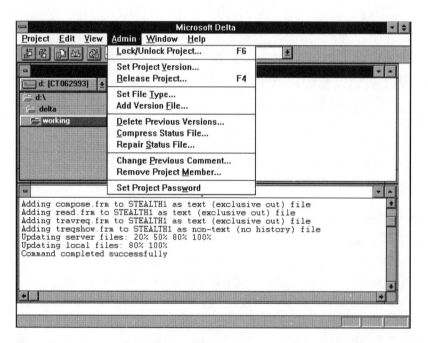

Two features you're likely to find extremely useful if you use Delta are its support for concurrent checkout and for side-by-side visual differencing. Concurrent checkout works thanks to a merge facility that automatically merges changes from multiple sources. The only major feature missing in Delta is support for branching versions. This is useful either when you want to maintain parallel development efforts or create customized versions of base applications for a variety of clients.

Other Development Issues

Once you've laid the foundations for your client/server project by deciding on programming and naming conventions and setting up project management, you'll face different issues.

As you saw in Figure 4-2, there are lots of ways to distribute the processing between the client and server processes. How you do it will depend on the back end server you use, performance requirements, and, to some extent, to your own preferences and conventions.

The "divide and conquer" metaphor for client/server application development is compelling but overly simplistic. In reality, you have to make decisions about *how* to divvy up the work—about how your application will be layered.

Data Validation

Most SQL databases store business rules and validation data on the server. However, is it logical to let an end user enter data that's invalid, have it shipped over the network to the server, be found invalid, and have the server return an error message? End users won't be happy if they have to re-enter all the data. But, by performing data validation locally, at the application level, you essentially defeat a major feature of client/server architecture: centralized, consistent data management. You run the risks of having different applications enforce different rules and of having applications that are out of sync with the server.

In other words, validation *should* be done on the server for security and consistency, but is should also be done at the client for performance and useability. The onus is on you to make sure your client validation mirrors *exactly* the validations that are built into the database on the server.

Data Buffering and Scrolling

Another sticky question is how to handle data buffering. Should you fetch data only as needed, a screen at a time? How do you handle monster SELECTs that risk flooding the network?

Cursors present another problem. Not all DBMSs even support cursors and most don't support backward-scrolling cursors. In other words, if the end user wants to scroll backward in the data, your application has to issue another SELECT. Obviously, though, users expect to be able to scroll backward without encountering inexplicable delays. Do you want to try to buffer the rows to avoid issuing new SELECTs? How do you write an application for end users that may have widely differing RAM on board?

Generic SQL

Another decision you'll face is whether to use generic SQL or SQL that takes advantage of server-specific features. If there's a chance you'll need to port the application to another back end, it may be worth your while to use generic SQL. In doing so, however, you're bound to sacrifice performance. In the case of ODBC drivers that promise to have short revision cycles, this will be an important decision.

Security and Error Handling

Different applications have different security needs. Most SQL databases have security built into them, as you saw in Chapter 2, where database access is strictly controlled via the GRANT statement. You may have to work with the DBA to make sure you understand the existing permissions. Some DBMSs have group permissions, for example, in addition to individual access rights. Some organizations may want additional security features like access logs and/or audit trails.

Finally, you'll need to master the back-end DBMS's error messages and code-robust error handling on the front end.

Summary

That should get you started. Think about your application's fundamental architecture and whether it's an OLTP or decision support application. Adopt VB standards and conventions if you haven't already, and investigate version control software, especially for team development.

We'll continue this thread later when we talk about testing and performance tuning. Now it's time to put theory into action.

Disk Files

PVCSVB.ZIP   Dan Rogers' VB interface to PVCS

5

The Database Connection

In the last four chapters, we've discussed relational databases and SQL, as well as client/server development issues. Now it's time to roll up your sleeves and put yourself into experimentation and exploration mode.

VB or Access?

We're asked frequently whether one should use Visual Basic or Access. Both products have a database engine, yet they are often seen as competitors. Both have Basic languages that Microsoft will apparently eventually merge into a common VBA (Visual Basic for Applications—see the Appendix for a comparison of VB, VBA, Access Basic, and Word Basic syntax). In general, VB has an edge when it comes to flexibility and performance, and Access has an edge when it comes to built-in ease of use for end-user reporting and querying.

Use Access if you want to do any of the following:

- Develop database applications that your clients can modify themselves.

- Use the RAD (rapid application development) approach to developing a prototype decision support client/server application. It's faster to create applications with Access.

- Print complex reports, or let users create their own reports. The Crystal Reports VBX and engine aren't nearly as easy to use.

- Create or let users create their own *ad hoc* queries in query design mode. Remember, though, that you can't take advantage of query design mode with the runtime version of Access. Access, unlike VB, also supports user-defined functions in queries.

- Embed or link BLOB objects in database fields. VB 3.0 doesn't support OLE objects in LongBinary fields directly.

- Create or modify databases interactively.

- Take advantage of Access's security system, which lets you to determine the rights of users to read and update data, as well as modify database objects.

Use Visual Basic when you want to do any of the following:

- Minimize computer resource requirements and obtain high performance. Almost all VB applications run well with 4MB RAM, while 8MB is required to run most Access applications satisfactorily.

- Change the properties of forms or subforms programmatically. Access requires that your application activate design mode in order to alter the design of Access objects and then return to run mode to display the object.

- Create graphs and charts programmatically or process graphics or other types of data in the LongVarBinary fields of client-server tables.

- Take advantage of VB's extensibility by writing your own DLLs or using as third-party custom controls.

- Create or modify databases and tables programmatically.

Similarities and Differences

We strongly recommend you have both VB 3.0 Professional *and* Access. There are certain tasks, like database definition and query design, where it's simply easier to use Access. You'll also find it much easier to report on database design and control Access database security from Access itself.

One of Access' gems is the ANALYZER.MDA database, which you can install and use by modifying your MSACCESS.INI file. If you chose a full installation, and if you had Access installed in the C:\ACCESS subdirectory, the ANALYZER.MDA file should be there. Add a line in the [Libraries] section that reads

```
[Libraries]
C:\ACCESS\ANALYZER.MDA
```

and a new section that will add Analyzer to Access' Help menu:

```
[Menu Add-Ins]
&Database Analyzer==StartAnalyzer()
```

Open any database and select Database Analyzer from the Help menu. You'll be able to select any number of tables, forms, queries, and so on for "analysis" (see Figure 5-1). What that means is that Access will create tables—adding them to any existing database— with pertinent information. You may find it useful to run Analyzer on queries in order to obtain and study the underlying SQL.

Figure 5-1: *Access includes the ANALYZER.MDA database, which you can use to inspect or document the structure of Access tables, forms, queries, and so on.*

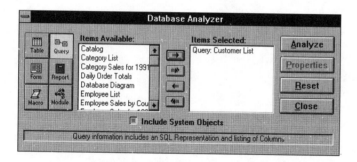

Microsoft has also released a "Security Wizard" MDA database, which you can install in the same fashion (SECWIZ.ZIP on your disk).

Unfortunately, the forms and reports aren't interchangeable—only the queries. As you do more database programming in VB, you'll find it both natural and easy to move back and forth between the two programs.

Access and VB have similar form design methodology. Access and VB's data access objects are virtually identical. Recordsets—table, dynaset, and snapshot objects—have identical properties and methods in both Basic dialects.

Access Basic and VB have a lot in common syntactically, too (see Appendix B). You even declare and call Windows API functions the same way in both Access and VB. Generally, about 75% of your Access Basic code will port to VB. Access DoCmds need to be re-written, and you won't be able to use Access' DLookup(), DAvg(), DMax() and other domain functions unless they're embedded in a SQL statement (one more reason to learn SQL). In VB there is no assumed "domain" database. In Access the domain is the "currentdb()".

Speaking of functions, Access lets you use your own custom functions in queries, but VB doesn't. A final significant difference is that Access' event-handlers need to have unique names since Access doesn't have VB's automatic event-handler naming feature.

Access Basic 1.1 and VB 3.0 are applications, on the average, about 75% code compatible.

The VB Database Universe

This may be a review for some of you, but it's important to understand the cast of characters in the VB database universe.

Objects

Let's start with the concept of an object. As a VB programmer, you use objects every day. But what *are* objects? VB, Access Basic, and VBA (Visual Basic for Applications) objects are all complex structures that include variables, called properties, and subprograms called methods. Database-related objects typically also include members—that is, data records—that are themselves objects.

Database Objects

Database objects are the highest-level objects that refer to databases where data records are actually stored. Think of a database object as the logical representation of a physical database. Unfortunately, although the idea of database objects makes it seem like all databases are created equal, that's not at all the case. Some of your biggest headaches come from assuming that, for example, Access MDBs act like dBASE, Paradox, Oracle, or SQL Server databases.

With the Standard Edition of VB3, you can open a database object only through the Data Control by specifying the `DatabaseName` and `Connect` properties. You need VB3 Professional Edition to use the `OpenDatabase` method or create object variables of type Database using the Dim and Set statements:

```
Dim MyDb As Database
Set MyDb = OpenDatabase("C:\VB\BIBLIO.MDB")
```

Database objects have these properties: `CollatingOrder`, `Connect` (for the connection string), `Name`, `QueryTimeout` (for ODBC), `Transactions`, and `Updatable`, these methods: `BeginTrans`, `Close`, `CommitTrans`, `CreateDynaset`, `CreateQueryDef`, `CreateSnapshot`, `DeleteQueryDef`, `Execute`, `ExecuteSQL`, `ListFields`, `ListTables`, `OpenQueryDef`, `OpenTable`, and `Rollback`. The following example uses database property of a data control and prints the name of each table in the Debug window.

```
Sub PrintTableNames ()
    Dim I
    Data1.DatabaseName = "BIBLIO.MDB"
    Data1.Refresh ' Open the Database
    ' Read and print the name of each table in the Database.
```

```
For I = 0 To Data1.Database.TableDefs.Count - 1
    Debug.Print Data1.Database.TableDefs(I).Name
Next I
End Sub
```

So what are TableDefs? They're special collection objects that contain table definitions, their *structure*. TableDefs themselves have interesting properties like Count and Fields you can access. Tables are different from TableDefs, since they contain the actual data. To list the fields in BIBLIO's Publishers table, for example, you could access the Fields collection:

```
Dim I
For I = 0 to Data1.Database.TableDefs("Publish-
...ers").Fields.Count - 1
 Print Data1.Database.TableDefs("Publish\
...ers").Fields(I).Name
Next I
```

A Database object's default collection is the TableDefs collection, and the default collection of a TableDef and all recordsets is the Fields collection. Since the default property of a TableDef is the Name property, you may want to simplify your code by taking advantage of these defaults. The following lines of code are functionally equivalent:

```
Print Data1.Database.TableDefs(0).Name
Print Data1.Database(0)
```

Other TableDef properties include DateCreated, LastUpdated, Updatable, Attributes (with basic info about the source of the underlying data), Connect, and SourceTableName.

VB lets you create desktop databases (Access, Paradox 3.x, FoxPro 2.0 or 2.5, dBASE III or IV, and Btrieve) with the DATAMGR program, but it's generally far easier to use the native DBMS to create new databases. That's another reason to own Access, not just the Access engine that comes with VB, if you're going to be using any Access databases. It's easier and faster to set up new Access databases using Access (see Figure 5-2) than DATAMGR (see Figure 5-3).

Figure 5-2: *Not only is it easier to define Access databases in Access, rather than with DATAMGR, you also have more options related to indexes and security.*

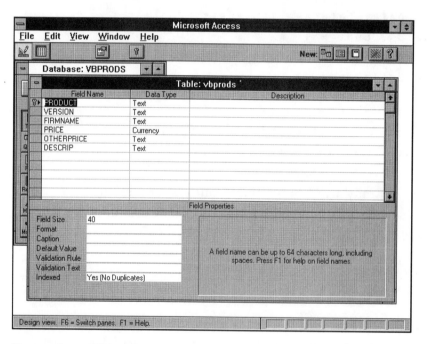

Recordset Objects

Dynaset, snapshot, and table objects are different flavors of what Microsoft calls *recordset* objects. Tables, of course, are a standard

Figure 5-3: *The DATAMGR.EXE program that comes with VB3 lets you define popular desktop databases.*

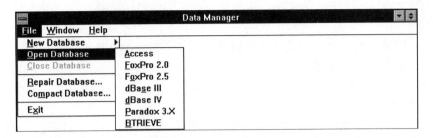

concept in the database world, but don't expect everyone to understand the Microsoft concepts of recordset, dynaset, and snapshot. They were introduced with Access, and will be understood by Access users, but not necessarily other database users. When you talk to MIS staffers who are familiar with traditional database terminology, you might want to say that recordsets are like SQL views.

Dynasets   Dynasets are basically special kinds of table objects that represent the result of a query. They may contain all the data from a table or only a portion of it. They can also contain data from multi-table queries. Dynasets can contain the data from tables that are "attached" to Access databases and from other external data accessed through ODBC connections, not just Access database data.

The Data Control automatically uses a Dynaset object.

Dynasets are updatable unless precluded by their underlying source table, but this poses some special challenges. For example, in multiuser situations, changes made to a table by other users won't automatically be reflected in your dynaset. Also, deletes don't work quite as you'd expect with a dynaset, since values in deleted dynaset records are simply changed to Null. On tables that have a unique index set up, this can cause problems if Access thinks it has two records with the same Null value in the index field. Adds cause another problem with indexed dynasets, since Access' Jet engine doesn't dynamically rearrange dynasets, as the name might lead you to believe. You'll use the `Refresh` method to solve most of these idiosyncrasies.

It may surprise you that you can't use database indexes directly with dynasets. Indexes are associated with tables and table objects, so even if your dynaset contains an entire table's worth of data, you still can't use indexes or the fast `Seek` method directly.

Dynasets create what's referred to as a local keyset index at the local PC. That's because the Access engine, Jet, is built around a *keyset-driven* cursor model. This means data is retrieved and updated based on key values. The keyset model was introduced to give Access some of the record-oriented functionality, such as, scrolling, that desktop users expect. Traditional relational database environments use a *dataset-driven* model, where individual records in a result set are simply part of the result set.

You need to understand that you're pretty much at Jet's mercy when it comes to scrolling through dynasets. Jet's goal is to return a screenful of data as quickly as possible, but typically brings back about a hundred keys preceding and following the records on the screen.

For the sake of performance, the keyset model doesn't fetch Memo data unless it's visible on the screen, so you can generally improve performance by designing your form so that, by default, Memo columns are *not* visible. Similarly, OLE objects are never fetched in bunches, nor are they stored in the dynaset caching window. When a row is displayed, the OLE objects are fetched if they are visible.

However, the current row's OLE objects are cached, so simple screen-repainting does not require refetching.

When you issue a query that results in a large result set, Jet only fetches the first row of that dynaset or snapshot and places the key to refetch that row in memory. Once a record is fetched or visited, it becomes a member of the recordset. As you visit additional rows of the recordset, the keys are stored in workstation memory in a temporary table. With snapshot objects, the data, as well as the keys, are stored in workstation memory. If you move back to previously fetched rows, Jet refetches the rows using the old key fetched from the temporary key table. If the database record has been deleted, you get a trappable error, and if the record's been changed, Jet fetches the new information.

As you move further into the recordset, more and more workstation RAM is taken up storing the keys. Eventually, this may get written out to disk cache as defined by your DOS TEMP environment variable, and if you run out of disk space, you will get a trappable error.

Bear in mind that moving to the end of the dynaset or snapshot forces Jet to visit all of the records in your recordset, saving *all* the keys—plus all the data if it's a snapshot—on the workstation. Obviously, you need to try to avoid operations that fetch more rows than your user or workstation can deal with. Another point to bear in mind is that dynaset or snapshot membership isn't set until the records are actually completely fetched for the first time. The only way to ensure that no changes are made while the recordset is built is to get exclusive access to the table or database before fetching, locking out other users.

Dynasets use Access' local keyset method for retrieving and buffering data.

Snapshots   Snapshots are read-only result sets. Snapshots are optimized for speed and are also the tool you *have* to use to retrieve information from Access collections. Recognize that the `MoveLast` method for a dynaset brings back the entire keyset into local workstation memory. That's bad enough, but for snapshots, `MoveLast` brings back all the data associated with those rows as well.

Tables 5-1 and 5-2 compare the properties and methods of the three types of recordsets.

Table 5-1:   *Properties available for Table, Dynaset, and Snapshot objects.*

Property	Datatype	Description	Table	Dynaset	Snapsho
BOF	Logical	Is record pointer at "beginning of file"?	Yes	Yes	Yes
Bookmark	String or Variant	Place location that uniquely identifies a record	Yes	Yes	Yes
Bookmarkable	Logical	Only tables with primary keys are bookmarkable	Yes	Yes	Yes
DateCreated	Variant	Datetime	Yes		
EOF	Logical	Is record point at "end of file"?	Yes	Yes	Yes
Filter	String	Optional SQL WHERE clause		Yes	Yes

Table 5-1: *(Continued)*

Property	Datatype	Description	Table	Dynaset	Snapshot
Index	String	Indicates which existing index to use	Yes	"Jet" decides whether to use indexes	
LastModified	Variant or String	Datetime	Yes		Yes
LastUpdated	Variant	Datetime	Yes		
LockEdits	Logical	For Access databases, indicates whether optimistic (False) or pessimistic (True) page locking is used. Access databases do not support record locking.	Yes		Yes
Name	String	Name of object	Yes	Yes	Yes
NoMatch	Logical	Indicates whether a Seek/Find method failed	Yes	Yes	Yes
RecordCount	Long	Number of records in recordset	Yes	Yes	Yes
Sort	String	Equivalent of SQL ORDER BY clause. Overrides QueryDef order, not needed if recordset defined via SQL.		Yes	Yes
Transactions	Logical	Indicates whether the recordset supports transaction processing	Yes		Yes
Updatable	Logical	True if a table is updatable	Yes		Yes

Table 5-2:   *Methods available for Table, Dynaset, and Snapshot objects*

Methods	Purpose	Table	Dynaset	Snapshot
AddNew	Add a new record by creating a new record in the copy buffer and setting all its fields to Nulls	Yes	Yes	
AppendChunk	Append string to end of field. Handy for memo, OLE data	Yes	Yes	
Clone	Creates shadow copy of a recordset Faster than creating a new dynaset	Yes	Yes	Yes
Close	Closes a database, recordset, or QueryDef	Yes	Yes	Yes
CreateDynaset	Creates a dynaset from a table, QueryDef or SQL string	Yes	Yes	Yes
CreateSnapshot	Creates a snapshot from a table, QueryDef or SQL string	Yes	Yes	Yes
Delete	Deletes the current record	Yes	Yes	
Edit	Copies the current record to the copy buffer for editing	Yes	Yes	
FindFirst	Finds the first record in a recordset satisfying the selection criteria. With a data control, if an Edit or AddNew operation is pending when you use one of the Find or Move methods, Update is automatically invoked unless you stop it with the Validate event		Yes	Yes
FindLast	Finds the last record satisfying the selection criteria		Yes	Yes
FindNext	Finds the next record satisfying the selection criteria		Yes	Yes
FindPrevious	Finds the previous record satisfying the selection criteria		Yes	Yes
GetChunk	Copies a portion of a memory or OLE field to a string variable	Yes	Yes	Yes

Table 5-2:   *(Continued)*

Methods	Purpose	Table	Dynaset	Snapshot
ListFields	Creates a snapshot with field info from the FieldDefs collection	Yes	Yes	Yes
ListIndexes	Creates a snapshot with index info from the Indexes collection	Yes		Yes
MoveFirst	Moves to the first record in the recordset	Yes	Yes	Yes
MoveLast	Moves to the last record in the recordset	Yes	Yes	Yes
MoveNext	Moves to the next record in the recordset	Yes	Yes	Yes
MovePrevious	Moves to the prior record in the recordset	Yes	Yes	Yes
Seek	Finds the first record in a table whose primary key or index 1-5 values match the selection criteria	Yes		
Update	Updates the current record with the contents of the record buffer	Yes	Yes	

Bookmarks   When recordsets are created or opened, each record will usually—inspect the value of the Bookmarkable property to make sure—already have a unique bookmark. You can save the bookmark for the current record by assigning the value of the Bookmark property to a variable. Bookmarks are extremely handy pseudo pointers into a recordset, but there are a few things to keep in mind. The value of the Bookmark property isn't the same as a record number and bookmarks can become invalid if the underlying record is deleted by another user.

Bookmark values between a dynaset and a duplicate dynaset created with the Clone method are identical and can be used interchangeably.

However, you can't use bookmarks from different dynasets, even if they were created from the same table or with the same SQL statement.

Data Control Methods

Bookmark properties are extremely useful, but you'll also want to understand how to use a handful of methods associated with the Data Control.

The Validate event might make you think of field-level data validation, but the Validate event is fired whenever the current row is changed—except when data is changed by the UpdateRecord method. In other words, Validate gets fired before an Update, and before a Delete, Unload, or Close operation. The Validate event's syntax is

```
Sub datacontrol_Validate ([ Index As Integer,] Action
...As Integer, Save As Integer)
```

when Index refers to a control array index and when Action is one of the following codes:

DATA_ACTIONCANCEL	0	Cancel the operation
DATA_ACTIONMOVEFIRST	1	MoveFirst method
DATA_ACTIONMOVEPREVIOUS	2	MovePrevious method
DATA_ACTIONMOVENEXT	3	MoveNext method
DATA_ACTIONMOVELAST	4	MoveLast method
DATA_ACTIONADDNEW	5	AddNew method
DATA_ACTIONUPDATE	6	Update operation
DATA_ACTIONDELETE	7	Delete method
DATA_ACTIONFIND	8	Find method
DATA_ACTIONBOOKMARK	9	Bookmark property has been set
DATA_ACTIONCLOSE	10	Close method
DATA_ACTIONUNLOAD	11	Form is being unloaded

The Save argument initially indicates whether bound data has changed, but Save can still be False if data in the copy buffer is changed. Only data from bound controls or from the copy buffer where the DataChanged property is True are saved by the UpdateRecord method.

The important thing to remember is that *the Validate event occurs even if no changes have been made to data in bound controls and even if there are no bound controls.* And during a Validate event, you can't use methods like MoveNext on the underlying-dynaset.

Updates and refreshes are handled with three methods: UpdateRecord, UpdateControls, and Refresh. UpdateRecord updates the recordset with data from any data-aware control, and UpdateControls updates data-aware controls with changes made on the underlying table data. This is useful when you need to reset the data in bound controls to the contents of the record after a user has requested to cancel any changes made.

UpdateControls is useful for resetting data in bound controls when a user has aborted changes.

Refresh is extremely important, because it causes the entire dynaset to be recreated from scratch. Changes made by other users will be displayed, and you can re-sort the dynaset.

Exploring Data Control

Let's see how some of these things work. There's an Access database called VBPRODS.MDB on your data disk with two tables. VBFIRMS contains about a hundred vendors of VB products, and VBPRODS contains brief descriptions and prices of the firms' VB products. Copy VBPRODS.MDB onto your hard disk. Our examples assume it is in a subdirectory C:\VB\SAM-PLES\VBDBBOOK.

The VBFIRMS table has the following structure:

FIRMNAME	Text	40	PrimaryKey
CONTACT	Text	25	
ADDRESS	Text	40	
CITY	Text	20	
STATE	Text	2	
ZIP	Text	10	
PHONE	Text	13	
PHONE2	Text	13	
FAX	Text	13	
CIS	Text	13	
COMMENTS	Text	70	

VBPRODS has these fields:

PRODUCT	Text	40	PrimaryKey
VERSION	Text	10	
FIRMNAME	Text	40	ForeignKey/Link Field
PRICE	Currency	8	
OTHERPRICE	Text	25	
DESCRIP	Text	60	

There is a one-to-many relationship between these tables, since each vendor can theoretically have more than one product. The common or "link" field is FIRMNAME. If you have Access, you can explore the tables in design mode and look at the Access VBSTUFF form that was created with Access' Form Wizard.

The VBFIRMS Form

In Chapter 1, you created this time a simple form using VB's Data Control. We'll use the same approach to create a new form, except for the VBPRODS database. Start with a blank form and add a Data Control near the bottom. Widen the control and change its `Caption` property to VB Vendors. Change the `DatabaseName` property to the location of your copy of the VBPRODS.MDB database, and set `RecordSource` as VBFIRMS. Accept the default name Data1 as the control's name:

Data Control

Caption: VB Vendors

DatabaseName: C:\VB\SAMPLES\VBDBBOOK\VBPRODS.MDB

Name: Data1

RecordSource: vbfirms

Now locate the Firmname label and text box (see Figure 5-4). Select the Firmname text box and select the `DataSource` property. Assign Data1, the only `DataSource` so far. Data1 is simply the default name for our first data source, and it serves as an alias for the VBFIRMS table in the VBPRODS.MDB database. Then select the `DataFields` property and use the drop-down listbox to select Firmname. Finally, change the `Name` property to be txtFirmname. Continue with the remaining 10 labels and their corresponding text boxes, and change the Name property of each of the text boxes to be txtFieldname, i.e., txtContact, txtAddress, and so on. Check your work and save your project.

Now have fun exploring! When you run the form, VB automatically loads the first record into the list boxes. Since the table has been indexed on FirmName, the records are in alphabetical order. Experiment with the VCR-style buttons. VB lets you change the data pretty indiscriminately. As long as you don't enter data that

Figure 5-4: *Start with a simple form containing 11 labels and 11 text fields corresponding to the 11 fields in the VBFIRMS table.*

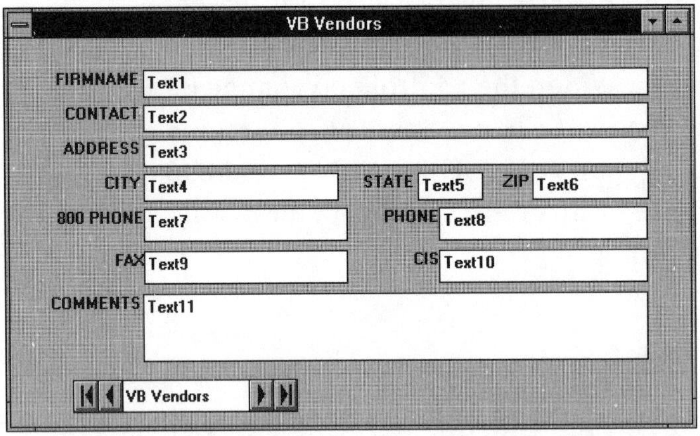

conflicts with the assigned data type—and in this case they're all text fields, so that's not a problem—or make a change that tries to break the unique index rule by creating a duplicate Firmname, VB saves the changes as soon as you move off the record or exit. Sorry, there's no undo.

That's not a bad set of functionality for a few minutes' work. Unfortunately, there are several missing elements. It would be nice to be able to use a Find feature, and it would be nice to be able to add new firms. We'll delay deleting firms until later, since that's more complex. When it comes to deleting firms, you're going to have to decide how to handle the referential integrity issue—that is, what to do with related records in the VBPRODS tables.

New, Find, Update, and Delete

Add four command buttons called cmdNew, cmdUpdate, cmdDelete, and cmdFind to the right of the Data Control. Assign captions of &New, &Update, &Delete, and &Find to permit hot key

access. Set the visible property of cmdUpdate to False. Then
enter this code for the cmdFind's click event:

```
Sub cmdFind_Click ()
    'Prompt for a firmname
    FindFirm = InputBox$("Please enter a vendor firmname: ",
    ..."Find a Firm")
    If Len(FindFirm) > 0 Then
        CurrRec = Data1.Recordset.Bookmark 'remember where
        ...we are
        Data1.Recordset.FindFirst "Firmname = '" &
        ...FindFirm & "'"
        If Data1.Recordset.NoMatch Then
            Data1.Recordset.Bookmark = CurrRec 'go back
            MsgBox "That firm doesn't seem to be on file",
            ...48, "Maybe it's spelled differently..."
        End If
    End If
End Sub
```

Test your code. ("AJS" is an easy hit for Firmname, but "Microsoft"
won't work. You need to enter "Microsoft Corporation".) Notice
how the Bookmark code works by returning you to the record you
were on in the absence of a hit.

There are lots of ways to beef up the Find routine. To permit
searches based on the beginning of the string only, for example,
you need to change the FindFirst line to read

```
Data1.Recordset.FindFirst "Firmname like '" & findfirm & "'
...& '*' "
```

This essentially uses the SQL LIKE clause. Another obvious
enhancement is to add FindNext.

Initial AddNew Routine   Next enter two lines of code in cmdNew's `Click` event and test them:

```
Sub cmdNew_Click ()
    Data1.Recordset.AddNew    'Clears form for new record
    txtFirmname.SetFocus      'Puts cursor in first field
End Sub
```

You're likely to run into more problems here, receiving VB error messages like "Can't have Null value in index" or "Can't have duplicate key; index changes unsuccessful." This is because VBFIRMS has been set up with Firmname as a primary key. That basically means no duplicates and no Nulls. Although the Jet engine provides error messages, you may want to provide your own.

The Initial Delete Routine   Enter the following in the cmdDelete button's Click event:

```
Sub CmdDelete_Click ()
    a% = MsgBox("Are you sure you want to delete this
    ...record?", 36, "Confirm Delete")
    If a% <> 6 Then Exit Sub
    On Error Resume Next
    Data1.Recordset.Delete
    Data1.Recordset.MoveNext
    If Data1.Recordset.EOF = True Then   'we deleted final
    ...record
    'final record may have been ONLY record
        Data1.Refresh      'see what's left
    End If
    If Data1.Recordset.BOF = True Then
        MsgBox "You must add a new record or exist", 48,
        ..."File is Empty"
```

```
            cmdNew.Value = True 'Turn on New Button
        End If
        If Err Then Data1.Recordset.MoveLast
End Sub
```

Test the Delete button by adding some junk records to delete rather than deleting "real" data!

Update   Before adding code to cmdUpdate, it's a good idea to think about the dynamics of adding and updating data. You want to preclude conflict between the New and Delete buttons so users can't click on Delete in the middle of an AddNew, crashing the program. You also want to hide New, showing Update instead, when the user is in the process of adding a new firm. Therefore, modify the cmdNew click event as follows:

```
Sub cmdNew_Click ()
    Data1.Recordset.AddNew    'Clears form to start a new
    ...record
    txtFirmname.SetFocus      'Puts cursor in first field
    cmdNew.Visible = False    'Hide the New button
    cmdUpdate.Visible = True  'Show Update
    Data1.Enabled = False     'Disable navigation until
    ...updated
    cmdFind.Enabled = False   'Disable Find
    cmdDelete.Enabled = False 'Disable Delete
End Sub
```

Finally, you're ready to tackle the Update button. Position the New and Update buttons on top of each other and enter the following to cmdUpdate's Click event:

```
Sub cmdUpdate_Click ()
    CurrFirm = txtFirmname.Text
```

```
    Data1.Recordset.Update
    Data1.Refresh
    Data1.Recordset.FindFirst "Firmname = '" & CurrFirm &
    ..."'"
    cmdNew.Visible = True
    cmdUpdate.Visible = False
    Data1.Enabled = True
    cmdFind.Enabled = True
    cmdDelete.Enabled = True
End Sub
```

Test your application so far and save it. At this point, your form should look something like that shown in Figure 5-5.

Figure 5-5: *This form handles adding, editing, and deleting vendors from the VBFIRMS table.*

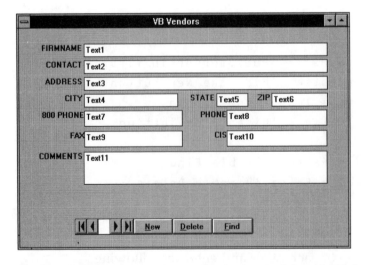

Empty Tables   Hopefully you haven't deleted all the records in the VPFIRMS table, but empty tables can present special problems. A bit of code, attached to the Data1 `Reposition` event, handles the problem:

```
'Add this to Global declaration
Dim JustStart As Integer
'Add this to Form's FormLoad event
JustStart = True
Sub Data1_Reposition ()
    If JustStart Then
        If Data1.Recordset.EOF = True And
        ...Data1.Recordset.BOF = True Then 'Empty table
            Show
            MsgBox "Either add a new record or exit", 48,
            ..."No records in table"
            'AddNew causes another reposition, so clear flag
            JustStart = False
            cmdNew.Value = True
        End If
        JustStart = False
    End If
End Sub
```

Intercepting Nulls and Duplicate Keys   You discovered in the
initial CmdNew routine that our program isn't too elegant in
handling records with either null or duplicate Firmnames. One
way to tackle the problem is to add the following to the
txtFirmname's LostFocus event:

```
Sub txtFirmname_LostFocus ()
   If Len(txtFirmname.Text) = 0 Then
      Msgbox "You must enter a Firm Name" , 16, "Required
      ...Field"
      txtFirmname.SetFocus
   Else
      If txtFirmname.DataChanged = True Then
          Dim Shadowset As Dynaset    'Set up clone
          Set Shadowset = Data1.Recordset.Clone()
```

```
        Shadowset.FindFirst "Firmname = '" &
        ...txtFirmname.text & "'"
        If Not Shadowset.NoMatch Then
            MsgBox "That Firm is already on file", 16,
            ..."Duplicate Firm Name"
            txtFirmname.SetFocus
        End If
        Shadowset.Close
    End If
  End If
End Sub
```

The trick to avoiding duplicates is to create a copy of the dynaset, where you can check for duplicates. Otherwise, you'd have to move the current record pointer in the "real" dynaset, and, as soon as you move the record pointer, Jet automatically saves the record. Sort of a Catch-22.

Another handy bit of code prevents users from changing the key Firmname field. The problem is that if they do, related records in the VBPRODS table can get orphaned. The following code does the trick:

```
If cmdNew.Visible = True Then
    SendKeys "{TAB}", -1      'Move cursor off Firmname
End If
```

Form Builders Abound

Although it's not *hard* to create a form from scratch, let's face it, it's tedious. I highly recommend you find a third-party add-in you like that has a form builder. Figure 5-6 shows a single-table form built in a matter of seconds with Sheridan's VBAssist 3.0. You can

Figure 5-6: *VBAssist has a Form Wizard that generates an instant form*

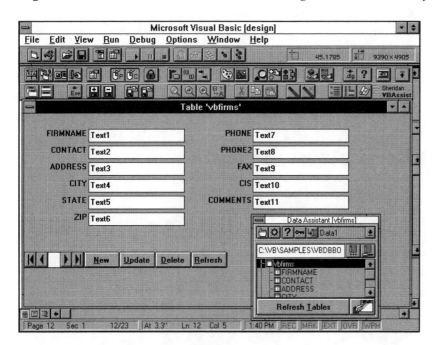

contact Sheridan Softwareat 65 Maxess Road, Melville, NY 11747. Phone: 516-753-0985: Fax: 516-753-3661.

Sheridan has another product, Data Widgets, that includes a data-aware grid control. Using Data Widgets, it's almost as easy to create a multi-table master-detail form.

I've also discovered some good shareware form builders on Compu-Serve, so I encourage you to check out the MSBASIC Forum if you're interested in seeing what's available.

Master-Detail Forms

Most relational database applications have to access data stored in more than one table. In the BIBLIO.MDB database that comes with VB3, for example, there are four tables: authors, titles, pub[lisher]s, and pubnotes. I encourage you to explore the \VB\SAM-PLES\DATACTRL\BIBLIO project (see Figure 5-7) if you haven't already.

Figure 5-7: *Data from three BIBLIO.MDB tables appear on this form, including multiple books associated with well-known relational database guru Chris Date*

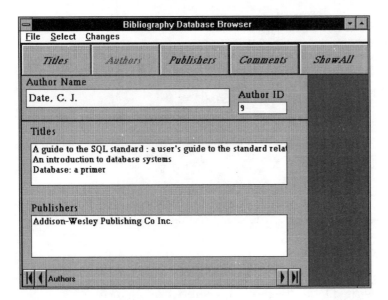

Visual Basic gives you a surfeit of tools for approaching the master-detail (or form-subform) issue. You can use the VB grid control or any of the myriad of third-party data-aware grid controls; you can use a MDI child window for the detail records; or you can picture boxes with control arrays containing the child records and use a vertical scrollbar if necessary. Depending on what resources you want to use, you can also instantiate the detail from code or simply draw the detail subforms at design time and .show them as necessary at runtime.

But those are mechanical issues related as much to personal preferences as anything else. You've seen the basic data handling techniques above. The basic idea is to locate additional Data Controls as needed and set their `RecordSource` properties programmatically with a SQL statement. Generally, you make the related Data Controls invisible and code the linking/refresh logic with a change in the contents of the common field. With the BIBLIO database, Au_ID is the common field that links AUTHORS and TITLES, for example. With the VBPRODS database, Firmname is the common field linking the VBFIRMS and VBPRODS tables.

ODBC

I'm convinced that the ODBC standard is going to be an increasingly important one. However, in late 1993, as the first ODBC drivers were hitting the market en masse, actually using ODBC posed real headaches. Microsoft itself tells you in a KnowledgeBase article that "there are four possible problem areas that can contribute to a failure to connect to a database server when using ODBC and Visual Basic." I think there are more. Problems include having correct .INI file settings (ODBC.INI, ODBC-INST.INI, yourdatabase.INI, and yourapp.INI—among others), having the correct DLLs in the right place (conflicting drivers, or redundant copies of ODBC program files), and having the server information needed to connect to a server correctly.

> Anticipate connectivity problems with ODBC. Potential culprits: PATH statements, multiple copies of driver DLLs, and multiple versions of other ODBC files.

Standards for file location—ODBC DLLs should all be installed in WINDOWS\SYSTEM, and ODBC good citizenship, such as not overwriting another vendor's driver—are emerging, but slowly. I have wasted many hours tracking down ODBC-related errors, and you probably will too. Be prepared for some heavy frustration as standards emerge.

One tool that I use to track which DLLs are actually loaded is the WPS.EXE program in your VB\CDK subdirectory. ODBC.INI contains the data for each installed driver. The driver manager uses this information to determine which DLL to use to access data from a particular database backend. Wrong entries in ODBC.INI can lead to illuminating error messages like the following:

```
ODBC - SQLConnect failure 'IM002[Microsoft][ODBC DLL]
...Data    source not found and no default driver specified'

ODBC - SQLConnect failure 'IM003[Microsoft][ODBC DLL]
...Driver
        specified by data source could not be loaded'

ODBC - SQLConnect failure '28000[Microsoft][ODBC SQL
...Server  Driver][SQL Server]  Login failed'
```

Managing ODBC

Only cowboys edit the ODBC INI files directly. Smart people use the ODBCADM (ODBC Administrator) program that Microsoft is now including as part of the Control Panel. There are two basic screens you have to work with when you set up ODBC drivers: Drivers (see Figure 5-8) and Data Sources (see Figure 5-9).

You may very well have more than one driver for a given DBMS like Oracle or SQL Server. Bear in mind that not all ODBC drivers are created equal. To find out which driver is which, click on the About box.

Figure 5-8: *ODBC Drivers*

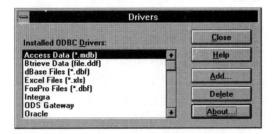

Figure 5-9: *ODBC Data Sources*

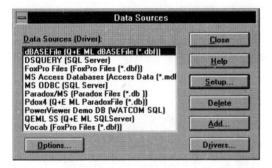

The names listed in Data Sources have already been defined. The name on the far left is a user-selected name. The part of the Data Sources names in parentheses refers to the ODBC driver being used.

SQL Server Tips   To use ODBC drivers, you need to add some special "stored procedures" to your SQL Server. Microsoft provides several versions of a SQL script called INSTCAT.SQL that you run using a command like this:

```
ISQL /U <sa login name > /n /P <password> /S <SQL
...server name> /i <drive: \path\INSTCAT.SQL >
```

Paradox Tips   If you use Microsoft's Paradox driver, which ships with VB, you need to set the Connect property of the Data Control to Paradox 3.5, not just Paradox. If you enter "Paradox" only—which is what the documentation tells you to do—you get a VB error message "Couldn't find installable ISAM." ISAM stands for indexed sequential access method and is associated with so-called "flat file" databases. If you use other vendors' Paradox drivers, you will probably have the option of choosing Paradox 3.5 or Paradox 4.0 file format. Make sure you select the correct one.

You need to use "Paradox 3.5," not just "Paradox," in the Data Control's Connect property, despite what the VB3 documentation says. Otherwise, you get an error message about not finding the installable ISAM.

Btrieve Tips   Btrieve data files must be in version 5.1x format, and your program needs to be able to locate the Btrieve data definition files FILE.DDF and FIELD.DDF, which are created by Xtrieve or another .DDF file-building program. You can't use Btrieve files that have Xtrieve security, and if you're using compressed Btrieve files, make sure the compression buffer Btrieve is using is adequate for your data. The buffer size must be at least as large as the largest record in your data files.

In VB, there are only two accepted methods for passing the key buffer parameter—as a string or as a user-defined TYPE structure. Attempting to access Btrieve integer keys by passing the key buffer as a string poses the problem of converting an integer to a two-byte string. Although VB doesn't support an MK$ function, you can use a Get Equal operation:

```
Type Index3Search
Age As Integer
```

```
End Type
Dim SearchOnKey3 As Index3Search
```

The Btrieve call might be

```
SearchOnKey3.Age = 38
KeyBufLen = LEN(SearchOnKey3)
KeyNum = 3
Status = btrcall(BGETEQUAL,
      PosBlk$,
      DataBuf,
      DataBufLen,
      SearchOnKey3,
      KeyBufLen,
      KeyNum)
```

Another approach is to write your own MKI$ function:

```
Function MKI$ (I%)
      TempI& = I%
      If TempI& < 0 Then
            TempI& + 65536
      End If
      Byte1% = TempI& / 256
      Byte2% = TempI& Mod 256
      C1$ = Chr$(Byte1%)
      C2$ = Chr$(Byte2%)
      MKI$ = C2$ + C1$
End Function
```

You might call the function like this:

```
SearchOnKey3$ = MKI$(38)
KeyBufLen = LEN(SearchOnKey3$)
KeyNum = 3
status = btrcall(BGETEQUAL,
```

```
PosBlk$,
DataBuf,
DataBufLen,
SearchOnKey3$,
KeyBufLen,
KeyNum)
```

Transaction Processing

You learned probably more than you wanted to know about
transaction processing back in Chapters 2 and 4, and here it is
again. While transaction processing, using VB's `BeginTrans`,
`CommitTrans`, and `Rollback` statements and methods certainly
isn't limited to ODBC, you're far more likely to want to use transaction processing with ODBC connections. Why? Performance.
You may find yourself packaging your transactions to minimize
network traffic.

Summary

You've seen how VB's Data Control object does a fine job as far as
it goes. It's an incredibly easy-to-use tool for accessing and navi-
gating data. However, code is needed to handle even rudimentary
tasks like adding new records, so there's plenty of job security for
VB database programmers. You've also seen that ODBC still has
some rough edges and is likely to cause you frustrating problems
that are very difficult to resolve. And if you think it's bad on a single
PC, wait until you try to deploy your application (Chapter 11).

Disk Files

DATAMGR.ZIP	Microsoft's VB source code for DATAMGR.EXE
SECWIZ.ZIP	Microsoft's Security Wizard program for Access MDBs
VBPRODS.ZIP	The database and related files

6

Accessing Enterprise Data

ODBC isn't the only way to connect to *enterprise data*—data that's generally in SQL databases on remote minis or mainframes. However, enterprise data takes many forms and may mean accessing anything from so-called "legacy data" to data in Lotus Notes databases.

Legacy data is usually non-SQL data on a mainframe or mini and is often associated with core vertical market production systems, e.g., accounting.

As ODBC gains momentum, you'll probably be able to find ODBC drivers for just about any data source. However, in the short term, you may want to explore other, more direct links. These usually offer better performance. There's also a big market for existing front-end 3270 terminal applications. IBM 3270s are character-based terminals that are used to access IBM mainframe applications, but vendors like DCA and Attachmate sell popular 3270 emulation programs that run on Windows PCs.

In this chapter, we demonstrate how to use Q+E Software's popular Q+E/MultiLink VB 2.0, the Lotus Notes API SDK, Oracle's Glue 1.0, Attachmate's EXTRA! for Windows, and DCA's QuickApp for Windows. We also talk briefly about "middleware" and gateways that offer other methods of connecting to host data.

Q+E/ MultiLink VB

Q+E Software's core technology is database connectivity based on its Q+E Database Library (QELIB) engine. Q+E Software has developed a line of products based on QELIB. In 4Q93, these were the current versions of Q+E's products:

- Q+E Database Editor 5.0

- Q+E Database Library 2.0

- Q+E Extend for Improv and Q+E Extend for Quattro Pro for Windows

- Q+E MultiLink/VB 2.0

- Q+E ODBC Pack 1.1

Microsoft helped popularize Q+E Database Editor by shipping an early version (Q+E Database Editor 2.7) with every copy of Excel between 1989 and 1993 before adding its own Microsoft Query to Excel. Microsoft isn't the only vendor that has licensed Q+E technology—so have Word Perfect (InForms), Lotus (Improv), MapInfo

(SQL DataLink), Pilot Software (LightShip Lens), Intersolv (PVCS and Excelerator), Computer Associates(CA-RET, CA-dbFAST, and CA-REALIZER), Concentric (R&R Report Writer for Windows, SQL Edition), Delrina (FormFlow), Cardiff (Teleform), ProtoView (SQLView), and others.

Q+E also ships a product called Q+E Database/VB. The difference between Q+E Database/VB and Q+E MultiLink/VB are that the earlier Q+E Database/VB only provided connectivity to XBase databases. Q+E Database/VB encountered plenty of competition from other vendors with XBase DLLs and was never wildly successful. Q+E Database/VB has been supplanted by Q+E Multi-Link/VB and is being phased out.

The product of interest for VB developers is Q+E MultiLink/VB, a much- enhanced superset of Q+E Database/VB. Q+E Multi-Link/VB ships with with ODBC-complaint drivers for over 20 databases. In this chapter, we focus only on Q+E's MultiLink/VB product and includes a VBX you can use with VB or Visual C++. Its greatest strength, a side from the impressive list of back ends it supports, is its query builder.

Because Q+E MultiLink/VB 2.0 ($399) was still in beta when we wrote the book, our examples may require small changes to work with the final release of Version 2.0. New to Release 2.0 are ODBC support, data dictionary functions, e.g., pFieldType and pFieldLength, edit masking, and the ability to search for strings in list and combo boxes.

For more information, contact Q+E Software at 800-876-3101 or 919-859-2220.

VB Wrapper

You might think of Q+E MultiLink/VB as a VB wrapper for QELIB. QELIB is Q+E's C language interface; you can see from the function declaration section of QELINK.TXT global declarations file that the VBX handles most common data access tasks.

```
'From Q+E Software's Q+E MultiLink/VB QELINK.TXT
Declare Function fDoQuery Lib "qelink.vbx" (queryCtl
...As Control) As Integer
Declare Function fEndQuery Lib "qelink.vbx" (queryCtl
...As Control) As Integer
Declare Function fNext Lib "qelink.vbx" (queryCtl As
...Control) As Integer
Declare Function fPrevious Lib "qelink.vbx" (queryCtl
...As Control) As Integer
Declare Function fRandom Lib "qelink.vbx" (queryCtl As
...Control, ByVal RecNumber&) As Integer
Declare Function fNew Lib "qelink.vbx" (queryCtl As
...Control, ByVal rowIndex%, ByVal before%) As Integer
Declare Function fEnterQBE Lib "qelink.vbx" (queryCtl
...As Control) As Integer
Declare Function fClearQBE Lib "qelink.vbx" (queryCtl
...As Control) As Integer
Declare Function fInsert Lib "qelink.vbx" (queryCtl As
...Control, ByVal rowIndex%) As Integer
Declare Function fUpdate Lib "qelink.vbx" (queryCtl As
...Control, ByVal rowIndex%) As Integer
Declare Function fDelete Lib "qelink.vbx" (queryCtl As
...Control, ByVal rowIndex%) As Integer
Declare Function fDiscard Lib "qelink.vbx" (queryCtl As
...Control, ByVal rowIndex%) As Integer
Declare Function fLock Lib "qelink.vbx" (queryCtl As
...Control, ByVal rowIndex%) As Integer
```

```
Declare Function fTranBegin Lib "qelink.vbx" (queryCtl
...As Control) As Integer
Declare Function fTranCommit Lib "qelink.vbx" (queryCtl
...As Control) As Integer
Declare Function fTranRollback Lib "qelink.vbx" (queryCtl
...As Control) As Integer
Declare Function fExecSQL Lib "qelink.vbx" (queryCtl As
Control, ByVal SQLStmt$) As Integer
Declare Function fLogon Lib "qelink.vbx" (connectionCtl
...As Control) As Integer
Declare Function fLogoff Lib "qelink.vbx" (connectionCtl
...As Control) As Integer
Declare Function fEnterFind Lib "qelink.vbx" (queryCtl As
...Control) As Integer
Declare Function fFind Lib "qelink.vbx" (queryCtl As
...Control, ByVal options%) As Integer
Declare Function fClearFind Lib "qelink.vbx" (queryCtl
...As Control) As Integer
```

Q+E MultiLink/VB's Connect and Query Controls

The Q+E VBX adds a dozen custom controls—to your toolbar. The all-important *Connect control* is Q+E's equivalent to the VB Data Control. It has the following custom properties, functions, and events:

- pAutoLogon

- pError

- pErrorDB

- pErrorOption

- pErrorText

- pEscEnabled

- pLogonInfo

- pLogonOption

- pMode

- pOneHstmtOptions

- pSource

- pTranPending

- fLogoff

- fLogon

- fTranBegin

- fTranCommit

- fTranRollback

- eError

You'll probably want to make sure pEscEnabled is set on so end users can abort out of long queries.

Q+E MultiLink/VB's biggest weakness is that its grid control is read-only.

MultiLink/VB's Query control creates links from the application to one or more database tables, and these links are used by every field control except the Query Grid. The *Query Grid* control is different from the Query control. The Query Grid control lets you display query results in a read-only, scrollable grid and links directly to database tables.

The basic Query controls, however, are invisible at runtime. Query controls *can* be referenced across forms. One quirk of Multi-Link/VB is that you can't load a form containing field controls that reference an already-active query. The *Query control's* custom properties, functions, and events are:

Properties	Functions
pAutoQuery	fClearFind
pConnectName	fClearQBE
pDistinct	fDelete
pError	fDiscard
pErrorDB	fDoQuery
pErrorOption	fEndQuery
pErrorText	fEnterFind
pMode	fEnterQBE
pQueryType	fExecSQL
pRecCount	fFind
pRecNumber	fLock
pRowIndex	fNew
pSelect	fNext
pTables	fPrevious
pTranPending	fRandom
pWhere	fTranBegin
	fTranCommit
	fTranRollback
	fUpdate

Errors

eError
eFetch
eRecLeave

Using Q+E MultiLink/VB

After adding the global variables (from QELINK.TXT) and QELINK.VBX control to your project, you insert the Connect and Query controls on your form to establish the basic data link, then add list box, radio button, and other data aware controls. Even though the Q+E MultiLink/VB doesn't have an *editable* grid object, the Query Grid object, along with radio buttons and check boxes, can be used very effectively for query and display routines. For example, you could have the user enter a firm name in a text box and return Paradox data (both 3.5 and 4 are supported) into a grid object:

```
Sub Q1dBase_eFetch (RowIndex As Integer)
Q2pdx.pWhere = "Firm_Name = '" + DB_Text9.Text + "'"
    Qgrid1.pWhere = "Firm_Name = '" + DB_Text9.Text + "'"
    res% = fDoQuery(Q2pdx)
    res% = fDoQuery(Qgrid1)
End Sub
```

A more complex routine that concatenates data entered into DB List Box controls, building WHERE and ORDER BY clauses might look like this:

```
Sub BuildWhereClause ()

whereclause = ""

' Step through all 3 list boxes building the WHERE clause
' to match the selected search values
For i = 0 To 2
    NumClause% = List1(i).ListCount

'Check if this list box has any clauses
    If (NumClause% > 0) Then
```

```
' If this isn't the first clause, add an 'AND'
     If (Len(whereclause) <> 0) Then
         whereclause = whereclause + " And "
     End If

     ' If the listbox has > 1 clause then we need (
        If (NumClause% > 1) Then
            whereclause = whereclause + "("
        End If

   ' Add each clause to the WHERE clause
      For X = 0 To NumClause% - 1              ' Add clause
         whereclause = whereclause +
DB_Combo1(i).pListQExpr + List1(i).List(X)
            ' Only add an 'or' if more are needed
            If (X <> NumClause% - 1) Then
                whereclause = whereclause + " Or "
            End If

      Next X
       ' Add the closing parentheses when needed.
         If (NumClause% > 1) Then
             whereclause = whereclause + ")"
         End If
      End If
   Next i

   orderby = ""

 ' Now check if any orderby clause is needed
    For i = 0 To 2          ' Check each check box.
       If (Check3D1(PanelPosition(i)) = -1) Then
            ' Check if a previous orderby has been set
```

```
        If (Len(orderby) = 0) Then
            orderby = "order by " +
DB_Combo1(PanelPosition(i)).pListQExpr
        Else
            orderby = orderby + "," +
DB_Combo1(PanelPosition(i)).pListQExpr
        End If
    End If
  Next i


    ' Add the orderby clause to the whereclause
    whereclause = whereclause + orderby
End Sub
```

To populate your grid, all you have to do is run the
BuildWhereClause subroutine, set the QGrid.pWhere to your
where clause, and assign the results of your fDoQuery
(QGrid) to a res%. You can also write your app so that end
users can construct their own queries with Q+E's Query Builder
(see Figure 6-1).

Error Handling

Q+E MultiLink/VB has good error handling routines. It defaults
to automatically displaying message boxes about any errors it
detects when your application runs (pErrorOption = 0), and this
is particularly useful during development. However, you can also
opt either for letting MultiLink/VB display design errors—like
setting an invalid pWhere expression—and writing your own code
to handle database errors, checking the result codes returned by
function calls (pErrorOption = 1) or by writing your own code
to handle both design and database errors (pErrorOption = 2).
The pErrorOption property is available for the Connect control, Query control, and Query Grid control.

Figure 6-1: *Q+E MultiLink/VB has its own query builder.*

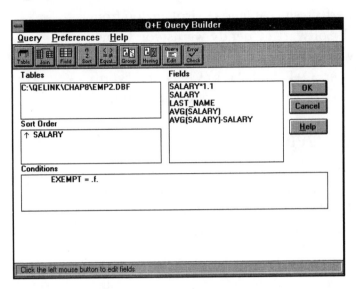

Here's an example where you provide your own error routine. If the result code returned by fDoQuery is anything but 0, then the query was unsuccessful, so the user is asked for a new path.

```
Sub cmdDoQuery_Click ()
    res% = fDoQuery(Query1)
    If res%  0 Then
        NewDir = InputBox ("Enter a valid path and filename
        ...for your database: )
        If NewDir  "" Then
            Query1.pTables = NewDir
            cmdDoQuery_Click
        End If
    End If
End Sub
```

Driver Options

Q+E MultiLink/VB isn't perfect, since it tends to isolate you from underlying functions. Q+E Software evidently wants you to buy its Q+E Database Library if you want lower-level control at the function-call level. However, Q+E MultiLink/VB is still worth investigating, especially since its drivers are ODBC compliant.

Distributing Q+E MultiLink/VB Applications

You'll probably want to use Microsoft's SetupWizard or Setup1 program to package your final application (see Chapter 11), but Q+E lets you distribute the QELINK VBX with your VB applications royalty free. You need to assemble these files:

QELINK.VBX
QEMLRUN.LIC
CTL3D.DLL
ODBC.DLL
QMUTL03.DLL
QMBAS03.DLL
ODBCINST.DLL
QMSQL03.DLL
QMGUI03.DLL
QMBLB03.DLL
QMMDS03.DLL
QMXXX03.DLL (database specific drivers)
QMFLT03.DLL (for "flat file" database access, e.g., Xbase, Paradox, or ASCII)

Lotus Notes

Although a Lotus Notes ODBC driver is bound to be available by the time you read this, some of you many prefer to use the Lotus

Notes Release 3.0 API toolkit (Lotus Part No. 37728, $495) to create your own DLLs. Lotus is also developing SQLNotes connectivity that should provide another tool VB programmers may want to add to their Notes toolbox. Finally, third-party vendors like Brainstorm Technology (Framingham, MA) have developed tools that let you access Notes databases from VB. In the meantime, Figure 6-2 shows a schematic view of connectivity options for Lotus Notes.

Figure 6-2: *A new NotesSQL is expected to join existing ODBC and DataLens links as an alternate way for Windows applications to access SQL data through Lotus Notes.*

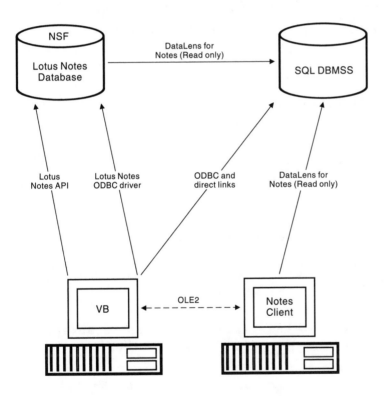

Lotus Notes API

The Lotus Notes Release 3.0 API contains almost 25MB of resources, including a small subdirectory of VB-specific files buried in the subdirectory \NOTESAPI\SAMPLES\MISC\VBASIC.

Lotus' sample VB application demonstrates how to call the Notes API from a VB program using "wrapper" functions around the API calls. Included in the Lotus Notes API toolkit are files for creating a Windows DLL in Microsoft C and a very simple VB program that calls the wrapper functions and retrieves the title of a Notes database. The "get started" wrapper functions provided in the Notes API samples include functions for starting and stopping Notes, for opening and closing a local Notes database, and for retrieving the title of a Notes database. Also included are some sample error routines.

```
/* Wrapper function to initialize Notes. */
int far pascal Start_Notes (void)

/* Wrapper function to exit from Notes. */
int far pascal Stop_Notes (void)

/* Wrapper function to open a Notes database. */
int far pascal Open_Notes_Database (char far *filename)

/* Wrapper function to close a Notes database. */
int far pascal Close_Notes_Database (void)

/* Wrapper function to get the title of a Notes database. */
int far pascal Get_Notes_Db_Title (char far *title)

/* Function to return the text associated with the last
...return code from an API call. */
int far pascal Get_Notes_Error_Message (char far
...*error_text)
```

DLL for Lotus Notes

Your disk comes with a ready-made DLL for accessing Notes databases. VBNOTES.DLL contains ten functions that let you read, update, and create Lotus Notes database records. Although you don't have to have the Notes API toolkit to *use* the DLL, you do have to have a Lotus Notes Windows client installed, along with a valid user ID in the workstation's path. You should install the DLL in the WINDOWS\SYSTEM subdirectory and make sure Notes is in your path.

Accessing a Notes Database   In order to access Notes, you must start a Notes "session" at the workstation. You do this by calling the NOTES_INIT function. To terminate the Notes session, call NOTES_TERM. To access a database, you must retrieve the database handle. You do this via the NOTES_DBOPEN function. Passing the server name and database filename to this function opens the database and returns the database handle. Once you have the database handle, you can access the data within the database, even if Notes isn't running. To close the Notes database, call the NOTES_DBCLOSE function.

Accessing a Notes Database Record   Each record in a Notes database has an associated note ID. This ID is a unique number for the note and does not change. To get one or more note IDs, call the function NOTES_GETNOTEID. You pass to this function a Notes selection formula (exactly like the one you would put in a view's selection formula). The function will return a list of note IDs for records that match your search criteria.

To get at a field within these notes, you must first get a note handle. The function NOTES_GETNOTEHANDLE takes the note ID as a parameter, opens the note, and returns the note handle. To access the value of a field, you call NOTES_DBNOTEGETFIELD, passing it the fieldname and the note handle.

To update a field within a note, take this note handle and call NOTES_DBNOTESETFIELD, passing it the fieldname, field type (text, time, or number), and new value for the field. This function will replace the current contents of the field with the value you passed or create a new field in that note if one did not exist before. As with the database, be sure you call NOTES_DBNOTECLOSE to close the note once you are done with it.

Creating a New Notes Database Record   To create a new record in Notes, call NOTES_DBNOTECREATE. This function creates a new note and passes the note handle back to you. Then simply call NOTES_DBNOTESETFIELD to set the field values. Be sure to close the database when you have finished.

The VB Declaration Section   Run the NOTESDEM sample application (see Figure 6-3) written by David Bourgeois, who also provided the C source code for his DLL. You'll see that the declaration section contains the following declarations:

```
Const FIELD_TEXT = 1
Const FIELD_NUMBER = 2
Const FIELD_TIME = 3

Declare Function Notes_Init Lib "VBNOTES.DLL" () As Integer
Declare Function Notes_Term Lib "VBNOTES.DLL" () As Integer
Declare Function Notes_DBOpen Lib "VBNOTES.DLL" (ByVal
...servername As String, ByVal filename As String) As
...Integer
Declare Function Notes_DBClose Lib "VBNOTES.DLL" (ByVal
...dbHandle As Integer) As Integer
```

```
Declare Function Notes_DBNoteCreate Lib "VBNOTES.DLL"
...(ByVal dbHandle As Integer) As Integer
Declare Function Notes_DBNoteClose Lib "VBNOTES.DLL"
...(ByVal noteHandle As Integer) As Integer
Declare Function Notes_DBNoteSetField Lib "VBNOTES.DLL"
...(ByVal noteHandle As Integer, ByVal fieldname As
...String, ByVal fieldtype As Integer, ByVal fieldvalue
...As String) As Integer
Declare Function Notes_DBNoteGetField Lib "VBNOTES.DLL"
...(ByVal noteHandle As Integer, ByVal fieldname As
...String, ByVal fieldvalue As String) As Integer
Declare Function Notes_GetNoteHandle Lib "VBNOTES.DLL"
...(ByVal dbHandle as Integer, ByVal noteID As Long) As
...Integer
Declare Function Notes_GetNoteID Lib "VBNOTES.DLL" (ByVal
...dbHandle As Integer, ByVal formula As String, ByVal
...returnString As String, ByVal returnStringLen As Inte-
...ger) As Integer
```

The functions are documented in detail, along with sample VB
code, in the VBNOTES.DOC file on your sample disk in
VBNOTES.ZIP.

Figure 6-3: *Using the VBNOTES.DLL on your sample disk to access a
Lotus Notes database*

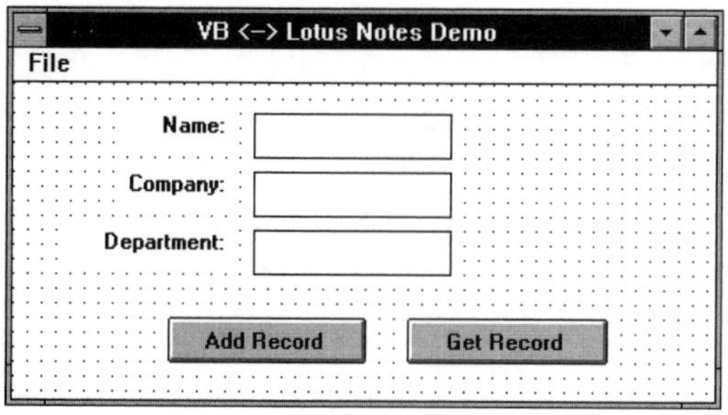

Oracle Glue

Oracle Glue is a "middleware" API that, in its first release, allows access to Oracle V6 and Oracle7 DBMSs, any other databases accessible from SQL*Connect, and Oracle*Mail. The first release of Oracle Glue wasn't available to VB programmers as a VBX, only as an application-specific DLL, VBGLUE.DLL.

The version of Oracle Glue we used, Release 1.0, provided support for DDE, but not ODBC or OLE. ODBC support should be available by the time you read this. The obvious question is, why use Oracle Glue when you can use ODBC drivers for Oracle directly from VB or third party tools like Q+E MultiLink/VB? The strongest argument for using Glue ($2,995) is for its tight integration with the Oracle product line that provides, for example, easy links to Oracle*Mail.

Using Oracle Glue

To use Oracle Glue, you add the necessary global declarations from the VBGLUE.BAS file to your project's declaration module. You have to call GlueInit—typically from your Form_Load subroutine—and register the controls that will be used as containers. The following code snippet shows how you might register controls:

```
Global G_Init_Flag As String

Sub Form_Load ()
   ' Check to see if already active
   ' If G_Init_Flag <> "Called" Then
      GlueInit
      G_Init_Flag = "Called"
   End If
' GlueInit for Schedule Downloader from Wizard Routine
GlueRegisterControl Combo1
GlueRegisterControl Combo2
```

```
GlueRegisterControl List1
List1.Clear
Combo1.Clear
' What kind of Sharp Wizard?
Combo1.AddItem "W8000"
Combo1.AddItem "W7000"
Combo1.AddItem "W6000"
Combo2.Clear
' Need to allow Wizard link to either serial port
Combo2.AddItem "COM1"
Combo2.AddItem "COM2"
End Sub
```

In Oracle Glue 1.0, you have to register each item in any control
arrays separately. Hopefully, this won't be necessary with later
versions.

Containers are data storage structures and must be embedded in
colons, much like embedded SQL references. With Release 1.0, you
can use Oracle Glue—but not VB—internal variables, files, or VB
controls that have text, list or picture properties as containers.

Execsql, Execmail, and Execlink are the functions you use to make
calls to back-end database, mail, and palmtop services, respectively. The functions all take a single-string argument. The meat of
your Oracle Glue routines typically involve making calls to these
services and using the `GlueSetString`, `GlueSetNumber`,
`GlueGetString`, and `GlueGetNumber` functions. These let you
transfer information between VB variables and Oracle Glue's internal
variables. The following code shows how you could populate a list
box with schedule data from Sharp Wizard.

```
Function dolink (cmd As String) As Integer
    screen.MousePointer = 11
    'Call the execlink function to access Sharp Wizard
```

```
    w = execlink(cmd)
    If w <> 0 Then
        LinkError (w)
        dolink = -1
    Else
        dolink = 0
    End If
    screen.MousePointer = 0
End Function

Sub Command1_Click ()
   temp# = dolink("connect to :Combo1.Text: at :Combo2.Text:")
   temp# = dolink("set rowindicator :ri:")
   temp# = dolink("open 'SCHEDULE1' for 'READ'")
   numrec = GlueGetNumber("ri", 0)

   For i = 1 To numrec
     temp# = dolink("read")
     syear$ = GlueGetString("YEAR", 0)
     smonth$ = GlueGetString("MONTH", 0)
     sday$ = GlueGetString("DAY", 0)
     sstart_hour$ = GlueGetString("START_HOUR", 0)
     sstart_minute$ = GlueGetString("START_MINUTE", 0)
     send_hour$ = GlueGetString("END_HOUR", 0)
     send_minute$ = GlueGetString("END_MINUTE", 0)
     sdescription$ = GlueGetString("DESCRIPTION", 0)
     List1.AddItem sday$ + "." + smonth$ + "." + syear$ + "
" + sstart_hour$ + ":" + sstart_minute$ + " - " +
send_hour$ + ":" + send_minute$ + "   " + sdescription$
     temp# = dolink("go to next record")
   Next i
End Sub
```

IBM Mainframe Terminal Emulation

As we all know, lots of end users are forced to access mainframe data using antiquated 3270 (or 5250 for AS/400 systems) character-based terminals. A handful of firms have developed VBXes that reduce the pain of dealing with client/host development.

APIs

IBM has defined several APIs that affect VB developers who need to write client/host programs that access mainframe data. High Level Language Application Programming Interface (HLLAPI) allows users to emulate multiple terminal sessions on their PCs while running a DOS session. A subset, confusingly known as EHLLAPI (the "e" for extended), only permits a single terminal session and lacks support for the concurrent DOS session. Windows applications that use EHLLAPI simulate multiple host sessions by logging in and out "under the hood." The EHLLAPI contains about 45 function calls that emulate what end users do from their 3270 terminals.

EHLLAPI is a subset of the IBM High Level Language API for terminal emulation. WinHLLAPI is the Windows version of that API.

IBM has also defined its Logical Unit Type 6.2 (LU 6.2) SNA (Systems Network Architecture) protocol for peer-to-peer communications between SNA devices, but since 3270 terminals are based on the older LU 2 master/slave protocol and because of low market acceptance of LU 6.2 and the related Common Program Interface for Communications (CPI-C) you probably won't have to worry about LU 6.2.

The final API you may run into is Distributed Remote Database Access (DRDA). It is IBM's newest API and theoretically allows transparent access across all of IBM's DBMSs. DRDA support is slowly being integrated into some front-end products, but as of 3Q93 there weren't any VBXs that supported DRDA.

There are also two relevant Microsoft APIs: Dynamic Data Exchange (DDE) and the newer WinHLLAPI. Dynamic Data Exchange represents another method of interacting with a mainframe. However, DDE links don't support all the functionality of HLLAPI terminal emulation, so it's not a popular choice with most VB developers. Furthermore, DDE is being supplanted by OLE 2.0, so it doesn't make much sense to use DDE for client/host development.

Microsoft's Windows Operating System Architecture (WOSA) has been extended to include APIs like ODBC, MAPI, and WinHLLAPI. The latter is a Windows-specific version of HLLAPI, and products supporting it have started entering the pipeline.

Commercial VBXes

By 3Q93, there were three major products providing VBXes for 3270 emulation applications:

EXTRA! Tools for Visual Basic ($195)
Attachmate Corporation
3617 131st Ave. SE
Bellevue, WA 98006
800-426-6283 or 206-644-4010; Fax 206-747-9924

QuickApp for Windows ($995, requires DCA IRMA Workstation for Windows, IRMA Workstation for INFOConnect, or IRMA/400)
Digital Communications Associates, Inc. (DCA)
Alpharetta, GA
800-348-3221 or 404-442-4000; Faxback 404-442-4035

Rumba Tools for Visual Basic ($195, requires Rumba terminal software)
Wall Data Inc.
17769 NE 78th Place
Redmond, WA 98052-4992
800-487-8622 or 206-883-4777; Fax 206-861-3175

Using any of those programs would allow you to write a snazzy front end that accessed Office Vision/MVS (OV/MVS), for example. OV/MVS is an IBM mainframe-based enterprise mail system that is replacing PROFS in many IBM shops. OV/MVS is a robust mail system, but it's character-based. No one has ever faulted OV/MVS for being overly user-friendly. A 3270 terminal address book screen developed to use OV/MVS might look like Figure 6-4 and be one of dozens of 3270 screens developed for a single applications (see Figure 6-5).

Figure 6-4: *A 3270 e-mail address book screen*

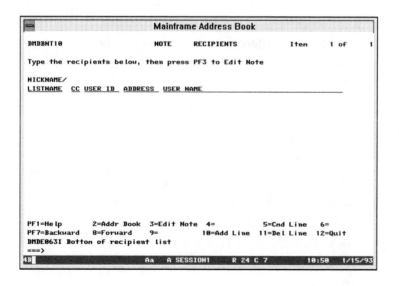

Figure 6-5: *A list of 3270 screens that might be developed as part of an Office Vision/MVS application*

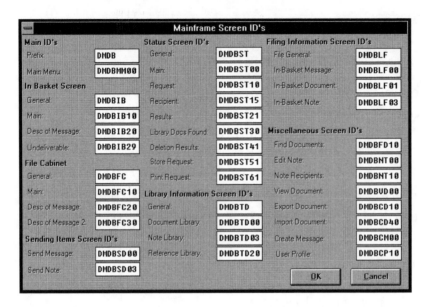

Mainframe Screen ID's					
Main ID's		**Status Screen ID's**		**Filing Information Screen ID's**	
Prefix:	DMDB	General:	DMDBST	File General:	DMDBLF
Main Menu:	DMDBMM00	Main:	DMDBST00	In-Basket Message:	DMDBLF00
In Basket Screen		Request:	DMDBST10	In-Basket Document:	DMDBLF01
General:	DMDBIB	Recipient:	DMDBST15	In-Basket Note:	DMDBLF03
Main:	DMDBIB10	Results:	DMDBST21		
Desc of Message:	DMDBIB20	Library Docs Found:	DMDBST30	**Miscellaneous Screen ID's**	
Undeliverable:	DMDBIB29	Deletion Results:	DMDBST41	Find Documents:	DMDBFD10
File Cabinet		Store Request:	DMDBST51	Edit Note:	DMDBNT00
General:	DMDBFC	Print Request:	DMDBST61	Note Recipients:	DMDBNT10
Main:	DMDBFC10	**Library Information Screen ID's**		View Document:	DMDBUD00
Desc of Message:	DMDBFC20	General:	DMDBTD	Export Document:	DMDBCD10
Desc of Message 2:	DMDBFC30	Document Library:	DMDBTD00	Import Document:	DMDBCD40
Sending Items Screen ID's		Note Library:	DMDBTD03	Create Message:	DMDBCM00
Send Message:	DMDBSD00	Reference Library:	DMDBTD20	User Profile:	DMDBCP10
Send Note:	DMDBSD03			OK Cancel	

Attachmate EXTRA! for Visual Basic

Since Attachmate is the 3270 terminal emulation market leader, we'll use an example from the Attachmate DLL to demonstrate how you might develop a VB application that replaces the 3270 terminal session.

The declaration section of your project needs to declare the Attachmate DLL and its global variables. The Attachmate DLL is consistent with the EHLLAPI specification that requires that all functions take four parameters: a function number, a data string, a length parameter, and a position parameter. Although not all EHLLAPI functions actually use all four parameters, they still require that your program pass them four values, even if some of them are simply place holders. The last parameter, the position parameter, is also used to store a return code.

```
'Attachmale EXTRA! for Visual Basic Function Declarations
Declare Sub EHLLAPI Lib "ACS3EHAP.DLL" Alias "HLLAPI"
...(Func%, ByVal DataString$, length%, RetCode%)
Global Const Connect = 1
Global Const Disconnect = 2
Global Const SendKey = 3
Global Const Wait = 4
Global Const CopyScreen = 5
Global Const Search = 6
Global Const GetCursor = 7
Global Const GetString = 8
Global Const QuerySessions = 10
Global Const LockKeyboard = 11
Global Const UnlockKeyboard = 12
Global Const QueryAttribute = 14
Global Const SendString = 15
Global Const WSCTRL = 16
Global Const Pause = 18
Global Const QuerySystem = 20
Global Const ResetSystem = 21
Global Const QueryStatus = 22
Global Const SendFile = 90
Global Const ReceiveFile = 91
Global Const Convert = 99
```

The most common EHLLAPI functions are `Connect` and `Disconnect`, `SendKey`, `Wait`, `Search`, `GetCursor`, `GetString`, `SetCursor`, `SendFile`, and `ReceiveFile`.

As you might expect, you have to establish the mainframe connection before your program can call any of the other EHLLAPI functions. A sample connection routine might be

```
Session$ =  A       'link to session A
Return% = 0         'initialize the return code
```

```
HLLAPI 1, Session$, 0, Return%
' To disconnect and issue the reset function, use these
...statements
HLLAPI 2, Session$, 0, Return%
HLLAPI 21,    , 0, Return%
```

The SendKey function sends a keystroke to the terminal as if an end user had typed it. To differentiate between characters and keystrokes, Attachmate uses a set of mnemonics—letters and numbers preceded by the @ symbol. @E, for example, stands for the Enter key, and @1 stands for a user pressing the PF1 function key.

To capture a string of data from the host screen, you use GetString, EHLLAPI function 8. To capture 10 characters starting at row 6, column 3, the VB code would be

```
DataString$ = String (10,  )
Position% = (6-1)*80 + 3
HLLAPI 8, DataString$, Len(DataString$), Position%
If Position% <> 0 then
   MsgBox  Error while capturing data
End If
```

In case you're wondering, Attachmate and other 3270 screen scraper applications have both keystroke recording utilities and programs that map mainframe screen field positions. Here's another example:

```
Function WaitForString (WaitString$) As Integer
   EHLLAPI Wait, temp$, 0, Ret%
   For counter% = 1 To 10   ' search up to 10 times
      DoEvents           ' allow other apps to run
      Ret% = 1           ' start searching a position 1
      length% = Len(WaitString$)
      ' call search function
```

```
      EHLLAPI Search, WaitString$, length%, Ret%
      If Ret% = 0 Then Exit For 'success
      If Ret% <> 24 Then     ' didn't find the string
        MsgBox "Parameter error in WaitForString"
        ExitApp        ' fatal error, exit
      End If
      DoEvents          ' allow other processing
      EHLLAPI Pause, temp$, 2, x%
    Next counter%
    If Ret% = 24 Then
      WaitForString = 0
    Else
      WaitForString = Length%
    EHLLAPI Wait, temp$, 0 Ret%' wait for host
    End If
End Function
```

By using Attachmate EXTRA! for Visual Basic, you can replace the 3270 screens with something like Figure 6-6. Attachmate EXTRA! for Visual Basic supports up to 26 "concurrent" sessions, memory permitting, and has a mainframe emulation mode that lets you do development offline, without using a live mainframe connection.

DCA's QuickApp for Windows and Wall Data's Rumba Tools for Visual Basic

QuickApp for Windows 1.1 requires that you use DCA's IRMA Workstation for Windows 2.1.2 or higher software that includes the QuickApp runtime. QuickApp for Windows comes with three custom controls: DCANavigate, DCALabel, and DCAText. QuickApp for Windows requires far less coding than Attachmate's EXTRA! does but, by the same token, doesn't give you direct access to the EHLLAPI functions.

Figure 6-6: *A Visual Basic interface to the Office Vision mail system created with Attachmate EXTRA! for Visual Basic*

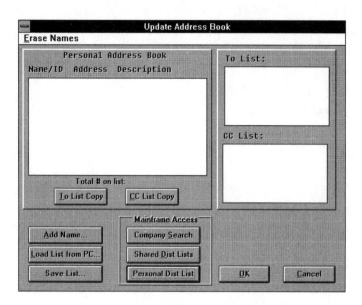

The DCANavigate control has the following custom properties and events:

- Action property

- Activate property

- ActualScrn property

- Direction property

- FTCmdOptions property

- FTParameters property

- RecorderFile property

- HostFileName property

- HostNextScrn property

- HostSess property

- PCFileName property

- ReturnCode property

- HostReturn event

- HostError event

- FileTransOK event

- FileTransErr event

The DCAText control has `AtCursor`, `AutoFill`, `QAFieldName`, `QAPassword`, and `QAScrnName` custom properties, and the `DCALabel` control has `QAScrnName` and `QAFieldName` custom properties. All three custom controls are contained in a single VBX that you can distribute with your application to DCA IRMA Workstation for Windows users.

With QuickApp for Windows Version 1.1, the keystroke recorder plays a more important role than it does in EXTRA! for Visual Basic. Once you've established your IRMA Workstation session—you can have up to five sessions—developing a QuickApp for Windows applications is a very simple two-step process. First you capture the screens, keystrokes, and paths between screens in the 3270 session and save them to a script file. The recorder takes care of mapping mainframe fields to your VB form and generates script files that look like this:

```
RECORDER
BEGIN
```

```
    CURSOR(ROW 23,COLUMN 1)
    SCREENIDENT
    BEGIN
        IDENT(ROW 1,COLUMN 1,TYPE ABSOLUTE,LITERAL "LOGON ")
        IDENT(ROW 3,COLUMN 1,TYPE ABSOLUTE,LITERAL "LOGON AT")
        IDENT(ROW 24,COLUMN 61,TYPE ABSOLUTE,LITERAL "RUN-
        ...NING    VMATL     ")
    END

NEXTSCREENID(5)
BEGIN
    USERINPUT("prof")
    AIDKEY(ENTER)
END
END

HOSTSCREEN
BEGIN
    SCREENID(5)
    SESSIONID(0)
    SCREENNAME(PROFS_MAIN)
    WINDOWNAME(TYPE MODAL)
    BEGIN
        LABEL(FIELDNAME QAPLABEL001,ROW 1,COLUMN 2,LENGTH
        ...75,ATTRIBUTES 0xE8)
        LABEL(FIELDNAME QAPLABEL002,ROW 1,COLUMN 78,LENGTH
        ...4,ATTRIBUTES 0xE8)
```

QuickApp's Control Pad has button (see Figure 6-7) that automates the recording process. Once you've recorded a typical mainframe session, you can log off the mainframe and continue development in VB. You use the QuickApp custom controls to move fields from the host screens onto your VB forms and to control file transfers from the mainframe using IBM IND$FILE, for example.

The QuickApp 1.1 VBX can also be used for Visual C++ or PowerBuilder development and is WinHLLAPI compliant. QuickApp also supports a 13-function QuickAPI that can be called without the VBX.

Figure 6-7: *QuickApp ships with three custom controls that help VB programmers create graphical interfaces to 3270 host applications.*

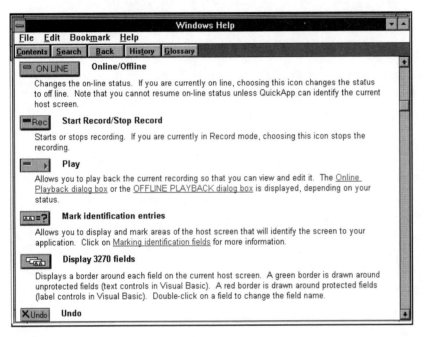

The central paradigm in Wall Data's Rumba Tools for Visual Basic isn't the recorder, it's the FormBuilder, which converts host mainframe (or AS/400 or VAX) screens into VB objects. Rumba Tools for VB also ships with an SDK Trace EHLLAPI utility that lets you view—and troubleshoot—the communications between your application and the host. Many developers also take advantage of Rumba Tools support for graphical icons on its command buttons. It may sound silly to Windows fans, but putting a PF1 on a command button can make it easier for some 3270 terminal users to make the transition to Windows.

Other Connectors

Sometimes you'll have to work with special-purpose gateways or routes that serve not only as links to back-end data—typically on a mainframe, but also serve as a type of gatekeeper. Many of these gateways are vendor-specific, but some are more general purpose and "open."

Some database gateways provide SQL gateways to non-SQL, or "legacy" data. That means the gateway takes care of mapping your SQL query to the mainframe data files. Other database gateways take the remote-procedure-call (RPC) approach and actually run existing applications on remote computers. Middleware is often harnessed for copy management, or replication services. Middleware might be used to do periodic downloads of mainframe data into a local database server for "real enough time" data access.

Popular gateways you should be aware of are

> Micro Decisionware Inc. (MDI) Micro Decisionware Gateway
> Information Builders Inc. (IBI) EDA/SQL
> Sybase OmniSQL Gateway
> Trinzic InfoPump

Summary

VB3 comes with a good set of data access tools, but you're not limited to using them or going through ODBC. In this chapter, we looked at how you might use Q+E Software's Q+E MultiLink/VB and introduced some of the more popular packages you can use to access Lotus Notes and mainframe data. In the next chapter, we show you how to *use* some of the data you've learned how to access and integrate report writing into your vb application.

Sample Disk Files

VBNOTES.ZIP   Simple DLL for accessing Lotus Notes databases. Includes C source and a sample VB application.

7

Crystal Reports:
The VBX and Engine

Real men don't use report writers, right? They'd rather hard code column-oriented reports themselves or use the Print or PrintForm methods. They don't really like tweaking tab and Format functions in Print statements but just can't get excited about hard copy. All their reports are printed out in Courier 12.

Times have changed. People expect nice-looking reports. Fortunately, all you have to do is open your toolbox and spend a few minutes exploring Crystal Reports.

Reports the Old Way

Prior to VB3, designing reports was not fun. You probably used the Print method:

```
Cobject.JPrint [expressionlist] C{ ; | , }]
```

as in

```
Printer.CurrentX = 0
Printer.CurrentY = 0
Printer.Print "This text is going to the printer."
```

For tabular reports, you may have experimented with the print zones that are built into Visual Basic. Each print zone is 14 columns wide, and each column is the width of the average character in the font and font size you specify. Print zones, unfortunately, are tedious to code and can be nasty to deal with if you use proportional fonts. This may look familiar:

```
Form1.FontName = "MS Sans Serif"
Form1.FontSize = 10
Form1.Print "First name", "Last name", "Phone number"
Form1.Print
Form1.Print "Jonathan", "Doe", "123-4444"
Form1.Print "Arlene", "DeLille", "123-5555"
Form1.Print "Joseph", "Buchanan", "123-3333"
```

To override the default tab positions, you use Tab(xx) in your Print statement as in

```
Form1.Print Tab(5);"First name", "Last name", "Phone number"
Form1.Print
Form1.Print Tab(5); "Jonathan", "Doe", "123-4444"
```

Formatting

Formatting is not point-and-click easy with the Print method, either. You use the Format (converts numeric to variant) or Format$ (numeric to string) functions and apply optional format strings. The fmt$ string consists of symbols that control formatting:

Symbol	Description
0	Digit placeholder; prints a trailing or a leading zero if appropriate
#	Digit placeholder; never prints trailing or leading zeros
.	Decimal placeholder
,	Thousands separator
+ $ ( ) space	Literals which are displayed as typed

VB also provides some stand formats you can use with the Format$ or Format functions instead of typing in your own formatting mask. The format name, such as Currency, Fixed, Scientific, or Short Date, must be enclosed in double quotes.

If you're a veteran VBer, you've probably also experimented with the related approach of printing text to a form and then printing the form with the `PrintForm` method which sends a bit-for-bit image of a non-MDI form to the printer. `PrintForm` prints all visible controls and bitmaps on the form and any graphics you may have added if `AutoRedraw` was `True` when the graphics were drawn.

Print and PrintForm aren't the only tools you've had. You may have crafted some reports with the Printer object, using `NewPage` or `EndDoc` methods to initiate printing. The TimeCard sample application (see Figure 7-1) that ships with VB3 has code that demonstrates some techniques for using the Printer object. It includes a series of general procedures that recreate selected portions of the data entry form on the Printer object drawing:

- The outline and title bar, but not the menu bar

- All the label controls (using a controls collection)

- The Print Card command button

- Lines that separate areas of information

- Icons that serve as column headings, but not the holiday, vacation, or sick-time icons

Figure 7-1: *Explore Microsoft's TimeCard application in the \VB\Samples\Print subdirectory*

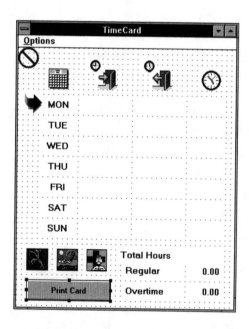

You may have even used DDE, MAPI, or some combination of SendKeys and the Clipboard to export or otherwise route your report for printing by the hapless recipient.

Crystal Reports

Fortunately, now there's an easier way. Microsoft addressed our complaints about how hard printing was in VB and VB2 by including a fine report writer from Crystal Services (1050 West Pender Street, Suite 2200, Vancouver, BC, Canada V6E3S7. Phone: (604) 681-3435; Fax (604) 681-2934).

Microsoft isn't the only firm to have licensed the technology: arch-rival Borland has bundled Crystal Reports with ObjectVision and the Paradox Engine, it's an integral part of Hewlett-Packard's HP Information Access, and Apex Software optionally bundles it with Agility/VB. Crystal Reports is the Windows report writer used by many XDB and NetWare SQL developers and Turbo Pascal programmers.

You may want to take advantage of the upgrade offer to get either the Crystal Reports 2.0 Standard Edition or the extensible DLL version of Crystal Reports Professional Edition. Both of them offer their own native data access drivers. In contrast, when you use Crystal Reports for Visual Basic, all data access is done through Access. One of the limitations of this approach, for example, is that you can't access Paradox 4.0 data. Armed with Crystal Reports 2.0, though, you can. The main differences between Crystal Reports for Visual Basic and Crystal Reports 2.0 Pro are as follows:

- Pro gives you direct access to the Crystal Report Engine API as well as the VBX interface to the Engine. The former supports about 20 more functions.

- Pro supports more SQL databases.

- Pro has a Report Compiler allowing you to compile reports into .EXE files.

- Pro has User Function Libraries (UFL) that let you add your own functions to the Crystal Engine. You have to write a DLL in C, C++, or anything else that can compile a DLL.

Sometime in early19 94, Crystal will be shipping a new Crystal Reports 3.0 and a new VBX that will add support for mail-enabled reports, a robust import/export API, and full support for OLE 2.0.

VB3 includes both an interactive standalone version of Crystal Reports and a VBX. You can use the standalone Crystal Reports to create reports based on Access, XBase, Paradox 3.5, Btrieve, or ObjectVision data. You can also access SQL databases through the Access engine's ODBC drivers. These selections are available from the File and Database menus respectively.

If you do opt for the full Crystal Reports 2.0 Standard or Professional Editions, bear in mind that Crystal Reports for Visual Basic will use its native DLLs for Crystal Report 2.0 in favor of going through Access. You may also run into problems if you create a report using the Crystal Reports that comes with VB and then try to open it with the standard version of Crystal Reports, since the former uses JET access routines.

Crystal Reports uses a standard, banded, report-writer interface with header, detail—or body—and footer sections. You can quickly access formatting options via the right mouse button (see Figure 7-2), perform calculations, group your data, and perform all the standard filtering and sorting activities you'd expect.

Figure 7-2: *Clicking on the right mouse button when a field is selected gives you fast access to formatting options.*

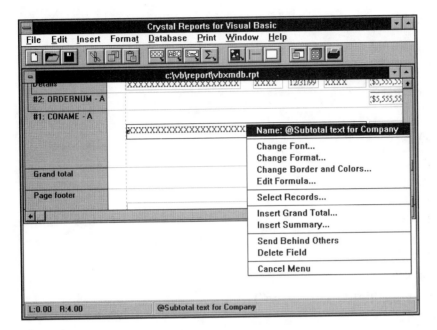

Lots of Functions

Take some time to explore Crystal's function language (see Table 7-1), because you can do a lot with it. It supports IF/THEN logic, a function for converting numbers to words, and statistical functions for variance and standard deviation.

Table 7-1: *Functions in Crystal Reports*

Abs(x)
Average([array])
Average(field, condField)
Average(field, condField, "condition")
Average(field)
BeforeReadingRecords

Table 7-1:   *(Continued)*

Count([array])
Count(field, condField)
Count(field, condField, "condition")
Count(field)
Date (yyyy, mm, dd)
Day (x)
DayOfWeek (x)
GroupNumber
IsNull
Length(x)
LowerCase (x)
Maximum([array])
Maximum(field, condField)
Maximum(field, condField, "condition")
Maximum(field)
Minimum([array])
Minimum(field, condField)
Minimum(field, condField, "condition")
Minimum(field)
Month (x)
Next
NextIsNull
NumericText(fieldname)
PageNumber
PopulationStdDev([array])
PopulationStdDev(field, condField)
PopulationStdDev(field, condField, "condition")
PopulationStdDev(field)
PopulationVariance([array])

Table 7-1: *(Continued)*

PopulationVariance(field, condField)

PopulationVariance(field, condField, "condition")

PopulationVariance(field)

Previous

PreviousIsNull

PrintDate

RecordNumber

Remainder(numerator, denominator)

ReplicateString(x,n)

Round(x, # places)

Round(x)

StdDev([array])

StdDev(field, condField)

StdDev(field, condField, "condition")

StdDev(field)

Sum([array])

Sum(field, condField)

Sum(field, condField, "condition")

Sum(field)

Today

ToNumber (x)

ToText (x, # places)

ToText (x)

ToWords(x, # places)

ToWords(x)

TrimLeft (x)

TrimRight (x)

Truncate (x)

UpperCase (x)

Table 7-1:   *(Continued)*

Variance([array])

Variance(field, condField)

Variance(field, condField, "condition")

Variance(field)

WhilePrintingRecords

WhileReadingRecords

Year (x)

Graphics, Mailing Labels, and CrossTabs

Crystal's button bar also has drawing tools and lets you insert BMP, PCX, TIF, GIF, and TGA files. There's also a File I New Mailing Labels report option—complete with Wizard—for creating mailing labels (see Figure 7-3). Version 3.0 of Crystal Reports will also have a graphical crosstab report generator, complete with Wizard.

Figure 7-3: *Crystal Reports for Visual Basic comes with a Wizard for setting up a mailing label report.*

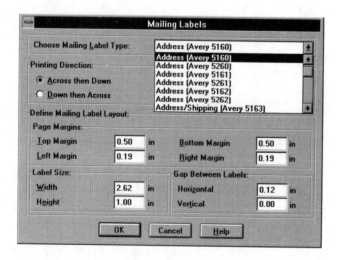

If you need crosstabs and haven't used VB's TRANSFORM (SQL) statement, you may want to compare it to Crystal's implementation of crosstab reports. TRANSFORM works a little like spreadsheet pivots. When you summarize data using a crosstab query, you select values from a specified field or expression as column headers so you can view data in a more compact format than a SELECT query would produce.

To use TRANSFORM, simply precede your normal SQL SELECT as follows:

```
TRANSFORM  aggregatefunction
   sqlstatement
   PIVOT  pivotcolumn
```

Your sqlstatement needs to include a SELECT statement that specifies the fields used as row headings and a GROUP BY clause that specifies row grouping. Pivotcolumn refers to the field, column, or expression you want to pivot (rotate) to form the column headings. When you pivot a field, the unique values of pivotcolumn become columns. For example, pivoting the sales figures on the month of the sale in a crosstab query would create twelve columns.

Crystal Reports has an easy-to-miss Browse feature. You'll see this option when you're doing database field-level actions like inserting fields into a report. Crystal's Browse lets you scroll through sample data, something that's especially handy when you inherit someone else's database. Crystal also reports the native field name and length (see Figure 7-4).

- Crystal also supports word wrap via the Format String dialog box. If you have a string field selected on-screen, you can access the Format String dialog box either by clicking on the right mouse button and selecting Change Format or by selecting Format | Field from the main menu. You'll also get it if you click the string button in the Field Formats box in the Options dialog box while using the File l Options command. To get word wrap, simply check the multiple lines box. You can limit the number of lines if you so desire, but a "0" entry uses as many lines as needed.

Tip: Use Crystal's Format String option to enable word wrap.

Figure 7-4: *Crystal's Browse Field Data option shows sample data and reports on native field definitions.*

But don't waste any time looking for OLE support or a SQL code editor in Crystal 2.0 or the VBX, because they aren't there. Both are planned for Release 3.0, though.

Custom Control Properties

CRYSTAL.VBX is the custom control that comes with VB3, and you can either File l Add it to your projects or add it directly to your AUTOLOAD.MAK file. The following properties are available on the Crystal Custom Control for Visual Basic (CRYSTAL.VBX). Note that many of the properties are only available at runtime.

About
Action (Runtime)
Connect
CopiesToPrinter
DataFiles (Runtime)
Destination
Formulas (Runtime, Read/Write)
GroupSelectionFormula
GroupSortFields (Runtime)
IndexLastErrorNumber (Runtime, Read/Write)
LastErrorString (Runtime, Read/Write)
Left
Name
Password
PrintFileName
PrintFileType
PrintReport (Runtime)
ReportFileName
SelectionFormula
SessionHandle (Runtime, Read/Write)
SortFields (Runtime, Read/Write)
Top
UserName
WindowBorderStyle
WindowControlBox
WindowHeight
WindowLeft
WindowMaxButton
WindowMinButton
WindowParentHandle (Runtime, Read/Write)

WindowTitle
WindowTop
WindowWidth

Using the Crystal VBX Properties   `Action` is the property that triggers the printing of the report. Set the `Action` property to 1 in your procedure code (`Report1.Action = 1`) to print the report in response to a user event. `Action` uses the integer data type.

`Connect` logs you onto a SQL server. Before you can use this property, you must install the ODBC driver for whatever SQL database you are planning to use and put the Database/BIN location in your path. The basic syntax for programmatic access to the connect string is

```
[form.]Report.Connect[=Name;UserID;Password;DBQualifier$]
```

To connect the "Admin" database on the "Accounting" server using the user ID #734 and the password "bigfoot," you could set the Connect property as follows:

```
DSN = Accounting;UID = 734;PWD = bigfoot;DSQ = Admin
```

The `CopiesToPrinter` property is self-explanatory: You enter the positive integer number of copies you want printed, assuming you're printing to a printer. The `Destination` property is where you specify the destination, and it defaults to 1 - Printer. `DataFiles` is an array property that's only available at runtime. You use `DataFiles` if you want to run the report with files or tables that are in different locations than specified in the report. As you can probably guess, `DataFiles` is an array of strings. The order of files in the array starts with 0 and must conform to the order of files in the report. If you can't remember, use Database | File Location to find out the order of files in your report.

You also need to use a separate line of code for each file for which you want to change the location. The property is reset after each print job. If you print a second time, the program reverts to the locations as originally specified in the report. The destination can be any of the following:

- 0 = Window, e.g. screen

- 1 = Printer

- 2 = File

If you set the destination to 2, you also have to set the `PrintFileName` and `PrintFileType` properties.

`Formulas` is an another array property that's only available at runtime. You use it to replace an existing string formula. Like the `DataFiles` property, Formulas is indexed from 0 and requires that you use a separate line of code for each formula you want to change. Like `DataFiles`, changes are purged after each print job. `Spaces` are significant in formula names, so the "=" must follow the formula name with no intervening spaces. You can't use this property to create new formulas, only to change existing formulas. The `GroupSelectionFormula` is basically a variation on the Formulas property, with one important difference. If you have created a group selection formula in your report at design time, any group selection formula you enter here will be appended to that group selection formula, connected by a logical "AND". Thus, your records will be selected based on a combination of the two formulas. If your group selection formula includes internal quotes, you'll need to change all of the internal double quotes to single quotes and then surround the entire selection formula in double quotes.

`GroupSortFields` is an array property available at runtime only. You need to use a separate line of code to specify each group sort field. The order in which you list the sort fields is significant, must be continuous, and the array starts at 0. Any sort fields you set up at design time will be overridden. To clear the group sort fields in your report, use an empty string (`Report1.GroupSort-Fields(0) = ""`). Descending order is specified with a "-", as in

```
Report1.GroupSortFields(0) = "-Count ({customer.
...CUSTOMER},{customer.STATE})"
```

Note the braces surrounding the file.fieldname. This non-standard notation is a major irritant.

`Index` is a standard Visual Basic property set automatically by the program when you create an array of controls.

`LastErrorNumber` and `LastErrorString` are runtime-only properties that return the error code and last error string, respectively, for the last runtime error. These properties must come after the `Action` call in order to display relevant values. After you've printed your report, you can refer to these properties to get an error number and error string (if any). No error returns a `LastErrorNumber = 0`.

```
If Result <> 0  Then
    MsgBox Report1.LastErrorString
EndIf
```

The `Left` property is where you enter the amount of space you want to appear between the left edge of the container (form, frame, etc.), and the left edge of the Crystal Custom Control. This value uses the same units specified for the form and lets you position the control icon numerically.

The `Name` setting lets you enter a new name for each of your reports. By default, the first control you activate for a form is given the name Report1, the second control is given the name Report2, etc. You can't change the `Name` property at runtime.

`Password` lets you designate passwords for restricted Access databases.

`PrintFileName` needs to be enclosed in quotes in your code if you set it at runtime.

`PrintFileType` can be any of the following:

0 - Record	Record style (columns of values). Doesn't use commas or separators. Outputs every record with a fixed field width.
1 - Tab separated	Tab separated values. Presents data in tabular form. Encloses alphanumeric field data in quotes and separates fields with tabs.
2 - Text	Text style. Saves the data in ASCII text format with all values separated by spaces. This style looks most like the printed page.
3 - DIF	Saves the data in DIF (data interchange format) format. This format is often used for the transfer of data between different spreadsheet programs.
4- CSV	Comma separated values. Encloses alphanumeric field data in quotes and separates fields with commas.
5 - Reserved	
6 - Tab separated text	Saves the data in ASCII text format with all values separated by tabs.

The `ReportFileName` property, like the `PrintFileName` property, needs to have the name enclosed in quotes in your code. The `SelectionFormula` property lets you enter a formula as if you were doing it in Crystal's Formula Editor, except that you have to enclose it in double quotes. For formulas that themselves contain internal quotes, such as {file.STATE} = "NY", you need to change all of the internal double quotes to single quotes and then surround the entire selection formula in double quotes. Like the GroupSelectionFormula property, any selection formula you enter here is appended to the existing selection formula connected by an "AND."

SessionHandle is a runtime-only property that sets the session handle for a user once the UserName and Password properties have been established to open an Access .MDB file. If you've already opened an Access/Jet session in your Visual Basic application, you can set this property to be the current session handle. Otherwise you have to use the Password and UserName properties to establish the Jet session.

SortFields is an array property available only at runtime, and it works like GroupSortFields: each sort field on its own line, in order, an so on. To clear sort fields set at design time, use an empty string. Otherwise, any sort fields specified override existing sort fields for the duration of the current print job. Field names need to be enclosed in braces. You can also use formula fields for sort fields by using the "@" sign before the formula name, as in @FORMULA-NAME. You use "+" or "-" signs to establish sort order, as in

```
Report1.SortFields(0) =  "+{orders.COMPANY}"
Report1.SortFields(1) = "-{orders.PODATE}"
```

Top sets the amount of space you want to appear between the top edge of the container (form, frame, etc.), and the top edge of the control.

UserName is the name associated with logging into a protected Access .MDB file.

WindowBorderStyle can be any of the following:

- 0 - None

- 1 - Fixed Single

- 2 - Sizable

- 3 - Fixed Double

WindowControlBox is the standard VB property for enabling or disabling the system menu. WindowHeight and WindowWidth refer to the external height (or width) of your window in pixels. WindowLeft and WindowTop reference the number of pixels you want between the left (or top) edge of the screen and the left (or top) edge of your window. WindowMaxButton and WindowMinButton are the standard VB properties for enabling or disabling the maximize and minimize buttons. You can use the WindowParentHandle property like this for MDI windows:

```
Report1.WindowParentHandle = Form1.hWnd
```

The WindowTitle property needs to be enclosed in quotes and is the title you want to have appear in the print window title bar.

The CRVBXSAM.MAK Project

Check out the sample project that comes with VB3. Form3, for example, is a "Print to File" form with code for outputting reports as CSV, tab-separated, DIF, or ASCII text files (see Figure 7-5).

Creating a Fast Report for VBPRODS

To create basic listing of VB add-in vendors from data in the VBFIRMS table in your VBPRODS database, heres how to get started.

Figure 7-5: *Look for the Crystal Reports sample application in the VB\REPORT subdirectory.*

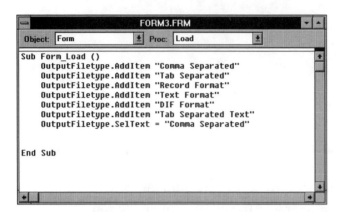

Open the VBPRODS.MAK project, or create a new one, but make sure the CRYSTAL.VBX is part of your project. Activate Crystal either from the Window | Report Designer menu or by selecting the Crystal icon. From the main menu, select File | New, and specify VBPRODS.MDB as the source database.

Crystal will display a stub report in its banded report writer. Youll also see a dialog box listing all the available database fields (Figure 7-6). To create a simple columnar, simply click on the fields you want and drop them into the details section. Crystal will automatically size them for you and add a header.

The next step will normally the shrink the fields, which is tedious, but at least you can select both the header and detail sections as a group. That means you can resize them at the same time, apply formatting, etc.

The next step is usually to select formatting, add computed columns, totals, and the like. Be sure to take advantage of the right mouse buttons when you do this, since they provide popup menus with field-related options.

Figure 7-6: *Selecting fields for a Crystal report*

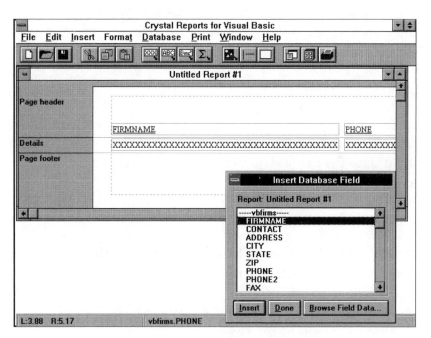

Crystal lets you preview your report by routing it to the screen (Print | Print to Window). Version 3.0 will probably also include a standard page preview option under the File menu. Once youre satisfied with the report, you can integrate it into your VB application as a command button option, or whatever makes sense.

Potential Irritants

Crystal's formula syntax and some of its notations are different from VB's, and this can be frustrating. The secret is to remember that formulas have to conform to Crystal Reports formula standards—for example, strings have to be embedded in quotes, but numbers don't. In VB, if you declare a string

```
charstr As String
charstr = "This is a string"
```

VB will recognize charstr as a string, but if you pass charstr to Crystal Reports, the string won't be recognized unless you embed the string in quotes. In VB, you can do that either by using two double quotes or a single quote.

```
charstr = """This is a string"""
charstr = "'This is a string'"
```

Dates are another source of irritation and require a little more work. To compare a date field to a date in Crystal Reports, you would use a formula like this

```
{datefield} = Date(1994,03,24)
```

To set up this formula from VB, you have to break down the date into components and set up formulas like this:

```
report1.Formulas(0) = "formulaname= {datefield} =
...Date("+Year+","+Month+","+Day+")"
```

Or, if you want to convert dates to text, youll have to use formulas like this:

```
ToText(Year(Date)) + "/" + ToText(Month(Date)) + "/" +
...ToText(Day(Date))
```

Print Engine and Custom Control

Crystal Reports Professional Edition, as opposed to the Crystal Custom Control, lets you call Crystal Print Engine functions directly. The print engine contains more functions than are available via the Crystal Custom Control, but you can't use the Crystal Custom Control and make direct calls to print engine functions at the same time; you must choose one or the other. Table 7-2 illustrates the differences.

If you have both Crystal Pro 2.0 and the VBX, the Crystal Engine will use its own DLLs in preference to the Access engine's. If you're not careful with your PATHs, it's easy to get confused about which version of Crystal is being used.

Tip: If you have Crystal Reports Professional 2.0, be aware that the Crystal Print Engine will use its own DLLs in preference to the Access engine's.

Table 7-2: *Crystal's Print Engine offers more granular control, but doesn't ship with VB3. The equivalencies in the chart are only approximate and there are some minor functionality variations between the direct call and the call via the Custom Control.*

Direct Print Engine Call Print Engine Management	Equivalent Property in Crystal Custom Control
PEOpenEngine	
PECloseEngine	
PEGetVersion	
Print Job Management	
PEPrintReport	Destination, WindowLeft, WindowTop, WindowWidth, WindowHeight, WindowTitle,WindowBorderStyle, WindowControlBox,WindowMaxButton, WindowMinButton, WindowParentHandle, PrintReport (or Action)
PEOpenPrintJob	
PEStartPrintJob	
PEGetJobStatus	
PECancelPrintJob	
PEIsPrintJobFinished	

Table 7-2:   *(Continued)*

Print Window Management	
PEGetWindowHandle	
PEPrintWindow	
PECloseWindow	
Print Destinations	
PESelectPrinter	
PEOutputToPrinter	CopiesToPrinter
PEOutputToWindow	WindowLeft, WindowTop, WindowWidth, WindowHeight, WindowTitle, WindowBorderStyle, WindowControlBox, WindowMaxButton, WindowMinButton, WindowParentHandle
PEOutputToFile	PrintFileName, PrintFileType
Print Format Management	
PEGetReportTitle	
PESetReportTitle	
PESetMargins	
PESetPrintOptions	
PESetMinimumSection-Height	
PESetLineHeight	
PESetFont	
PESetNDetailCopies	
PESetSectionFormat	
Sorting	
PEGetNSortFields	
PEGetNthSortField	
PESetNthSortField	SortFields
PEDeleteNthSortField	SortFields
PEGetNGroupSortFields	
PEGetNthGroupSortField	

Table 7-2: *(Continued)*

PESetNthGroupSortField	GroupSortFields
PEDeleteNthGroupSortField	GroupSortFields
Formulas	
PEGetFormula	
PESetFormula	Formulas
PEGetSelectionFormula	
PESetSelectionFormula	SelectionFormula
PEGetGroupSelectionFormula	
PESetGroupSelectionFormula	
Server Management	
PELogOnServer	Connect
PELogOffServer	
Table Management	
PEGetTables	
PEGetNthTableType	
PEGetNthTableLogOnInfo	
PESetNthTableLogOnInfo	Connect
PEGetNthTableLocation	
PESetNthTableLocation	DataFiles
PETestNthTableConnectivity	
Error Management	
PEGetErrorCode	LastErrorNumber
PEGetErrorText	LastErrorString
Miscellaneous	
PEGetHandleString	
PESetGroupCondition	
SelfRegister	

Implicit vs Explicit Logons with the Print Engine

When logging on to a SQL Server you can choose from the options: an explicit logon using `PELogOnServer` or an implicit logon using `PESetNthLogonInfo`. The explicit API call is used to log on to a specified server. You might use this for your runtime routine. For example, a user could input a specified `ServerName`, `DatabaseName`, `UserID`, and `Password`. However, when a report is created using SQL Tables, all of the previous information is stored in your report except for the password. Therefore, when you initialize the structure, you can leave each structure blank, except for the password:

```
Dim DLLName As String
Dim LogOnInfo As PELogOnInfo


DLLName = "PDSSYBAS.DLL"
'the DLLName is the name of the Crystal Reports DLL
'for the Server you want to log onto
'DLLName for SQL/Sybase is PDSSYBAS.DLL
'DLLName for Oracle(Q+E) is PDSORACL.DLL
'DLLName for NetWare SQL is PDSNETW.DLL
'DLLName for Gupta is PDSGUPTA.DLL
'DLLName for SQL Sever or ODBC connections is PDSODBC.DLL


'Initialize the structure
LogOnInfo.Structsize = PE_SIZEOF_LOGON_INFO
LogOnInfo.ServerName = "ServerName" + Chr$(0)
LogOnInfo.DatabaseName = "DatabaseName" + Chr$(0)
LogOnInfo.UserID = "UserID" + Chr$(0)
LogOnInfo.Password = "Password" + Chr$(0)


'if you want to use the logoninfo stored in your report,
'leave everything except password blank, i.e. " "
```

```
'PELogOnServer can be called at any time but requires user
...know DLL name

If PELogOnServer(DLLName, LogOnInfo) = false then
  MsgBox("Connection to Server was unsuccessful")
Else
  MsgBox("Connection to Server was Successful")

  ' make other Print Engine calls

If PELogOffServer (DLLName, LogOnInfo) = false then
  MsgBox("Unable to disconnect from Server")
End if
```

The Print Engine's implicit logon allows the user to access the appropriate logon information from a report table with `PEGetNthTableLogOnInfo` and then lets the user set the password or change any of the logon parameters via `PESetNthTableLogOnInfo`.

Using the Print Engine with Dates   The following code fragment illustrates how you pass date or date range information from your VB app to the Crystal Print Engine.

```
' open a print job and assign the print job handle to a
...variab;e
JobHandle% = PEOpenPrintJob (C:\CRW\CUSTOMER.RPT)

' create variables for start and end year, month, and day
...values
StartYear$ = 1993
StartMonth$ = 09
StartDay$ = 01
EndYear$ = 1994
```

```
EndMonth$ = 3
EndDay$ = 31

' build a string to pass to the record selection formula
' note the required use of braces around field names
StrtSelect$ = "{filea.StartDate} < Date (" + StartYear$ +
...", " + StartMonth$ +
", " + StartDay$ +")"
EndSelect$ = "{filea.EndDate} < Date (" + EndYear$ + ", " +
...EndMonth$ + ", " +
EndDay$ +")"

' build the selection formula using StartSelect$ and
...EndSelect$
Recselect$ = StrSelect$ + " AND " + EndSelect$

'set the record selection formula for the report:
RetCode% = PESetSelectionFormula (JobHandle%, RecSelect$)

' finally, print the report.
RetCode% = PEStartPrintJob (JobHandle, 1)
RetCode% = PEClosePrintJob (JobHandle, 1)
```

Using the Crystal Print Engine is obviously more code-intensive than using the VBX, but the Print Engine has lots of features not available in the VBX.

Distributing Crystal Reports

All versions of Crystal Reports give you the right to distribute a runtime version of the Crystal Reports Print Engine with your Visual Basic applications at no charge. You should be able to find all these files in the \VB\REPORT subdirectory. The following files are mandatory:

CRPE.DLL	Interface to the print engine
COMMDLG.DLL	Help with printer selection, etc.
PDIRJET.DLL	Crystal Access Engine DLL
PDBJET.DLL	Crystal Access Engine DLL
MSAJE110.DLL	Microsoft Access Engine DLL
MSAES110.DLL	Microsoft Access Engine DLL
MSABC110.DLL	Microsoft Access Engine DLL
CTL3D.DLL	Microsoft Access Engine DLL
VB.INI	Visual Basic initialization file
CRXLATE.DLL	ToWords(x) or ToWords(x, # places) function support

To use ODBC links, end users need the following files:

- PDSODBC.DLL

- ODBC.DLL

- ODBCINST.DLL

- SQLSRVR.DLL

- SQLSETUP.DLL

- ODBC.INI

- ODBCINST.INI

Paradox, XBase, and Btrieve databases need the PDX110.DLL, XBS110.DLL, and BTRV110.DLL files, respectively.

All the Crystal Print Engine files should be placed in the same directory, where Windows can find them. Windows will look first in the current directory, then in the WINDOWS subdirectory, then in the WINDOWS\SYSTEM subdirectory, and finally in your PATH. It's easiest if you can put database files in the same directory as the report files. Again, if Crystal doesn't find the database files in this directory, it will look in the current directory, then in the WINDOWS subdirectory, then in the Windows\SYSTEM sub-directory, and finally in your PATH.

The executable version of a shareware program, VBPRINT, which prints VB program listings, is available on your diskette. To get the VB source, you have to register.

Another VBPRINT program, one that first appeared on the Microsoft Developer CD Disc 3, lets you test graphic, text, and tab-delimited output (see Figure 7-7). It includes both VB and C source code. Look for these on your code disk in the \PRINT subdirectory.

Figure 7-7: *A TESTAPP application provides good sample code. Accompanying TESTAPP is a VBPRINT.DLL and support files written in Quick C for Windows.*

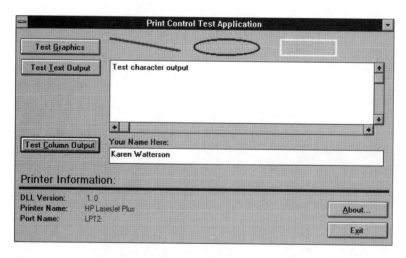

Crystal has also provided several real world examples; look for them in the \CRYSTAL subdirectory. VBXMDI is a nifty little program that shows you how to use a Windows API call to create

MDI child windows when printing a report to the screen. Look for it in the \CRYSTAL subdirectory.

Summary

The Crystal VBX that ships with VB3 will satisfy most of your printing needs, including combining data from multiple databases. Since the Crystal VBX works through the Access engine, however, you're limited to whatever data access is available from Access. If you need additional connectivity or want more granular control, you may want to get the Crystal Reports Pro version.

Disk Files

PRINTVB	Shareware program for printing VB program listings
VBPRINT	C and VB source for testing printer output
VBXMDI	Crystal Report Writer sample for screen reports

8

E-Forms and Other Mail-Enabled Applications

Life would be a lot simpler if end users weren't so demanding. Blame it on Bill Gates. He told them they were entitled to "information at their fingertips," and life hasn't been the same since. Now they want workgroup and workflow applications. What all that amounts to is a giant convergence of e-mail, e-forms, and databases. Your VB program, of course, is what ties it all together. In this chapter, we show you how to do that. We start out by giving you a fast-paced overview of the key concepts associated with MAPI, Microsoft's Messaging API.

If you're like most VB programmers, you've studiously avoided DDE, SQL, and MAPI like the plague because you heard they were "hard." The truth is, none of them is that bad. DDE and Simple MAPI consist of about a dozen functions each. *Only a dozen?* Of course, DDE is being supplanted by OLE 2.0, and SMAPI is really only a transitory subset of MAPI, but the point is, it doesn't take a rocket scientist to get up and running with DDE or SMAPI today.

In this chapter, we focus on using VB3 with Microsoft's Electronic Forms Designer (EFD). Electronic Forms Designer is basically a VB add-in that goes one step beyond the MAPI example that comes with VB. It's more than a VBX—it's what Microsoft calls a "Generic Template" that will give you a jump on creating message-enabled smart forms with VB. If you want to create mail-enabled forms, you'd be crazy not to buy EFD ($395). Unlike most forms packages, EFD doesn't have separate form "fillers," just runtime files you can distribute freely.

The main advantage of using the Electronic Forms Designer is that you get libraries that support e-form initialization and caching, enumeration of tagged controls, validation of e-mail recipient lists, error handling, and form resizing and scrolling. Microsoft also provides a "browser" program available from MSMail, Windows for Workgroups, Excel, and Word for Windows from which users can select e-forms.

To work through the examples in this chapter, you'll need Visual Basic Professional 3.0, Microsoft Electronic Forms Designer, and Microsoft Mail or Windows for Workgroups.

E-Forms

To understand all the excitement associated with workgroup and workflow computing, think about all the routine forms you fill out at work. You probably have forms for scheduling vacation, requesting supplies, changing your benefits or withholding, and so on. Travel requests and expense reports are another common category of forms. Once firms get a critical mass of about 15 employees, they seem impelled to invent "Travel Request" and associated "Travel Expense Reimbursement Request" forms.

Let's say you need to go to Fall Comdex (bet you can hardly wait). In the paper forms world, the first step is to locate a copy of the travel request form—there's never one in your drawer when you need it or else it's out of date, right? You fill it out—studies show the average form takes 20 minutes to fill out—and get your manager's approval (read signature). Finally, depending on your organization and the urgency of your request, your manager (1) routes the form through company mail to the travel coordinator or the human resources department, (2) gives it to you, signed, to hand-deliver to the appropriate people, or (3) gives you back the signed form, leaving you to make your own travel arrangements. In all cases, though, the filled-out, approved travel request form constitutes the first step in a paper trail related to your Comdex trip. Ultimately, the form will be filed in someone's file cabinet, where it will languish for several years until someone decides it's probably okay to throw it out or archive it.

An increasingly popular alternative, one that's not only environmentally correct but also more efficient, is to use electronic forms. E-forms, when combined with database technology and e-mail, are a good example of workgroup computing. The idea is to post a travel request form on the mail server, where it's easy for employees to find and fill out. Then, instead of pushing papers, you push electrons. You fire up MSMail (or Windows for Workgroups), select Mail | Form, fill out the travel request e-form, and route it to the appropriate chain of recipients. Somewhere along the line, the person who's responsible for tracking travel requests and/or expenses stuffs the info into a database.

MAPI, SMAPI, and VIM

Before jumping into the hands-on stuff, let's spend some time at the chalkboard. If you're a little confused about MAPI (Extended MAPI), Simple MAPI (SMAPI), VIM, CMC, and MEF, here's the lowdown.

MAPI, Microsoft's Messaging API, is a two-sided API that's part of the Windows Open System Architecture (WOSA). MAPI is really a messaging *subsystem*, since it's a set of code that's a subset of the entire operating system, in this case Windows. MAPI's two sides are the client APIs with the client-to-MAPI link and the service-provider interfaces that complete the MAPI-to-messaging system link.

The Messaging Subsystem

Simple MAPI and Extended MAPI both provide the required API calls for messaging applications. These calls work with a second level of MAPI features that are actually built into the Windows operating system: the *messaging subsystem*. The MAPI messaging subsystem and a MAPI dynamic-link library (DLL) are responsible for dividing the tasks of handling multiple transport-service providers. Drivers for each transport exist in the form of a Windows DLL to provide the interface between the MAPI messaging subsystem message spooler and the underlying back-end messaging system(s) or services. The message spooler is similar to a print spooler except that it assists with the routing of messages instead of print jobs. The spooler, MAPI.DLL, and the transport drivers work together to handle the sending and receiving of messages.

When many different transport drivers are installed on a Windows-based desktop, messages from client applications can be sent to a variety of transport services. When a message is sent from a client application, the MAPI.DLL responds to the Simple or Extended

MAPI calls first, routing the message to the appropriate message store and address book service providers. When a message is marked for sending, it is handled by the message spooler, where it is delivered to the appropriate transport driver.

The message spooler looks at the message's address to determine which transport to use to send the message. Depending on the recipients, the message spooler may call on more than one transport provider. The spooler performs other message-management functions as well, such as directing inbound messages to a message store and catching messages that are undeliverable because no transport provider can handle them. The spooler also provides an important store and forward function, maintaining a message in a store if the needed messaging service is currently unavailable. When connection to the service is reestablished, the spooler automatically forwards the message to its destination.

Except for dialog boxes at the initial transport login, provided both in the VBMAPI example and Electronic Forms Designer template, the spooler and transport providers operate in the background, transferring messages among various messaging services. The spooler does its work and makes its calls to the transport providers when the foreground applications are idle, so users don't have to wait while they are working with the messaging application. In addition to the common functions for sending and receiving messages, MAPI and its subsystem can support file attachments and Windows OLE objects.

The subsystem also supports unified logons and encrypts any security information it stores for a service provider. Information from a variety of services, including fax, bulletin boards, and host e-mail, can be used with any MAPI client application.

Messaging subsystems like MAPI don't replace messaging systems like cc:Mail, MSMail, Novell MHS, X.400, or IBM PROFS. To borrow a term from the database world, messaging subsystems are like middleware. They act like central clearinghouses or go-betweens that shield users and programmers from their differences. Messaging subsystems provide common user interfaces for routine message tasks and manage different message stores, address books, and the different transports required to send messages to different messaging systems. They should also be able to handle store and forward tasks and to notify applications when events such as mail delivery or mail sending occur.

Simple MAPI (SMAPI) contains the 12 most common messaging API calls from the "real" MAPI. Armed with this subset, you can create applications like forms routing programs for purchase or travel requests or even workgroup calendar and scheduling programs. SMAPI can also be used to add messaging to capabilities to Windows applications like spreadsheets and word processors. SMAPI includes an optional common user interface (dialog boxes) that can be used as the basis for a consistent "look and feel" to their applications. Although SMAPI includes a user interface, the APIs can be called non-interactively.

MAPI is Microsoft's Messaging API, a fundamental middle-man between applications and the underlying mail transport systems. Simple MAPI, sometimes called SMAPI, is a subset of MAPI.

The idea is that SMAPI (and even MAPI) insulates us from the nitty gritty communications details of the underlying messaging systems or the network platforms. SMAPI functions let you send, address, and receive messages, including messages with data attachments and OLE objects. These functions are listed in Table 8-1.

Table 8-1:   *Microsoft's Simple MAPI functions*

SMAPI Functions	
MAPILogon	Begins a MAPI session.
MAPILogoff	Ends a MAPI session.
MAPIFree	Frees the memory allocated by the messaging subsystem.
MAPISendMail	Sends a standard mail message, either unattended or interactive.
MAPISendDocuments	Sends a standard mail message, but always prompts with a Send Note dialog box for the recipient's name and other sending options. Intended primarily for use with a scripting language such as a spreadsheet macro.
MAPIFindNext	Allows an application to enumerate messages of a given type. This call is targeted at incoming mail.
MAPIReadMail	Reads a mail message.
MAPISaveMail	Saves a mail message.
MAPIDeleteMail	Deletes a mail message.
MAPIAddress	Allows the user to create or modify a set of recipient entries using a common address dialog box.
MAPIDetails	Presents a dialog box that provides the details of a given address-book entry based on information provided by the address-book provider to which the entry belongs.
MAPIResolveName	Resolves a friendly name (an alias) to an address-book entry and offers the option of prompting the user to choose between ambiguous entries if necessary.

Simple MAPI includes routines intended for use by applications that want to become mail-aware, such as spreadsheet programs and word processors: in fact, both Excel and Word for Windows are MAPI compliant. Simple MAPI is also robust enough to build custom messaging applications such as calendaring and scheduling programs that focus on the easy exchange of datafiles and sending simple messages generated by these applications. Simple MAPI uses three Visual Basic types:

- MapiMessage

- MapiRecip

- MapiFile

MapiMessage

MapiMessage is the main part of a message containing information about the message itself, such as message text and subject. Two entries, RecipCount and FileCount, provide a value that indicates the size of both the Recipient and Attachment arrays. The MapiMessage type contains—bet you can guess—basic information about a message and has the following structure:

```
Type MapiMessage
        Reserved as Long
        Subject as String
        NoteText as String
        MessageType as String
        DateReceived as String
        ConversationID as String
        Flags as Long
        RecipCount as Long
        FileCount as Long
End Type
```

Each field in the MapiMessage structure translates to the VBMAPI custom control property as follows:

Reserved	Not Available
Subject	Mapimessages.MsgSubject
NoteText	MapiMessages.MsgNoteText
MessageType	MapiMessages.MsgType
DateReceived	MapiMessages.MsgDateReceived
ConversationID	MapiMessages.MsgConversationID
Flags	MapiMessages.MsgRead
	MapiMessages.ReceiptRequested
	MapiMessages.MsgSent
RecipCount	MapiMessages.RecipCount
FileCount	MapiMessages.AttachmentCount

MapiRecip

Each message as indexed by the MapiMessage.RecipCount has a corresponding record of MapiRecip with the following structure:

```
Type MapiRecip
      Reserved as Long
      RecipClass as Long
      Name as String
      Address as String
      EIDSize as Long
      EntryID as Long
End Type
```

Fields in the MapiRecip structure map to the following custom control properties:

Reserved	Not Available
RecipClass	MapiMessages.RecipType
Name	MapiMessages.RecipDisplayName
Address	MapiMessages.RecipAddress
EIDSize	Not Available
EntryID	Not Available

Information about the message originator can be found in the following custom control properties:

```
MapiMessages.MsgOrigAddress
MapiMessages.MsgOrigDisplayName
```

Recipients are indexed from 0 to `MapiMessages.Recipient-Count -1`.

MapiFile

Each file attachment is indexed by the field `MapiMessages.`FileCount has a corresponding record of type MapiFile with the following structure.

```
Type MapiFile
        Reserved as Long
        Flags as Long
        Position as Long
        PathName as String
        FileName as String
        FileType as String
End Type
```

Fields in the MapiFile type translates to the following custom control properties:

Reserved	Not Available
Flags	MapiMessages.AttachmentType
Position	MapiMessages.AttachmentPosition
PathName	MapiMessages.AttachmentPathName
FileName	Mapimessages.AttachmentName
FileType	Not Available

Attachments are indexed from 0 to `MapiMessages.AttachmentCount 1`.

SMAPI lets you embed three different kinds of attachments:

- A data file attachment

- An editable OLE object attachment that has been rendered in the message body

- A static OLE object file attachment that's not editable

Real MAPI

So what's MAPI, or Extended MAPI, or whatever the "full" MAPI is being called, and how does it differ from SMAPI? Extended MAPI goes beyond Simple MAPI to provide even greater interaction with the messaging services. Extended MAPI is the additional API set, intended for complex messaging-based applications such as advanced workgroup programs that use the messaging subsystem extensively. Such applications are likely to handle large and complex messages in large numbers and require sophisticated addressing features, including directory synchronization. Other functions that Extended MAPI is poised to handle include easy data collection, unattended message filtering, and agent-based retrieval.

Expect "full" MAPI in Windows 4.0 sometime in 1994. If you're interested in finding out more about MAPI, you'll find the spec on the Microsoft Developer CD Disc 4 or later—in the Specs and Strategy section. CD5 has the MAPI 1.08 spec details both for MAPI clients and servers. You may also still find a half meg file in Help file format on CompuServe (GO MSWRKGRP) in Section 17.

VIM, Vendor Independent Messaging, is a competing API backed by Lotus, Borland, and others. VIM, as you would expect, is supported by Lotus Notes, cc:Mail, and a growing number of mail-enabled applications. Fortunately, efforts are being made to bridge the gap. At press time, Lotus' VIM to SMAPI converter is reportedly near completion. And the X.400 Application Program Interface Association (XAPIA) has given its blessing to a compromise API called, Common Messaging Call (CMC).

With any luck, all of this will have been papered over by the time you read this. Lotus is working on a VIM to MAPI driver and Borland is adding VIM support to its products. All indications are that MAPI or something like it will continue to be a desktop messaging standard for a while.

MSMAPI.VBX vs. MEF

Electronic Forms Designer is essentially an extension of the MAPI example that ships with VB. If you want to check out the latter or don't have EFD yet, look in the SAMPLES\MAPI subdirectory. You'll find a program that uses the MSMAPI.VBX and CMDIALOG controls and consists of five forms (see Figure 8-1):

VBMAIL.FRM	The main form
MAILLST.FRM	Form for displaying the list of mail messages
MAILOPTF.FRM	Form for setting options
MSGVIEW.FRM	Form in which a viewed message is displayed
NEWMSG.FRM	Form for creating a new message

Remember that, although you'll be able to sniff around even without MSMail support (just ignore the warning messages when you open the project), you'll need a MAPI mail system if you want to actually run the app.

If you open the VBMAIL.FRM form, you'll see a general purpose form for messaging that includes two special MAPI controls: MapiSession and MapiMessage.

Figure 8-1: *The MAPI sample project that ships with VB3 is a precursor to Electronic Forms Designer (EFD)*

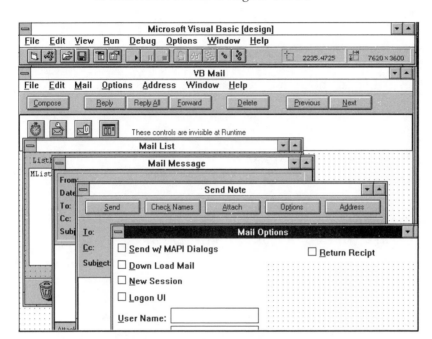

MSMAPI's The MAPI Session Control

The MAPI session control is used to establish a valid session to the mail system. On doing so, it returns a long value that can be used by the MAPI messages control. In addition, the session control can be used to end a session and to download any new message contained within the mail server into the local-user message store. Properties that apply specifically to this object are as follows:

- Action

- DownloadMail

- LogonUI

- NewSession

- Password

- SessionID

- UserName

The following piece of code shows how to use the MAPI session control:

```
Sub Logon ()
      On Error GoTo MAPILogonError
      Form1.MapiSession1.Action = SESSION_SIGNON
      Exit Sub
      MAPILogonError:
      MsgBox Error$ + ".", MB_OK, "MAPI Error"
      Resume Next
End Sub
```

Note that Microsoft Mail only allows one session. It's shared among all mail-enabled applications, so setting the `MapiSession.NewSession` has no effect. If a Valid session already exists (Microsoft Mail), the Logon UI is not displayed.

When the application terminates, it's important to sign off to remove the existing mail session with code similar to this:

```
Sub Logoff ()
   On Error GoTo MAPILogoffError
   Form1.MapiSession1.Action = SESSION_SIGNOFF
   Exit Sub
MAPILogoffError:
   MsgBox Error$ + ".", MB_OK, "MAPI Error"
   Resume Next
End Function
```

The value returned in `MapiSession.SessionID` should now be used to set the `MapiMessages.SessionID`.

The MAPI Action Property

This property is used to select an action for the MAPI messages control. It is not available at design time. The available settings are as follows:

MESSAGE_FETCH   Creates a message set from selected messages in the Inbox. The message set includes all messages of type `FetchMsgType` found in the Inbox, sorted as selected by the `FetchSorted` and qualified by `FetchUnreadOnly`. Any attachment files in the read buffer are deleted when a subsequent fetch action occurs. Works in Compose and Read buffers. Value=1.

MESSAGE_SENDDLG   Sends a message inside a dialog box. Prompts the user for the various components of a message (subject, recipients, text, and so on) and submits the message to the mail server for delivery. All message properties associated with a message being built in the compose buffer (an outgoing message with `MsgIndex = 1`) form the basis for the displayed message dialog box. Changes made in the dialog box, however, do not alter information in the compose buffer. Value=2.

MESSAGE_SEND   Sends a message without using a dialog box. Submits the outgoing message to the mail server for delivery. No dialog box is displayed, and an error occurs if a user attempts to send a message that has no recipients or if attachment path names are missing. Works in Compose buffer. Value=3.

MESSAGE_SAVEMSG   Saves the message currently in the compose buffer (with `MsgIndex =  1`). Works in Compose buffer. Value=4.

MESSAGE_COPY   Copies the currently indexed message to the compose buffer. Sets the `MsgIndex` property to –1. Works in Read buffer. Value=5.

MESSAGE_COMPOSE   Composes a message. Clears all of the components of the compose buffer. Sets the `MsgIndex` property to –1. Works in Read buffer. Value=6.

MESSAGE_REPLY   Replies to a message. Copies the currently indexed message to the compose buffer as a reply and adds RE: to the beginning of the Subject line. The currently indexed message originator becomes the outgoing message recipient, then text is copied, and so on. Sets the `MsgIndex` property to –1. Works in Read buffer. Value=7.

MESSAGE_REPLYALL   Replies to all message recipients. Same as Reply, except that all other To: and CC: recipients are maintained. Sets the `MsgIndex` property to –1. Works in Read buffer. Value=8.

MESSAGE_FORWARD   Forwards a message. Copies the currently indexed message to the compose buffer as a forwarded message and adds FW: to the beginning of the Subject line. Sets the `MsgIndex` property to –1. Works in Read buffer. Value=9.

MESSAGE_DELETE   Deletes a message. Deletes all components of the currently indexed message, reduces the `MsgCount` property by 1, and decrements the index number by 1 for each message that follows the deleted message. If the deleted message was the last message in the set, this action decrements the MsgIndex by 1. Works in Read buffer. Value=10.

MESSAGE_SHOWADBOOK   Displays the mail Address Book dialog box. The user can use the address book to create or modify a recipient set. Any changes to the address book outside of the compose buffer (when `MsgIndex` does not equal –1) are not saved. Works in Compose and Read buffers. Value 11.

MESSAGE_SHOWDETAILS   Displays a dialog box that shows the details of the currently indexed recipient. The amount of information presented in the dialog box is determined by the message system. At a minimum, it contains the display name and address of the recipient. Works in Compose and Read buffers. Value=12.

MESSAGE_RESOLVENAME   Resolves the name of the currently indexed recipient. Searches the address book for a match on the currently indexed recipient name. If no match is found, an error is returned. (No match is not considered ambiguous.) The AddressResolveUI property determines whether to display a dialog box to resolve ambiguous names. This action does not provide additional resolution of the message originator's name or address. This action may cause the `RecipType` property to change. Works in both buffers. Value=13.

RECIPIENT_DELETE   Deletes the currently indexed recipient. Automatically reduces the `RecipCount` property by 1, and decrements the index number by 1 for each recipient that follows the deleted recipient. If the deleted recipient was the last recipient in the set, this action decrements the `RecipIndex` by 1. Works in Compose buffer. Value=14.

ATTACHMENT_DELETE   Deletes the currently indexed attachment. Automatically reduces the `Attachment Count` property by 1, and decrements the index by 1 for each attachment that follows the deleted attachment. If the deleted attachment was the last attachment in the set, this action decrements the `AttachmentIndex` by 1. Works in Compose buffer. Value=15.

The MAPI Message Control

All other simple MAPI functions are handled using the MAPI Messages custom control which lets you

- read messages currently in the Inbox

- compose new messages

- add and delete message recipients and attachments

- send messages

- save, copy, and delete messages

- display the Address Book dialog box

- display the Details dialog box

- resolve recipient names

- perform reply and reply-all and forward actions to messages

Reading Messages   To read messages you must first fetch all of the required messages from the inbox into a message set like this, where IPM.Microsoft Mail.Note refers to the form name as registered in MSMail.INI:

```
Sub MessageFetch ()
   MapiMessage.FetchMsgType = "IPM.Microsoft Mail.Note"
   MapiMessage.Action =  MESSAGE_FETCH
End Sub
```

Messages are now indexed from 0 to `MapiMessages`.MsgCount and can be accessed by setting the `MsgIndex` property to the appropriate value.

Creating Messages   The compose buffer is active when the `MapiSession.MsgIndex` property is set to -1.

```
Sub Message_Compose ()
   MapiMessages.Action = MESSAGE_COMPOSE
End Sub
```

Adding an attachment requires that you first set the Attachment Index to the value for this attachment.

Wait, you're not finished yet—four more pieces of information must now be supplied: the short name (DOS filename) used by the application to display the attachment, the full pathname, the position (in bytes) at which to render the attachment, and, finally, the way to render the attachment, either as an Icon or as an OLE object. For example:

```
MapiMessage.AttachmentName = "generic.doc"
MapiMessage.AttachmentPathName = "c:\data\generic.doc"
Mapimessage.AttachmentPosition = Len(MapiMess-
...age.MsgNoteText) - 2
MapiMessage.AttachmentType = ATTACHTYPE_DATA
```

Finally, a completed message can be sent by setting the action property to either of the following:

```
MapiMessage.Action = MESSAGE_SEND or
MapiMessage.Action = MESSAGE_SENDDLG
```

The first choice fails if any part of the message is incorrect, such as an invalid recipient or invalid attachment. The second displays a Send dialog box containing any of the properties that have already been completed or partially completed.

What Does EFD Bring to the Table?

Okay, what does Electronic Forms Designer give you that the VB MAPI examples don't? Aside from the generic template with ready-to-use Compose and Read forms, you get over 50 higher-level functions (see Table 8-2).

Table 8-2:   *The Electronic Forms Designer includes high-level functions that go beyond the 12 included in SMAPI.*

Packing Management	
MEF Functions	Packaging Management
MEFCreatePackage	Creates e-form package you attach to a mail message
MEFOpenPackage	Opens a package
MEFSavePackage	Saves a package
MEFFreePackage	Frees the resources used by a package
Data Management	
MEFWriteText	Writes a String to a package
MEFWriteLong	Writes a Long to a package
MEFWriteItem	Writes an item of data to a package
MEFReadText	Reads a String from a package
MEFReadLong	Reads a Long from a package
MEFReadRecipientList	Reads a recipient list from a package
MEFReadItem	Reads an item of data from a package
MEFDeleteItem	Deletes an item of data from a package

Table 8-2:   *(Continued)*

Recipient List Management	
MEFAddRecipientsToListBox	Adds recipient names to a list box
MEFDoResolveNames	Validates recipient names
MEFDoListDetails	Lists information about a recipient
Printing	
MEFBeginPrinting	Starts a printing session
MEFEndPrinting	Terminates a printing session
MEFPrintRecipient	Prints a recipient's name
MEFPrintLabel	Prints a label in bold
MEFPrintLabelAndValue	Prints a label plus a value associated with the label
MEFPrintMultiLineText	Prints word-wrapped text
MEFPrintCheckBox	Prints a check box.
MEFPrintOptionButton	Prints an option button.
MEFPrintBlankLines	Prints blank lines.
MEFHandlePrintingError	Deals with printing errors.
File Management	
MEFAddFile	Adds a file to a package
MEFDeleteFile	Deletes a file from a package
MEFSaveFile	Copies a file from a package and saves it
MEFGetFileCount	Determines the number of files in a package
MEFGetFileName	Determines the friendly name of a file in a package
MEFGetFileIndex	Returns the index of a file in a package
MEFAddAttachment	Attaches a file to a mail message
MEFDeleteAttachment	Deletes a file attached to a mail message
MEFFindAttachment	Locates a file attached to a mail message
MEFFreeAttachments	Deletes all files attached to a mail message

Table 8-2:   *(Continued)*

Message and Form Management	
MEFDoFormUnload	Frees the package and attachments, then determines whether a form should exit or remain in the e-form cache
MEFDoDelete	Deletes the current mail message
Performance Cache	
MEFRegisterInstance	Registers an instance of an e-form
MEFQueryExit	Queries the MEF cache to determine whether an e-form should deactivate or terminate
MEFExecEForm	Executes an e-form, using a given command line
Utility	
MEFWhoAmI	Identifies the logon name associated with a Mail session.
MEFFormatMAPIDate	Returns the date in international long-date format and the time in medium time format
MEFWriteMessageToFile	Writes a MAPI message to a file
MEFReadMessageFromFile	Reads a MAPI message from a file
MEFGetTempFile	Returns an unused filename in the Windows TEMP directory
MEFGetToken	Returns a token from a String
MEFMax	Returns the higher of two values
MEFMin	Returns the lower of two values
MEFSetEditReadOnlyState	Sets a text box control for Read only or Read/Write accesss
Error Handling	
MEFCheckMEFError	Determines if an MEF error occurred
MEFCheckMAPIError	Determines if a MAPI error occurred

The main advantage of using the Electronic Forms Designer is that you get all these high-level functions, which support e-form initialization and caching, enumeration of tagged controls, validation of e-mail recipient lists, error handling (sigh), and form resizing and scrolling. You also get Microsoft's Form "browser" program, which works with MSMail, Windows for Workgroups, Excel, and Word for Windows.

Forms—which are actually just *viewers*—can be stored on local drives or on the Mail server. This architecture means that only the actual form data needs to travel across the network. The main MEF functions you'll use are the ones that handle message packaging.

Messaging Alternatives

Although routing e-forms with MAPI is the focus of this section, it's not the only game in town, and Electronic Forms Designer may be downright overkill. Plain e-mail may accomplish the task. Or you may prefer to use MSMAPI.VBX or even DDE. If you're comfortable using Access, you'll be surprised what you can accomplish with a combination of Access Basic's SendKeys and the clipboard.

If you're considering EFD, spend an extra $39 and get Microsoft's Workgroup Template.

Creating a Form

To demonstrate how Electronic Forms Designer works, let's to create a simple travel request form with a few fields that correspond to data in an Access database. The form will be attached to an EFD Read Note Compose form (see Figure 8-2) as a modal subform. Then we'll suggest how you could customize it with data-aware controls that allow a recipient to add data to a travel request database you'll set up in VB3 as an Access database.

Figure 8-2: *Part of the Electronic Forms Designer's "generic template" are stock forms for posting and receiving messages and their attached forms.*

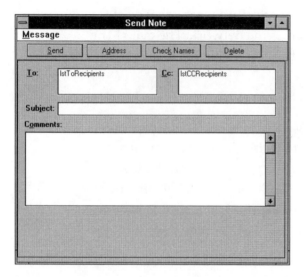

Preliminaries

There's a fair amount of housekeeping to do, mainly since we're really working with four programs: VB3 and its built-in Access engine, EFD, and MSMail. We need to begin with the following five steps.

1. Install EFD Designer on your own system. (You'll want to use the MSMail administrator to install EFD in Server mode on the Mail server.) Make sure you aren't running MSMail, Word for Windows, or Excel when you install EFD. If you do use WinWord or Excel, you may as well

have the installation routine mail-enable those programs for you—adding File | Route menu options. Test your installation to make sure you can run the sample applications where you mail forms to yourself. Then create a new subdirectory to contain your Travel Request project, such as VB\EFORMS\PROJECTS\TRAVREQ, and copy all the nine files—a mere 68K—from the VB\EFORMS\TEMPLATE subdirectory into your new subdirectory.

2. Open the EFORM project and create a new project called TRAVREQ. Edit the EFORM.BAS file and create a unique message type for your form. Change the line

```
Global Const MESSAGE_CLASS = "IPM.Microsoft.Template"
```

to something like

```
Global Const MESSAGE_CLASS = "IPM.KLW.TravReq"
```

and change the subject prefix to replace "Generic" with "Travel Request":

```
Global Const SUBJECT_PREFIX = "Travel Request:"
```

3. Save the edited EFORM.BAS and select File | MakeEXE to create an EXE file called TRAVREQ.EXE.

4. Run MSMail and edit the MSMAIL.INI file by selecting Mail | Edit Msmail.ini.
   You need to register your form, so add a new, 3-screen-wide line to the [Custom Messages] section. The easiest way to do this is to copy an existing line and edit it consistent with the message class and EXE names you have already created above. For example, ours reads

```
IPM.KLW.TravelReq=3.0;;Travel Request Form;;
...C:\windowS\SYSTEM\MEFLIB.DLL;
...<MC:IPM.KLW.TravReq>C:\VB\EFORMS\PROJECTS\
...TRAVREQ\TRAVREQ.EXE -MSG <COMMAND>
...<MESSAGEID>;1111111000000000;Travel Request
...Form;;;
```

While you're at it, you may as well disable the E-Form Cache setting in MSMAIL.INI to make sure you're always working with the most current version of a form. You'll probably want to enable caching for the production version, but during development no caching is highly recommended.

```
[E-Form Cache]
Maximum=0
```

5. Once you're sure the TravReq form has been successfully registered via step 4, consider modifying the [Custom Messages] section again, this time for debugging. To debug a "Read" or "Compose" e-form used to display an unsent message, it's useful to have MSMail start Visual Basic in design mode on the e-form's project so you can set break points and step through your e-form code. You'll need to modify the [Custom Messages] section of MSMAIL.INI shown above to include a path to VB.EXE, the path to the project file, e.g. EFORM.MAK or TRAVREQ.MAK, rather than the EXE, and a /CMD flag before the other command line arguments passed to Visual Basic.

```
IPM.KLW.TravelReq=3.0;;Travel Request Form;;
...C:\windowS\SYSTEM\MEFLIB.DLL;
...<MC:IPM.KLW.TravReq>C:\VB\VB C:\VB\EFORMS\
...PROJECTS\TravReq\EFORM.MAK /CMD -MSG
...<COMMAND> <MESSAGEID>;1111111000000000;
...Travel Request Form;;;
```

Creating the Database

Let's start by creating the kind of database travel request information might go into. Here's a reasonable relational database design for a travel request database:

Employees Table	
EmployeeID	Integer
	Indexed (EmpID) as unique and primary
EmpLastName	Text, 40
EmpFirstName	Text, 20
JobTitle	Text, 20
Dept	Text, 20
SupervisorID	Integer
TravelRequest Table	
TravelRequestID	Long Integer, Counter,
	Indexed (TravReq) as unique and primary
Event	Text, 30
EmployeeID	Integer
RequestDate	Date/Time
DepFrom	Text, 20
DepDate	Date/Time
ArriveNLT	Date/Time
Destination	Text, 20
DestHotel	Text, 30
HotelNights	Integer
RetFrom	Text, 20
RetDate	Date/Time
RetDest	Text, 20
EstTotCost	Currency
SupOK	Integer
OKDate	Date/Time

Remember, you can run Datamgr either from VB or directly from the File Manager. Datamgr is a primitive database table builder that comes with VB3 and has the distinction of being written in VB—source code available on your disk. Default installation locates DATAMGR in your main VB directory, which is where it will create new databases, too, unless you specify otherwise.

Select File | New Database and pick Access 1.1 as the target database. Call your new database EFDTest, and click on Tables | New. Create tables called Employees and TravelRequest, along with their indexes. EmployeeID will serve as the primary key in the Employee table, and we'll take advantage of Access' ability to generate a serial counter type to maintain a primary key in the TravelRequest table. Because employees can have many travel requests, this is a one-to-many relationship, with the key from the "one" side (Employee ID from the Employee table) existing as a foreign key in the table from the "many" side. Using EmployeeID in the TravelRequest table makes it a link field that also forms the basis for referential integrity.

Testing

Once you'll defined the TravReq database, you've planted the seeds for what could become a sophisticated Expense Tracking system. Our goal here is more modest—to show you what's required to create modal forms attached to the EFD's Compose and Read templates.

First, open the TravReq project and create a new form called frmTravReq with the Control Box property set to False. Give it a caption like Travel Request. Open the Load event procedure and add the line

```
ReadTaggedControls Me, gPackage
```

in order to load the values of any tagged controls you'll be adding.

Design Decision: SubPanel or SubForm?

You've got two basic options if your form needs more real estate than the COMPOSE.FRM gives you: use one or more subpanels or display modal or modeless subforms in separate window(s). Subpanels are probably easiest if you have several pages of forms.

Add a command button with the caption OK. Open the Click event procedure for the OK button and add this code:

```
WriteTaggedControls Me, gPackage
Unload Me
```

Add a few controls for the TravelRequest table, such as labels and text boxes for EmployeeID, Event, and Destination. Set the tag property for the text boxes by assigning unique names and add

```
gModified = True
```

code to the Change event procedures for the tagged controls.

Remember to set up your controls with a *Tag property* if you want the data in them included in the e-mail package. The WriteTaggedControls and ReadTagged Controls functions are responsible for packaging and unpackaging the data for shipment with the e-mail message.

Add controls for the Supervisor's signature and Date Approved fields and save the form. Now open the Compose form and add a command button that will display the form you just created. Add code to the command button's click event

```
frmTravReq.Show MODAL
```

Do the same thing for the Read form and update the .EXE.

To see the results of your handiwork, test the form in Debug mode. If you're not logged into MSMail, you'll be prompted to do so. Try to send a copy of the Travel Request form to yourself. Once you're convinced that part works, exit debug mode and log out of MSMail. Start MSMail again, and test the new form starting from there like an end user would. Select your form from the Mail | Select e-form menu, and fill out another travel request that you mail yourself (see Figure 8-3). This is what the end user will see, thanks to EFD's Browser. Only forms that have been "registered" in the MSMAIL.INI and/or SHARED.INI files will appear on the list.

The next step is to link your form to the EFDTest (travel request) database, and you may choose one of several approaches. You may want to add another form and let the user select the target database. You may want to set that up in an .INI file. You may want to define a data control and hard code record source properties for each of the data fields. You'll probably want to add a command button "Save Travel Request."

There are all kinds of enhancements you may want to experiment with. Use masked edit controls if that makes sense. Set up pre-defined distribution lists either with EFD's gRecipients or in your form's .INI file.

Microsoft sells a Workgroup Templates ($39) package with 13 sample applications you can use as a model for your own E-mail enabled applications. One of the samples is a Supply Request E-form. It uses a grid control where users can enter requests for office supplies (see Figure 8-4). A master Supply database is provided in Access format.

Figure 8-3: *Testing the Travel Request e-form*

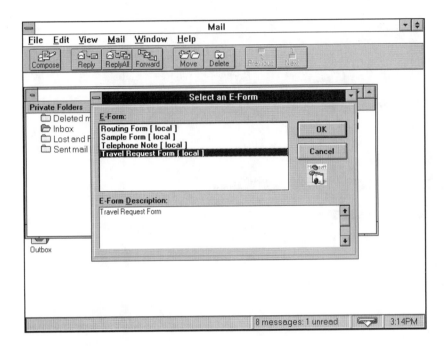

Summary

Our goal in this chapter was to provide you with a gentle introduction to MAPI and to get you thinking about mail-enabled VB applications in general. Microsoft's Electronic Forms Designer is a natural add-in for VB programmers who are creating applications for shops that use a MAPI-compliant mail system like MS Mail or Windows for Workgroups.

Figure 8-4: *A sample supply application built with Electronic Forms Designer*

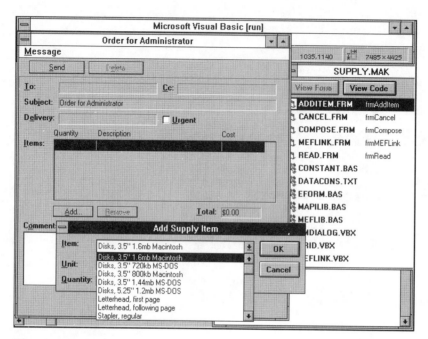

Resources

Simple MAPI

   SDK: SMAPI.ZIP (296K) CompuServe MSWRKGRP, Liv 17

   Spec: Microsoft Developer Network CD Disc 5 (Specs & Strategy, Specs, MAPI)

   Reference: MSMail Technical Reference (Microsoft Document WG-39442-0193)

   Sample application: VB3\SAMPLES\MAPI subdirectory

MAPI

   Help File: MAPIHL.ZIP (491K) CompuServe MSWRKGRP, Lib 17

   Spec: Microsoft Developer Network CD Disc 5 (Specs & Strategy, Specs, MAPI)

Common Messaging Call (CMC)

SDK: CMCSDK.ZIP (158K) CompuServe MSWRKGRP, Lib 17

Spec: CMCSPC.ZIP (61K) CompuServe MSWRKGRP, Lib 17

Microsoft Workgroup Templates ($39). Order from 800-426- 9400, 800-227-4679, or 206-882-8080.

Sample application: CMC SDK sample on Microsoft Developer Network CD Disc 5 (Sample code, Product Samples, CMC SDK Sample)

9

Using OLE 2.0

Why talk about OLE 2.0 in a database programming book? It's a good question. Here's our rationale. First, as data and applications become more entwined, users are going to want the flexibility that OLE, and especially OLE 2.0, offers. You're going to be expected to make your VB database applications OLE-aware. Second, if an OLE 2.0 object support in-place editing and OLE Automation (more about which later), it effectively becomes an additional VB control. OLE objects seem destined to replace VBXes.

In this chapter, we go over the basic OLE technology and talk about using the new OLE 2.0 control in VB3. We also provide some sample code that illustrates how you might use OLE 2.0 with a drawing program like VISIO 2.0.

OLE 2.0 vs. OLE 1.0

Microsoft introduced OLE 1.0 in 1989 as a document-centric set of services that was typically used to create documents with graphics or charts in them. In OLE 1.0 parlance, you had OLE servers, programs like Excel or Corel that could provide OLE objects and registered themselves as such, and OLE clients, programs that could accommodate linked or embedded OLE objects.

> OLE 2.0 is destined to replace DDE and maybe even VBXes. The OLE 2.0 world is divided into objects (formerly OLE servers) and containers (formerly OLE clients).

With OLE 2.0, the terminology has changed. Instead of OLE "clients" and "servers," there are OLE "containers" and OLE "objects." Applications can be containers, objects, or both. Word for Windows documents, for example, are containers most of the time, but they could be objects in PowerPoint presentations or in your VB application. In the initial release of Visual Basic 3.0, VB3 functions only as an OLE container (client), not as an OLE object (server).

You might think of OLE 2.0 in terms of a continuum that started with the Clipboard. We've had DDE and Network DDE, OLE 1.0. Now we've got OLE 2.0.

In-place Activation

In-place activation lets users directly activate objects within documents without switching to a different window. In OLE 1.0, you double-click to activate an embedded object. That action visibly launches the application that created the object, assuming it's present on the PATH and assuming you have enough memory. The user is transferred to a different application window to interact with the object and is switched back to the original document when the interaction is completed.

OLE 2.0 updates the object activation paradigm with *in-place activation* or visual editing. With in-place activation, the user can double-click an object in a compound document and interact with the object right there, without switching to a different application or window. The menus, toolbars, palettes, and other controls necessary to enable the temporary interaction replace existing menus and controls of the active window. The called application partially takes over the document window. Although in-place activation supports a variety of operations, such as editing, playback, displaying and recording, only embedded objects can be *edited* in place.

OLE Automation

Some applications provide objects that support OLE Automation. This basically means you can run and control other Windows applications from within VB, using Visual Basic to programmatically manipulate objects in the other programs.

Some objects that support OLE Automation also support linking and embedding. If an object in the OLE control supports OLE Automation, you can access its data using the Object property. You can create an OLE Automation object without the OLE control using the CreateObject function. You can still use the Data and DataText properties to send data to and from an OLE 1.0 object that doesn't support OLE Automation, but since using these usually requires in-depth understanding of the file format, you may need to resort to DDE.

OLE Automation lets you create *compound applications*, not just compound documents, where OLE objects function like Lego blocks.

OLE Automation is like DDE on steroids.

Drag and Drop

Another big improvement over OLE 1.0 is OLE 2.0 support for drag and drop. Drag and drop basically is an alternative to the Clipboard, letting you drag objects from one application window to another, or to drop objects inside other objects.

The OLE 2.0 drag-and-drop model supports inter-window dragging, inter-object dragging, where objects nested within other objects can be dragged out of their containing objects to another window or to another container object, and, where appropriate, dropping over icons, such as dragging an object and dropping in on top of a system resource icon such as a printer or mailbox.

Synchronous Function Completion

In OLE 1.0, many functions were completed asynchronously. Instead of doing their work immediately, these functions finished their operations at a later, unspecified time. That meant that OLE 1.0 container applications needed to have a message loop to manage function completion and handle the container-object connection.

In OLE 2.0, functions complete synchronously. This means you don't need to implement the traditional message loop, since it has been internalized within the OLE 2.0 infrastructure. The completion of function calls is managed transparently.

Component Object Model

Microsoft's Component Object Model (see Figure 9-1) promises to be the foundation of the next generation of Windows, sometimes referred to as Cairo or Windows 4. The fact that the core of the Component Object Model is built into OLE 2.0 is yet another incentive for exploring the new OLE 2.0 VBX and object functions.

Figure 9-1: *Microsoft's Component Object Model forms the basis of OLE 2.0.*

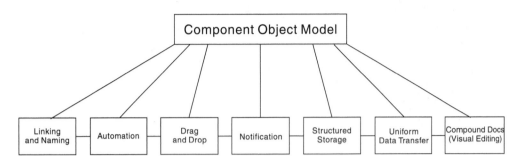

Ideally, the Component Object Model acts as a broker for all objects—OLE 2.0 and the distributed objects—thanks to the binary-level standard for components. OLE 2.0 objects follow a four-stage life cycle: creation of the object supplier process, negotiation between the container and object processes, manipulation of the OLE object, and mop-up, where the object supplier process is terminated and resources are released.

Structurally, an OLE 2.0 object contains pointers to functions, just like C++ objects. Interestingly, however, OLE 2.0 objects adhere to even stricter notions of class than C++ objects, since OLE 2.0 programs access OLE objects through indirection via the object's interface. This extra level of indirection provides the binary standard that makes OLE 2.0 language independent, that is, available to VB as well as C++ programmers.

OLE's big weakness has always been that it's essentially limited to a single PC. You'll need to wait for Cairo to get network OLE 2.0 functionality.

Other Changes

OLE 2.0 supports nested objects. It also supports version management, which allows objects to contain information about the application and version of application that created them, and object conversion, supporting interoperability among different brands of spreadsheets, for example.

OLE Objects

OLE objects are discrete units of data supplied OLE applications. An application can expose one or more types of objects. Excel, for example, exposes entire worksheets, ranges of cells, macros, and charts. Other programs expose sound or video clips, and graphic images.

In VB2, you used the OLE control to create linked or embedded objects, and you can still do that in VB3. Those linked or embedded objects contain the name of the application that supplied the object, either the actual data or a reference to it, and an image of the data. The OLE control can contain only one object at a time.

There are several ways to create standard linked or embedded objects. You can use the standard Insert Object (see Figure 9-2) or Paste Special dialogs either at design time or runtime. At design time, you can set the `Class` property in the Properties window, then click the OLE control with the right mouse button and select the appropriate command. Or, at runtime, you can set the `Action` property of the OLE control.

OLE Control Basics

You use the OLE control to create linked and embedded objects. When a linked or embedded object is created, it contains the name of the application that supplied the object, its data (or, in the case of a linked object, a reference to the data), and an image of the data. An OLE control can contain only one object at a time. You can create a linked or embedded object by:

- using the Insert Object or Paste Special dialog (run time and design time),

- setting the Action property of the OLE control (run time only), or

- using the OLE control's pop-up menus (design time only).

Figure 9-2: *Inserting a standard OLE object from the list of registered OLE object (server) applications*

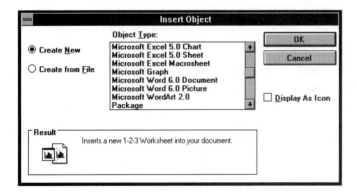

Linked Objects

When you create a linked object, the data displayed in the OLE control exists only in the linked file which is accessible—and editable—by basically anyone. The OLE control maintains the object's link information, such as the name of the application that supplied the object (its Class property), the name of the linked file (the SourceDoc property), and an image of the linked data. To create a linked object using the Insert Object dialog, complete the following steps.

1. Draw an OLE control on the form. VB displays the Insert Object dialog. Registered OLE servers/objects are listed.

2. Select the application/object you want.

3. In the Insert Object dialog, check Link and select the Create-from-File button.

4. Click on the Browse button, and use the Browse dialog to select the file you want to link. Click OK to return to the Insert Object dialog.

5. In the Insert Object dialog, select the Link check box and click OK to create the object.

Remember that when you use a linked object, anyone using your application must have access to the linked file. Otherwise, when your application is run, an image of the *original* data is displayed, but the user won't be able to modify the data or see changes others may have made to the linked data.

An object's image defaults to being automatically updated (UpdateOptions = Automatic) when the form containing the object is loaded. You'll also want to pay attention to the SizeMode property: The default is 0 for Clip. Select 1 to have the object stretched to fit or 2 for autosizing.

Embedded Objects

When you create an embedded object, you can either create an object from a file or create a new object. When you create an object from a file, a copy of the specified file's data is displayed in the OLE control. You display existing data in an embedded object by creating the object using an existing file as a template. The OLE control then contains an image of the file along with a copy of the embedded file's data. Since the OLE control contains the embedded data, an application that displays data using an embedded object will be larger than an application that displays the same data using a linked object. To create an embedded object using an existing file, complete the following steps.

1. Display the Insert Object dialog.

2. In the Object Type list box, highlight the type of object you want to create.

3. In the Insert Object dialog, choose the Create from File option button and click on the Browse button.

4. Select the file you want to embed and click OK.

Data in an embedded object is not persistent. If the user can modify the object's data, you must write code to save the data so that the changed data appears the next time the application is run.

General OLE Tips

Figure 9-3 shows some of the properties associated with the OLE 2.0 control.

The OleTypeAllowed property determines the type of object you can create. You set the OleTypeAllowed property to OLE_LINKED, OLE_EMBEDDED, or OLE_EITHER. For most situations, setting OleTypeAllowed to OLE_EITHER (the default) will suffice.

When the AutoVerbMenu property is set to True, a pop-up menu showing all the object's available verbs is displayed whenever the user clicks the OLE control with the right mouse button. The list of verbs an object supports may vary, depending on the state of the object.

Figure 9-3: *The OLE 2.0 control's properties*

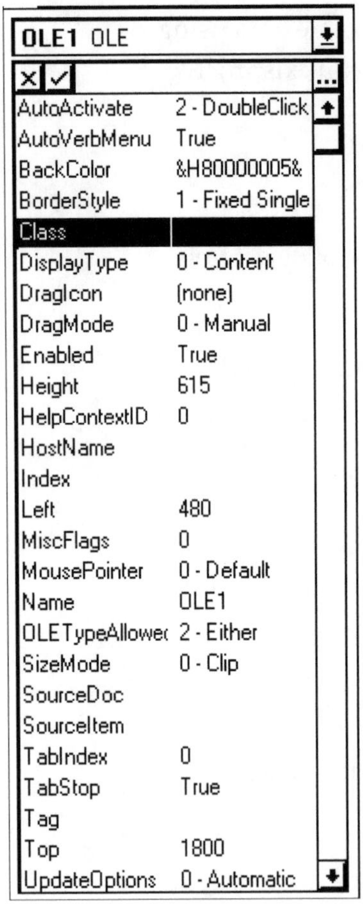

OLE1 OLE	⬇
☒ ✓	...
AutoActivate	2 - DoubleClick ⬆
AutoVerbMenu	True
BackColor	&H80000005&
BorderStyle	1 - Fixed Single
Class	
DisplayType	0 - Content
DragIcon	(none)
DragMode	0 - Manual
Enabled	True
Height	615
HelpContextID	0
HostName	
Index	
Left	480
MiscFlags	0
MousePointer	0 - Default
Name	OLE1
OLETypeAllowec	2 - Either
SizeMode	0 - Clip
SourceDoc	
SourceItem	
TabIndex	0
TabStop	True
Tag	
Top	1800
UpdateOptions	0 - Automatic ⬇

Data associated with an OLE object is not persistent; that is, when a form containing an OLE control is closed, any data associated with that control is lost. To save the data from an OLE object to a file, you use the `Action` property. Once this data has been saved to a file, you can open the file and restore the OLE object. Objects in the OLE control can be saved only to open, binary files. For example:

```
Sub SaveObject_Click ()
    'Get file number
    FileNum = FreeFile
    'Open file to be saved
    Open "TESTFILE.OLE" For Binary As #FileNum
    'Set the file number
    Ole1.FileNumber = FileNum
    'Save the file (OLE_SAVE_TO_FILE = 11)
    Ole1.Action = OLE_SAVE_TO_FILE
    'Close the file
    Close #FileNum
End Sub
```

The OLE 2.0 Control's Properties

The Action property determines an OLE operation to be performed on the OLE object by the OLE container application, e.g., saving its data to a file. Don't confuse this property/method with the OLE Verbs which are actions to be performed by the OLE application on the object like Play, Edit, delete. The Action property is only available at runtime.

AppIsRunning indicates whether the OLE application is already running. It occurs at runtime only and returns true or false. Usage: [form.]ole.AppIsRunning.

AutoActivate activates the OLE Object whenever user double clicks on OLE Object if it has been set to the default 2. Setting the property to 0 establishes a manual activation: 1 setting it to activates the object whenever it gets the focus.

AutoVerbMenu activates the OLE Object verb popup menu when the user clicks the right mouse button over the OLE Object.

BackColor and BorderStyle are standard VB properties.

`Class` determines the type of data the object contains and the name of the OLE application associated with the data. This information is kept in an OLE registration database (see Figure 9-4) on each system, and OLE products that support OLE 2.0 must register themselves with Windows. Registration includes the Class name, OLE application name, verbs supported, and default verb, executed whenever the user double-clicks on the OLE object.

Figure 9-4: *When you run REGEDIT from the Program Manager, you can examine details about the OLE objects registered for a given system. You can also clean up your object database!*

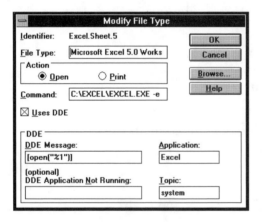

`DisplayType` determines whether the OLE object displays its actual content (0, the default) or merely an icon (1) of the data provided by the OLE application.

`DragIcon`, `DragMode`, `Enabled`, `Height`, and `HelpContextID` are the standard VB properties.

`HostName` sets the OLE displayed name of your application while in the OLE application.

`Index` and `Left` are standard VB properties.

MiscFlags has two settings: 1 (OLE_MISCFLAG_MEMSTOR-AGE), which causes the control to use memory to store the object while it is loaded, and 2 (OLE_MISCFLAG_DISABLEINPLACE), which overrides the control's default behavior of allowing in-place activation for objects that support it.

MousePointer and Name are the standard VB properties.

ObjectVerbFlags and ObjectVerbs are runtime read-only properties that contain flags and verbs supported by the OLE application. Flags determine the state of each verb, that is, greyed or checked. The verbs can be loaded onto a menu for selection by the user. To update this list, issue Action=17 (fetch Verbs). The VB OLE 2.0 control automatically builds a pop-up menu over the OLE Object with each verb listed. Press the right mouse button over the OLE Object to get this menu.

OLETypeAllowed refers to the type of OLE Link in OLE Object: 0=Linked, 1=Embedded, or 2=Either.

PasteOK indicates that the clipboard contains an OLE object.

SizeMode determines how the OLE control is sized. A 0 setting represents actual size but clipped if necessary, 1 will stretch to fill the control, and 2 autosizes the OLE control.

SourceDoc identifies the file used to create the OLE object, if applicable.

SourceItem is used to identify the data within the SourceDoc to be linked, e.g., a range of cells in a spreadsheet. SourceItem must be supplied as a string, for example: [form.]ole.SourceItem = "R2C10:R3C10".

TabIndex, TabStop, Tag, and Top are the standard VB properties.

`UpdateOptions` determines how the OLE Object will be updated when linked data is changed, either as 0, for automatically updated, 1 for frozen until OLE Application does a save, or 2 for manually updated by `Action=6` (Update).

`Verb` determines the action to be taken when OLE Object is activated (`Action=7`). A 0setting is for Default Action, -1 is for Edits Object and supports in-place editing, -2 is for Edits in its own window, and -3 is for Embedded Objects, which hides OLE application from the user.

The `OLE Object's Action` Property performs these functions as well as other operations on the object:

- `CreateEmbed(0)`. Calls the OLE application to create a new embedded object.

- `CreateLink(1)`. Creates an OLE Linked object from the OLE application's file.

- 2, 3 reserved for future use

- `Copy(4)`. Copies the linked or embedded object to the Clipboard.

- `Paste(5)`. Pastes a linked or embedded object from the Clipboard. Checks the `PASTEOK` property for TRUE first. Used to implement Edit-Paste menu command. if the paste was successful the `OLEType` property will be set to 0 (Linked) or 1 (Embedded).

- `Update(6)`. Retrieves current data from OLE application.

- `Activate(7)`. Activates the OLE application with the verb in the Verb property.

- 8 is reserved for future use

- `Close(9)` - Closes the OLE Object's link to the OLE application and terminates the OLE Application.

- `Delete(10)`. Deletes an OLE Object.

- `SaveToFile(11)`. Saves the OLE Object's data to a file.

- `ReadFromFile(12)`. Reloads the OLE Object with the previously saved OLE data using the `OLE_SAVE_TO_FILE`.

- 13 is reserved for future use

- `InsertObjDialog(14)`. Displays the Insert Object Dialog Box. Allows the user to create an OLE object and type. Use the `OLETypeAllowed` property to limited types.

- `PasteSpecialDlg(15)`. Displays the Paste Special Dialog Box. Allows the User to paste a clipboard object and choose the Type of OLE Object to create. Use the `OLETypeAllowed` property to limited types.

- 16 is reserved for future use

- `FetchVerbs(17)`. Updates the objects set of verbs supported by the OLE application.

- `Convert(18)`. Saves an OLE 2.0 object in an OLE 1.0 format.

`Visible` and `width` are standard VB properties.

OLE Automation

OLE Automation is an emerging industry standard that applications use to expose their OLE objects to development tools, macro languages, and container applications that support OLE Automation. For example, a spreadsheet application may expose a worksheet, chart, cell, or range of cells, all as different types of objects. A word processor might expose objects such as applications, paragraphs, sentences, bookmarks, or selections. A drawing package might expose drawings, portions of drawings, or shapes.

When an application supports OLE Automation, the objects it exposes can be accessed by Visual Basic. You use Visual Basic to manipulate these objects by invoking methods on the objects, or by getting and setting the objects' properties just as you would with Visual Basic's own objects. If you've used DDE, you'll see there's a lot of overlap between the two. In fact, OLE 2.0 is expected to supplant DDE.

Accessing OLE Objects

You can manipulate other applications' OLE objects remotely, without creating a linked or embedded object, using the `CreateObject` function. Before creating an object, you define a variable that can be used to reference the object. You do this by dimensioning a variable of type Object. For example:

```
Dim Spread As Object
Dim appVisio As Object
```

Then you use the `CreateObject` function to create the object. This function requires a single parameter—a string that indicates the application name and the type of object you want to create. You specify the object to create with syntax like *application.ObjectType*. For example:

```
Excel.Sheet.5
appVisio.ActiveDocument
```

To get a list of objects that an application supports, you'll have to refer to the application's documentation. Next, you use the Set keyword to assign the object returned by the CreateObject function to the object variable. For example:

```
Set Spread = CreateObject("Excel.Sheet.5")
Set appVisio = CreateObject(visio. application)
```

When this code executes, the application providing the object is started (if it is not already running) and an object is created. Unlike the image displayed when you create a linked or embedded object with the OLE control, the object's image is not displayed anywhere in Visual Basic, nor is the object's data maintained by Visual Basic. The object is part of the application that created it and can be referenced in Visual Basic code using the object variable you defined.

Visual Basic code using the object variable you defined. For example, you might use code like this to change the current cell, insert text, and save your work as a new file:

```
Dim Spread As Object
Set Spread = GetObject("vbtest.xls", "excel.sheet.5")
Spread.Cells(2, 1).Value = "Hello, world!"
Spread.SaveAs "C:\EXCEL\OLETEST.XLS"
```

Creating and Using Invisible Objects

Some applications may provide objects that are never displayed to the user. For example, a word processing application may expose its spelling checker engine as an object. Let's say this object supports a method called CheckWord that takes a string as an argument. If the string is spelled correctly, True is returned; otherwise, the method returns False. The code might look something like this:

```
'Hypothetical listing
Sub CheckSpelling ()
    Dim ObjVar As Object
    Dim MyWord, Result
    MyWord = "potatoe"

    'Create the object
    Set ObjVar = CreateObject("WP.SpellCheck")

    'Run the spell checker
    Result = ObjVar.CheckWord (MyWord)
    'If False, get suggestion or process error message
End Sub
```

Many OLE Automation applications allow the user to save objects in files, and GetObject is the flip side of CreateObject. You use the GetObject function to activate an object that's been saved to a file by first dimensioning an object variable. Then you call the GetObject function using the following syntax:

```
GetObject (filename[, class])
```

as in

```
GetObject ("C:\EXCEL\VBTEST.XLS", "Excel.Sheet.5")
GetObject ("C:\VISIO\ORGCHART.VSD", "Visio.Application")
```

where filename contains the full path. If the filename argument is set to an empty string (""), the GetObject function returns the currently active object of the specified class, and if there isn't one, you get an error. To specify just *part* of a file, use an exclamation point (!) or a backslash (\) to the end of the file name, followed by a string that identifies the part of the file you want to activate.

Using Objects' Properties and Methods

Assigning and retrieving object property values is standard VB fare. Keep in mind that all arguments to OLE Automation objects use the Variant data type.

In addition to getting and setting properties, you can manipulate an object using the methods it supports. Some methods return a value, and methods that don't return a value essentially behave like subroutines. If you assign such a method to a variable, an error occurs. With Visio, for example, you can use Copy, along with related Cut, Paste, Delete, and Duplicate methods. This demonstrates the Copy method:

```
Sub TestEdits()
   Dim appVisio As Object, DrawPage As Object, shp
   ...As Object
   Set appVisio = CreateObject("visio.application")

   'Set up Visio with a document and page to draw on
   If appVisio.ActiveDocument is Nothing Then
       appVisio.Documents.Add ("")
   End If

   Set DrawPage = appVisio.ActivePage
   If DrawPage Is Nothing Then
      SetDrawPage = appVisio.ActiveDocument.Pages(1)
   End If

   'Draw a demo rectangle.
   ' Copy, paste to clipboard, copy to drawing page
   Set shp = DrawPage.DrawRectangle (1,5,5,1)
   shp.Copy        'Copy to Clipboard
   DrawPage.Paste              'Paste to drawing page
   shp.Cut         'Remove original
```

```
    Set shp = DrawPage.Shapes.Item(DrawPage.Shapes.Count)
    shp.SetCenter 3,5
End Sub
```

Table 9-1 illustrates the properties and methods by object available in Shapeware's Visio.

Some objects contain subobjects. You can include multiple objects, properties, and methods on the same line of code using the dot syntax, just as you would with a Visual Basic object (for example, Form.Control.Property).

OLE Memory Use

All OLE Automation objects support some method that closes the object and the application that created it, and since OLE objects can use a significant amount of memory, it's virtually mandatory to explicitly close an object when you no longer need it. To close an object, use the appropriate method, such as Close or Quit:

```
'Closes the object
ObjVar.Close
'Closes the application that created the object
ObjVar.Quit
```

The user can also close an object using the application that created the object. When an object has been closed, either programmatically or by the user, any object variables that refer to the object are set to Nothing.

Collections

A collection is an object that contains zero or more objects of a specified type. Excel 5, for example has collections called Charts,

Table 9-1: *Properties and methods by object in OLE-enabled Visio 2.0*

Identifier	Application	Cell	Connect	Connects	Document	Documents	Master	Masters	Page	Pages	Selection	Shape	Shapes	Style	Styles	Window	Windows
Activate																●	
ActiveDocument	●																
ActivePage	●																
ActiveWindow	●																
Add										●							
AddGuide									●								
AddRow												●					
AddSection												●					
AddToGroup											●						
AlignName							●										
Application	●	●	●	●	●	●	●	●	●	●	●	●	●	●	●	●	●
Arrange																	●
Background									●								
BackPage									●								
Cells												●					
CellsSRC												●					
Close																●	
Combine											●						
Connects												●					
Copy											●	●					
Count				●		●		●		●	●		●		●		●
Creator					●												
Cut												●					
Data1												●					
Data2												●					
Data3												●					
Delete												●					
DeleteRow												●					
DeleteSection												●					
Description					●												
DeselectAll																●	
Document							●		●			●					
Documents	●																
DrawLine									●								
DrawOval									●								
DrawRectangle									●								
Drop					●							●					
Duplicate											●	●					
Error		●															
FillStlyeKeepFmt												●					
FillStyle												●					
Formula		●															
FormulaForce		●															
Fragment											●						
FromCell			●														
FromPart			●														
FromSheet			●		●												
FullName					●												
GeometryCount												●					
GlueTo		●															
GlueToPos		●															
Group											●						
IconSize							●										
IconUpdate							●										
Index					●		●		●			●					●

Table 9-1:   *(Continued)*

Identifier	Application	Cell	Connect	Connects	Document	Documents	Master	Masters	Page	Pages	Selection	Shape	Shapes	Style	Styles	Window	Windows
Keywords					o												
LineStlyeKeepFmt												o					
LineStyle												o					
Master												o					
Masters					o												
Name					o		o		o			o		o			
NameID												o					
NewDocument	o																
OneD							o					o					
OpenDocument	o																
Page																o	
Pages					o												
Paste									o								
Path					o												
Print					o				o								
Prompt							o										
Quit	o																
ReadOnly					o												
Redo	o																
Result		o															
ResultForce		o															
ResultIU		o															
ResultIUForce		o															
RowCount												o					
RowsCellCount												o					
RowType												o					
Save					o												
SaveAs					o												
Saved					o												
Select																o	
SelectAll																o	
Selection	o															o	
SetBegin												o					
SetCenter												o					
SetEnd												o					
Shapes									o			o					
StlyeKeepFmt												o					
Style												o					
Styles					o												
Subject					o												
Text												o					
TextStlyeKeepFmt												o					
TextStyle												o					
Title					o												
ToCell			o														
ToPart			o														
ToSheet			o														
Type												o				o	
Undo	o																
Union											o						
Value				o		o	o			o	o		o		o		o
WindowHandle	o																
Windows	o																
Zoom																o	

Sheets, Worksheets, and so on. Most collections support a property called Count. This property returns the number of elements in the collection. You specify an individual element of a collection using an index. You can run into two problems when iterating through a collection of an OLE object. First of all, there's no guarantee the subscripts of the collection are numeric. Further complicating matters is the fact that even if the collection returns a numeric subscript, there's no guarantee the subscripts are contiguous.

Some objects provide methods that allow you to iterate through collections. If an object doesn't explicitly provide methods for doing this, you may not be able to cycle through an object's collections in your Visual Basic program. In any case, you should provide error trapping in case the subscripts aren't contiguous.

Here's a simple example that shows how to print information about Visio's active documents to the debug window:

```
Sub ShowNames ()
' Prints names and pages of open Visio documents
' Assumes Visio is running
Dim iDoc As Integer, iPag As Integer
Dim appVisio As Object
Dim pag As Object, doc As Object
Dim docs As Object

Set appVisio = GetObject(, "visio.application")
Set docs = appVisio.documents
    For iDoc = 1 To docs.count
        Set doc = docs(iDoc)

        Debug.Print doc.name
        For iPag = 1 To doc.pages.count
            Set pag = doc.pages(iPag)
```

```
            Debug.Print pag.name
        Next iPag
    Next iDoc
End Sub
```

Here's an example from Visio that will return the master stencil
collection for a document:

```
Sub DumpMasterNames ()
' Prints the name of the masters in the current document to
' the debug window

    Dim I As Integer
    Dim appVisio As Object, CurDoc As Object, Mstrs As
    ...Object

    ' Assume Visio is running and has an active document
    Set appVisio = GetObject(, "visio.application")
    Set CurDoc = appVisio.ActiveDocument

    If CurDoc Is Nothing Then
        Debug.Print "No Active Document"
        Exit Sub
    End If

    'Get the master colleciton from the document
    Set Mstrs = CurDoc.Masters
    Debug.Print "Master Name Dump for Document ";
CurDoc.name
    If Mstrs.Count  0 Then
        For I = 1 To Mstrs.Count
            Debug.Print "  "; Mstrs(I).name
        Next I
    Else
```

```
        Debug.Print "    No Masters in current document"
    End If
End Sub
```

Limitations

OLE 2.0 isn't perfect. It's really not set up for distributed applications, since you need to hard code PATHs into your code. VB3 also has some limitations when it comes to using arrays with OLE objects. You can't use an array or a user-defined type as an argument to a method, use an array to set a property, or assign an array variable or a variable of a user-defined type to the return value of a property or method. However, when a property or method returns an array, you can use the LBound and UBound functions to determine the size of an array and then access the individual array elements. You cannot use named arguments when calling an object's methods in Visual Basic. When calling a method that supports named arguments, you must specify each argument in the correct order

Distributing OLE Applications

When you create and distribute applications that use the OLE control, you should install the following files in the customer's Microsoft Windows \SYSTEM directory:

- COMPOBJ.DLL

- MSOLE2.VBX

- MSOLEVBX.DLL

- OLE2.REG

- OLE2.DLL

- OLE2CONV.DLL

- OLE2DISP.DLL

- OLE2NLS.DLL

- OLE2PROX.DLL

- STORAGE.DLL

- VBOA300.DLL

You also need to make sure OLE 2.0 is registered on the user's machine and that SHARE.EXE is installed in the user's AUTOEXEC.BAT file. SHARE.EXE is *not* required, however, if the user is running Microsoft Windows for Workgroups. You can use the SetupWizard to create distribution disks that do this.

Summary

Microsoft and many vendors are committed to OLE, and Visual Basic is clearly poised to serve as the mega container for any number of OLE objects. Although we weren't able to show you any OLE-enabled DBMSs—they simply weren't available at this writing—it's only a matter of time before we start using them.

References

OLE 2.0 SDK, Microsoft Developer Network CD Disc 5

OLE 2.0 Design Specification.

Product Tools & Utilities I OLE 2.0 Tools. For information on the Developer Network, call 1-800-227-4679 ext. 11771 or 206-635-7033.

OLE 2 Developer's Guide by Kraig Brockschmidt, Microsoft Press, 1993. ISBN 1-55615-618-9, $39.95. 1-800-MSPRESS to order. 1-800-888-3303 for catalog.

Visio 2.0 from Shapeware, 1601 Fifth Ave, Suite 800, Seattle, WA 98101-1625. Phone: 206-521-4500, Fax 206-521-4501.

10

Microsoft's Programmer's Toolkit for SQL Server

We'll be honest—if you don't use Microsoft or Sybase SQL Server, you don't need to read this chapter. However, if you have applications that access any flavor of SQL Server, you can use Microsoft's SQL Server Programmer's Toolkit, previously known as VBSQL, to your advantage. It provides both VB and C/C++ programmers with tools to access SQL Server's client library API, DB-Library (DBLIB). You also get Microsoft's Open Data Services (ODS) C libraries for developing your own server-based gateway, should you be so inclined.

What You Get

The Programmer's Toolkit for SQL Server ($695) weighs about seven pounds and includes not only the Programmer's Reference for Visual Basic, but also the Microsoft SQL Server Transact-SQL Reference, the Microsoft SQL Server Programmer's Reference for C, and the Open Data Services Programmer's Reference. Transact-SQL (T-SQL) is SQL Server's own dialect of SQL, and the SQL Server Programmer's Reference for C documents the DB Library API. The ODS manual shows you how to create a custom gateway.

VB programmers will be most interested in the VBSQL functions and routines and the VBX custom control that supplies error handling routines, but the sample projects and good on-line help file provide invaluable time-saving models. VB for DOS programmers will also be happy for DOS-specific sample files, good documentation that flag commands routines that are Windows- or DOS-specific, plus an entire chapter on strategies for creating cross-platform applications.

The Visual Basic for SQL Server library, sometimes referred to as VBSQL or VBPTK, is actually an "augmented" subset of DB-Library. How's that for doublespeak?

ODBC or DBLIB

With point-and-click ODBC access from VB to SQL Server, there's been a good deal of confusion about the need for lower-level direct access to SQL Server's API. ODBC has the advantage of being a standard that promises interoperability. DBLIB, on the other hand, is best for performance and control.

ODBC (Open Database Connectivity), as you know by now, is a C-language API that defines database connectivity for the

Windows world. The ODBC interface permits maximum inter-operability—a single application can theoretically easily access diverse database management systems without changing much code. You can develop, compile, and ship an application without targeting a specific DBMS, assuming, of course, that the back-end data is the same. ODBC achieves interoperability by forcing all clients to adhere to a standard interface. The ODBC driver acts as a black box that interprets the command for a specific data source.

DBLIB, on the other hand, is a set of C functions and macros that allow an application to access and interact with SQL Server. DBLIB offers a rich set of APIs for opening SQL Server connections, formatting queries, sending query batches to the server and retrieving the resulting data, bulk-copying data from files or program variables to and from the server, performing two-phase commit (2PC) operations, and executing stored procedures on remote servers.

DBLIB is an API that has been designed for one database backend only: SQL Server. ODBC has been designed to be a general-purpose Call Level Interface (CLI) for any database back end, including non-relational DBMSs. The challenge of the ODBC API is to strike a balance between interoperability and support for DBMS-specific features. There are several specific ramifications. DBLIB doesn't need to include elaborate APIs for extracting catalog information. Nor does it need to define a canonical set of scalar functions like ODBC does. DBLIB also offers better error-handling routines. Overall, because DBLIB doesn't have all the overhead associated with supporting multiple back-ends, it offers better performance than the ODBC API.

DBLIB is SQL Server's Clanguage API.

The Functions and Routines

The following tables list the functions and routines provided with the VBPTK (VBSQL).

Initializing VBSQL	
SqlInit$	Initializes Visual Basic for SQL Server Library (VBSQL)
Setting Up a Log-in Record	
SqlFreeLogin	Frees the memory allocated for a log-in record
SqlLogin%	Allocates a log-in record for use with `SqlOpen%`. ODBC doesn't have the concept of a log-in record; with ODBC you use its `SQLConnect` or `SQLDriverConnect` functions.
SqlSetLApp%	Sets the application name in the SQL Server log-in record
SqlSetLHost%	Sets the workstation name in the SQL Server log-in record
SqlSetLNatLang%	Sets the name of the national language in the SQL Server log-in record
SqlSetLPwd%	Sets the user's SQL Server password in the SQL Server log-in record
SqlSetLUser%	Sets the log-in identification string in the SQL Server login record
Establishing a SQL Server Connection	
SqlChange$	Determines whether a command batch has changed the current database to another one
SqlIsAvail%	Determines whether a `sqlconn%` connection is available for general use
SqlGetMaxProcs%	Determines the current maximum number of simultaneously open `sqlconn%` connections
SqlName$	Returns the name of the current database

Initializing VBSQL

SqlOpen%	Allocates and initializes a SQL Server connection. An application can open multiple connections to SQL Server.
SqlServerEnum%	Lists the server names of SQL Server computers on the network
SqlSetAvail	Marks a `sqlconn%` connection as being available for general use
SqlSetLoginTime%	Sets the number of seconds VBSQL waits for SQL Server to respond to a request by `SqlOpen%` for a connection
SqlUse%	Sets the current database for a particular SQL Server connection. This function is equivalent to the Transact-SQL `USE` statement and can be called repeatedly in an application.

Command Processing

SqlCmd%	Adds Transact-SQL text to the command buffer. You can call `SqlCmd%` repeatedly to add multiple statements or parts of statements to the command buffer; the text added with each successive call is appended to the previous text.
SqlFreeBuf	Clears the command buffer. The command buffer is auto-matically cleared when your application calls `SqlCmd%` after a call to `SqlExec%` or `SqlSend%`. Use `SqlFreeBuf` to clear the buffer at other times or when the SQLNOAUTOFREE option has been set.
SqlGetChar$	Returns the value of a character in the command buffer
SqlGetOff%	Checks for the existence of Transact-SQL statements in the command buffer
SqlStrCpy%	Copies a portion of the command buffer to a program variable Helpful for debugging, since it tells you exactly what was sent to SQL Server

Initializing VBSQL	
SqlStrLen%	Returns the length, in characters, of the command buffer
SqlDataReady%	Indicates whether SQL Server has finished processing a statement
SqlExec%	Sends the statements in the command buffer to SQL Server for execution. Once `SqlExec%` returns SUCCEED, `SqlResults%` must be called to process the results. Calling `SqlExec%` is equivalent to calling `SqlSend%` followed by `SqlOk%`
SqlOk%	Verifies the correctness of statements in the command buffer. You must call this function after a successful return from `SqlSend%`. Once `SqlOk%` returns SUCCEED, `SqlResults%` must be called to process the results.
SqlSend%	Sends the statements in the command buffer to SQL Server for execution. Unlike `SqlExec%`, this function doesn't wait for a response from SQL Server. When `SqlSend%` returns SUCCEED, `SqlOk%` must be called to verify the correctness of the statements in the command buffer
SqlClrOpt%	Clears an option set by `SqlSetOpt%`
SqlIsOpt%	Checks the status of an option set by `SqlSetOpt%`
SqlSetOpt%	Sets a VBSQL option, e.g.,`SQLSHOWPLAN`
Results Processing	
SqlResults%	Sets up the next statement in the command buffer for processing and indicates whether there are more results pending. This function must be called once for each statement in the buffer

Initializing VBSQL	
SqlAData$	Returns a string containing data for the result column for a compute row. A compute row is the result of a SELECT statement that contains a COMPUTE clause
SqlData$	Returns a string containing data for the result column for a regular row
SqlClrBuf	Drops rows from the row buffer
SqlGetRow%	Sets the current row in the row buffer to a specific row number and reads it. This function reads buffered rows that were previously read by SqlNextRow%
SqlNextRow%	Reads the next data row from the row buffer. The return value from SqlNextRow% indicates whether the buffer is full and whether the last result row has been read.
SqlPrHead	Displays the column headings for a set of results on the default output device. Used in conjunction with SqlPrRow%
SqlPrRow%	Displays the rows for a set of query results on the default output device. If you use this function, your application doesn't need to call SqlNextRow%
SqlCancel%	Cancels the execution of statements in the command buffer and flushes any pending results
SqlCanQuery%	Cancels any rows pending from the most recently executed statement
SqlGetTime%	Returns the number of seconds that VBSQL waits for a SQL Server response
SqlSetTime%	Sets the number of seconds that VBSQL waits for a SQL Server response
Retrieving Information	
SqlColLen%	Returns the maximum length of the data, in bytes, converted to a string in a regular column

Initializing VBSQL	
SqlColName$	Returns the name of a regular result column
SqlColType%	Returns the SQL Server datatype for a regular result column
SqlDatLen&	Returns the actual length, in bytes, converted to a sting, of the data in a regular column This function is often used in conjunction with `SqlData$`. The value returned by `SqlDatLen&` can be different for each row that `SqlNextRow%` reads
SqlNumCols%	Returns the number of columns in the current set of results
SqlPrType$	Converts a SQL Server token value to a string
SqlADLen&	Returns the actual length of the data in a compute column in the form of a string. This function is often used in conjunction with `SqlAData$`. The value returned by `SqlADLen&` can be different for each compute row that `SqlNextRow%` reads
SqlAltColId%	Returns the identification number in a compute column
SqlAltLen%	Returns the maximum length of the data, in bytes. The length is converted to a string in a compute column
SqlAltOp%	Returns the type of aggregate function of a compute column
SqlAltType%	Returns the datatype of a compute column
SqlByList$	Returns the bylist of a compute row
SqlNumAlts%	Returns the number of columns in a compute row
SqlNumCompute%	Returns the number of `COMPUTE` clauses in the current set of results
SqlCurRow&	Returns the number of the row currently being read
SqlFirstRow&	When the SQLBUFFER option has been set, returns the number of the first row in the row buffer

Initializing VBSQL	
SqlLastRow&	When the SQLBUFFER option has been set, returns the number of the last row in the row buffer
SqlRowType%	Indicates whether the current result row is a regular row or a compute row
SqlCmdRow%	Indicates whether the current statement can return rows. Rows can be returned by SELECT statements or by stored procedures containing SELECT statements.
SqlCount&	Returns the number of rows affected by the current (most recently executed) statement
SqlCurCmd%	Returns the number of the current statement in the command buffer
SqlMoreCmds%	Indicates whether there are more statements in the command buffer to be processed
SqlNumOrders%	Returns the number of columns specified in the ORDER BY clause of a SELECT statement
SqlOrderCol%	Returns the number of a column specified in the ORDER BY clause of the current SELECT statement
SqlRows%	Indicates whether the current (most recently executed) statement has returned rows
Using Cursors	
SqlCursor%	Updates, deletes, inserts, and refreshes the rows in the fetch buffer
SqlCursorClose	Closes a cursor
SqlCursorColInfo%	Returns a column's name, type, length, and user-defined type for a specified column
SqlCursorData$	Returns the value of the data in a specified row and column from the cursor buffer
SqlCursorFetch%	Scrolls the fetch buffer
SqlCursorInfo%	Returns the number of columns and rows in a keyset

Initializing VBSQL	
SqlCursorOpen%	Declares and opens a cursor, specifies the size of the fetch buffer and the keyset, and sets the concurrency control option
Browse Mode	
SqlColBrowse%	Indicates whether the source of a result column can be updated using browse mode
SqlColSource$	Returns the name of the database column from which a result column was derived
SqlQual$	Returns a string containing the WHERE clause for the current row in a specified table
SqlTabBrowse%	Indicates whether a specified table can be updated using browse mode
SqlTabCount%	Returns the number of tables involved in the current SELECT statement
SqlTabName$	Returns the name of a table based on its number
SqlTabSource$	Returns the name of the table from which a particular result column was derived, and returns the number of a table based on the table's order in the SELECT list
SqlTsNewLen%	Returns the length of the new value of the timestamp column after a browse-mode update
SqlTsNewVal$	Returns the identifier of the new value of the timestamp column after a browse-mode update
SqlTsPut%	Puts the new value of the timestamp column into a specified table's current row in the row buffer
Special Text and Image Handling	
SqlMoreText%	Sends part of a large text or image value to SQL Server
SqlTxPtr$	Returns the identifier for a text or image column in the current row

Initializing VBSQL	
SqlTxTimeStamp$	Returns the text timestamp for a column in the current row
SqlTxTsNewVal$	Returns the new value of a text timestamp after a call to `SqlWriteText%`
SqlTxTsPut%	Puts the identifier for the new value of a text timestamp into a specified column of the current row in the row buffer
SqlWriteText%	Sends text or image values to SQL Server
Bulk Copy Routines	
SqlBCPColfmt%	Specifies the format of an operating system file for bulk copy purposes
SqlBCPColumns%	Sets the total number of columns found in an operating system file to be used with the bulk copy operation
SqlBCPControl%	Changes various default settings for the control parm
SqlBCPSetL%	Sets the `loginrec%` for bulk copy operations
SqlBCPInit%	Initializes a bulk copy
SqlBCPExec%	Executes a bulk copy
Stored Procedure Processing	
SqlHasRetStat%	Determines whether the current Transact-SQL statement or stored procedure generated a return status number
SqlNumRets%	Calculates the number of returned parameter values generated by a stored procedure
SqlRetData$	Returns a value generated by a stored procedure
SqlRetLen&	Determines the length of a return parameter value generated by a stored procedure
SqlRetName$	Returns the name of a stored procedure parameter associated with a particular return-parameter value

Initializing VBSQL	
SqlRetStatus&	Returns the stored procedure status number returned by the current command or stored procedure
SqlRetType%	Determines the datatype of a return-parameter value generated by a stored procedure
SqlRpcInit%	Initializes a remote stored procedure
SqlRpcParam%	Adds a parameter to a remote stored procedure
SqlRpcSend%	Signals the end of a parameter list for a remote stored procedure and sends it to the server to be executed
SqlRPwClr	Clears all remote passwords from the login% record
SqlRPwSet%	Adds a remote password to the login% record
Clean-Up	
SqlClose	Closes and frees a single connection
SqlDead%	Indicates whether a particular connection is inactive. When a connection is inactive, the current VBSQL function fails
SqlExit	Closes and frees all connections
SqlWinExit	Informs VBSQL that the Windows application calling it is about to exit. This call releases the memory that VBSQL allocated to keep track of an app, making it available to other apps
Miscellaneous Utilities	
SqlBCPColumnFormat	Sets up the column format for an input file in a bulk copy operation
SqlOpenConnection%	Allocates a log-in record, opens a connection to the server, and deallocates the log-in record
SqlSendCmd%	Sends Transact-SQL text from the command buffer and sets up the statement for processing

Initializing VBSQL	
SqlGetColumnInfo%	Sets the type, length, name
SqlGetAltColInfo%	Sets the column ID, datatype, maximum length, type of aggregate function, and aggregate type name of a specific column in the current set of results
SqlTsUpdate%	Updates the value of a timestamp column in a specified table
SqlTextUpdate1Row%	Updates one row of results in a text column. All subsequent rows, if any, are removed from the results buffer
SqlTextUpdateMany-Rows	Updates all rows of results in a text or image column, starting from the current row

Writing a VB Program

As the VBPTK manual points out, to write a VB program that accesses SQL Server, you'll typically follow these steps:

1. Set up an error and message handler

2. Call SqlInit$ to initialize the VBSQL library

3. Open one or more connections to SQL Server

4. Send Transact-SQL (T-SQL) statements to SQL Server

5. Process the results

6. Close the connection(s)

Error Handling

The VBSQL error handler custom control icon is a Stop sign. It receives error and message information from SQL Server and is necessary since VB doesn't allow callback functions. So the first thing you'll want to do when you write a VBSQL program is to add the VBSQL VBX to your project and locate the error handler on your startup form. You will then get two event handlers, VBSQL1_Error and VBSQL1_Message. You also need either to include the VBSQL.BI declaration file to your project or copy the declarations into your own declaration file, such as GLOBAL.BAS. VBSQL1_Error takes five parameters:

- `sqlconn%`: the SQL Server connection that encountered the error

- `severity%`: an integer between 1 and 11 (worst) indicating the severity of the error

- `errornum%`: a five-digit VBSQL error code

- `errorstr$`: a brief string corresponding to the VBSQL error

- `retcode%`: an output parameter that determines how VBSQL will handle the error

VBSQL1_Message also takes five parameters:

- `sqlconn%`: the SQL Server connection that encountered the error

- `message&`: an integer with the SQL Server error message number

- `state%`: the current message's error state number

- `severity%`: an integer between 1 and 11 (worst) indicating the severity of the error

- `msgstr$`: string with SQL Server error message

ODBC and DBLIB differ substantially as far as error handling goes. DBLIB's error handling is based on the concept of asynchronous error and message handlers. In ODBC, every function call returns SQL_SUCCESS when it executes successfully. Alternately, you'll probably get a SQL_SUCCESS_WITH_INFO or SQL_ERROR, and it's your program's responsibility to retrieve the buffered message with a call to SQL_ERROR and subsequent calls to the appropriate handlers to handle these errors. The driver buffers errors or messages one call at a time, with subsequent calls overwriting existing error message information.

SqlInit$

This function takes no parameters but is necessary to "register" your application with the VBSQL library. You typically call it from the Form_Load event of your application's primary form. `SqlInit$` returns the DBLIB version number as a string, such as DB-Lib Version 4.2, so be sure your error and message handlers are available before you call `SqlInit$`.

Logging in and Opening a Connection

To open a SQL Server connection, you can either use a combination of `SqlLogin%` and `SqlOpen%` or `SqlOpenConnection%`. `SqlLogin%` allocates a log-in record; note that ODBC doesn't have a log-in record. Initialization with ODBC consists of calling the ODBC functions `SQLAllocEnv` and `SQLAllocConnect` to allocate memory for maintaining global information about all connections and information local to each connection and then calling `SQLConnect` and/or `SQLDriverConnect`. You can open multiple connections by issuing multiple SqlOpen% statements.

You'll typically also want to call `SqlSetLUser%` and `SqlSetLPwd%` to pass the user's login ID and password to SQL Server:

```
SqlSetLUser%(loginrec%, loginid$)
SqlSetLPwd%(loginrec%, pwd$)
```

For `SqlSetLPwd%` to have any effect, it must be called before `SqlOpen%`. Note that `SqlSetLPwd%` is required only if the user has a SQL Server password. If you don't call `SqlSetLPwd%`, the password is set to an empty string. You can use a subroutine like the following to have the user's password entered as a series of asterisks:

```
Sub password_field_KeyPress (KeyAscii As Integer)

'This will keep the password from being seen
If (KeyAscii >= 65 And KeyAscii <= 90) Or (KeyAscii >= 97
And KeyAscii <= 122) Then
    Password$ = Password$ + Chr$(KeyAscii)
    KeyAscii = Asc("*")
End If

End Sub
```

Figure 10-1 depicts a typical, if uninspired, log-in form.

Figure 10-1: *Standard log-in form*

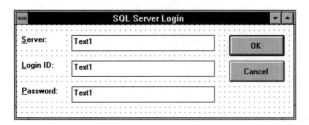

As far as connections go, you may want to keep in mind the difference between ODBC and DBLIB. In ODBC, every connection handle corresponds to one network-level connection between the server and the application. A connection handle might be associated with multiple-statement handles, meaning that each connection might have multiple-statement streams. To multiplex virtual-statement streams on a single connection in the case of DBLIB, however, you have to use cursors. And DBLIB requires that cursors be explicitly declared and given a name. With ODBC, every SELECT statement is automatically associated with a cursor.

T-SQL has a USE database command, which you can use to set the active database. If your application doesn't know what databases are available or wants to let the user choose one, you can use a routine from the VBSQLGEN.BAS code that comes with VBSQL to retrieve the database names and fill a combo box:

```
Function GetDatabases (Database_Control As Control) As
Integer

'Gets the names of all the databases on the SQL Server

If ExecuteSQLCommand("Select name from master..sys-
databases") = FAIL% Then
    GetDatabases = FAIL
    Exit Function
Else
    If SqlResults(SqlConn%) = FAIL% Then Exit Function
        While SqlNextRow(SqlConn%) <> NOMOREROWS%
            Database_Control.AddItem SqlData(SqlConn%, 1)
        Wend
End If

'If it's a combobox we're filling, display the first
database in the list to start with

If TypeOf Database_Control Is ComboBox Then
```

```
    Database_Control.Text = Database_Control.List(0)
End If

GetDatabases = SUCCEED
End Function
```

The GetDatabases function is only one of about a dozen useful routines you can cut and paste into your own applications (see Figure 10-2).

Figure 10-2: *The VBSQLGEN.BAS module has over a dozen useful routines like LoginToServer and GetDatabases.*

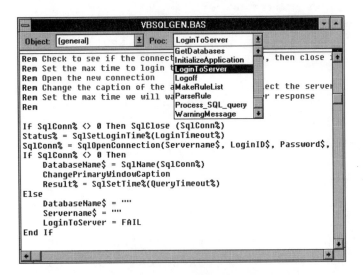

Sending T-SQL Statements to SQL Server

As you can see from the Command Processing section of the table, the `SqlCmd%` and `SqlExec%` functions are the workhorse functions for building T-SQL statements and having them sent to SQL Server. Likewise, `SqlResult%`, `SqlNextRow%`, and `SqlData$` are the commands you'll use most often to return information to the user.

SqlResults% is called after SqlExec% returns SUCCEED. Once SqlResults% returns SUCCEED, you typically process any result rows using SqlNextRow%. You have to call SqlResults% for each statement in the command buffer, whether or not the statement returns any rows. If you don't know how many statements are in the command buffer, you can call SqlResults% until it returns NOMORERESULTS. To determine whether a particular statement returns rows and needs results processing with SqlNextRow%, call SqlRows%. For example:

```
'Put a statement into the command buffer
Result% = SqlCmd%(Sqlconn%, "SELECT * FROM sometable")


'Send the statement to SQL Server and start execution
Result% = SqlExec%(Sqlconn%)
DO UNTIL Result% = NOMORERESULTS
    Result% = SqlResults%(Sqlconn%)

    'Retrieve and process the data in each row
    DO UNTIL SqlNextRow%(Sqlconn%) = NOMOREROWS
        'Do work---code to print or process row of data
    LOOP
LOOP
```

You can close SQL Server connections either with SqlExit, which closes all connections, or with SqlClose, to close one connection at a time. To free memory allocated by VBSQL, your application should also call SqlWinExit. None of these routines requires any parameters.

Browse Mode

Relational DBMSs like SQL Server return data in result sets, and most queries your application sends to SQL Server will return more than one row. You have to decide how to handle the multiple rows. Basically, you can have your application control row buffering, by buffering, say, three screens of data (one for display, plus the previous and next), you can buffer the entire result set, or you can use cursor-based queries. Think of browse mode as a special case of row buffering and bear in mind that it's not standard SQL and there's no ODBC equivalent.

> In order to implement SQL Server's browse mode—a SELECT statement ending with FOR BROWSE—the target table needs to have a TIMESTAMP column. The column's name and data type should both be "timestamp".

There are several prerequisites to using browse mode. Most crucial is that you can only use it with tables that have a TIMESTAMP column and a unique index. But you also need to remember to set up two SQL Server connections—one for selecting the data and another for performing updates. The final point to remember about browse mode is that you have to transfer each row of data into program variables as it is being browsed if you want your user to be able to update the rows. You'll probably want to use an array for this. For all intents and purposes, browse mode means you're dealing with copies of data, not the original table data. Browsing routines basically consist of these steps:

1. Set up connections

2. Check for timestamp column

3. Set up array or other variables

4. Build and execute a SELECT statement with the FOR BROWSE option

5. Copy values from result column(s) into program variables

6. Display the results

7. If desired, let the user make changes and post the updates

The VBPTK comes with a good BROWSE sample program that accesses data from the Authors table in the classic SQL Server's pubs database (see Figure 10-3). The Authors table has the columns

Column name	Data type
au_id	id
au_lname	varchar(40)
au_fname	varchar(20)
phone	char(12)
address	varchar(40)
city	varchar(20)
state	char(2)
zip	char(5)
contract	bit
timestamp	timestamp

where au_id is used for a unique, clustered index. The timestamp column, by the way, should simply be called timestamp. You can change the capitalization, but be careful, since SQL Server is usually installed in its default mode, which is case-sensitive.

Cursors

Cursors are a construct used by set-oriented relational DBMSs to mimic record-based DBMSs, which allow useful actions like "next row" and "previous row." Cursors permit scrolling—usually forward and backward—and positioned updates. To be effective, they typically can be "tuned" with settable locking options.

Figure 10-3: *Study Microsoft's BROWSE sample to see how to work with browse mode.*

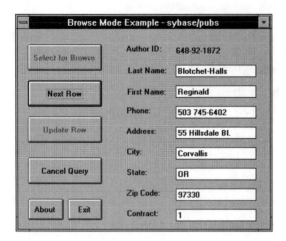

Microsoft SQL Server 4.2 and above include support for cursors, but earlier versions of Microsoft SQL Server as well as Sybase SQL Server 4.2 and earlier don't offer intrinsic support for cursors. To use cursors, you have to run the widely available INSTCAT.SQL script, which creates some special stored procedures developed by Microsoft that provide cursor support. This implementation of cursors is not engine-based, though, and is sometimes criticized for being slow.

If you want to use cursors, the target SQL Server tables need to have a unique index, just as it does when you use browse mode. Unlike browse mode, however, cursors don't require either a timestamp column or multiple open connections.

The Microsoft cursor API defines three kinds of cursors: static, keyset, and dynamic. *Static* cursors are like read-only snapshots and can't be updated. The advantage to static cursors is that they're fast. In *keyset* cursors, row values can be changed, but not the order or membership of the result set. (The term *keyset* refers to the fact that all keys for the resulting set are kept locally.) When you use a *dynamic* cursor, values, order, and membership can all be changed dynamically.

To open a cursor, specifying the scroll option, concurrency option, and size of the fetch buffer—that is, the number of rows retrieved with a single fetch—you use `SqlCursorOpen%`

```
SqlCursorOpen%(sqlconn%, statement$, scrollopt%,
...concuropt%, numrows%, pstatus&( ))
```

where `statement$` is the `SELECT` statement that defines the cursor. `Scrollopt%` specifies the desired scrolling technique:

CURFORWARD   Forward scrolling only
CURKEYSET   Keyset driven
CURDYNAMIC   Fully dynamic
intn   Keyset-driven cursor within (n*`numrows%`) blocks,
                  but fully dynamic outside the keyset

Concurrency control is set with `concuropt%`

CURREADONLY   Read-only cursor
CURLOCKCC   Intent to update locking
CUROPTCC   Optimistic concurrency control
CUROPTCCVAL   Optimistic concurrency based on values

and the number of rows in the fetch buffer is controlled by the all-important `numrows%`. The final parameter, `pstatus&()`, identifies an array of row status indicators. The array must be large enough to hold one long integer for every row in the buffer to be fetched.

Both DBLIB and ODBC support Microsoft cursors, but there are some important differences in the functionality of the cursor APIs between ODBC and DBLIB. DBLIB requires that a cursor be explicitly declared and given a name. In ODBC, though, every `SELECT` statement is automatically associated with a cursor. The reason

why the APIs for handling cursors are different in ODBC and
DBLIB is the fact that all cursor operations in DBLIB use a special
cursor handle, while ODBC uses the same statement handle for
cursor and non-cursor operations alike. Another difference is how
ODBC and DBLIB handle positioned updates and inserts. DBLIB
gives you a single function that lets you specify a row in the fetch
buffer for insertion, deletion, updating, refreshing, or locking.
ODBC is slightly different. First that application tags a row as the
current row. To do positioned updates, inserts and deletes, ODBC
relies on the special positional insert, delete, and update statements provided in the ANSI SQL standard, that is WHERE CUR-
RENT OF cursor-name.

If you're thinking about using cursors, take a look at the sample
CURSORS application included with VBPTK (see Figure 10-4).
Creating applications that scroll cursors in VB is done with a
vertical scroll bar control where you synchronize mouse clicks on
the scroll bar with cursor fetches. Here's the subroutine for scrolling
from the CURSORS example:

```
Sub VScroll1_Change ()
If VScroll1.Value = 0 And CursorSliderValue% = 0 Then
...Exit Sub

    '
Define <Page Up> and <Page Down> values
    '
Get the current scroll value

PAGEUP = CursorSliderValue% - VScroll1.SmallChange
PAGEDOWN = CursorSliderValue% + VScroll1.SmallChange

x = VScroll1.Value
```

```
'Based on the scroll value, call the appropriate routine
'If "Mixed" scroll and scrolling within the keyset, then
just do a random

If x > CursorSliderValue% And x < PAGEDOWN Then
    If x > VScroll1.SmallChange Then
        Fetch_Random (x)
    Else
        Fetch_Relative (x)
    End If
Else
    If x < CursorSliderValue% And x > PAGEUP Then
        If x > VScroll1.SmallChange Then
            Fetch_Random (x)
        Else
            Fetch_Relative (x)
        End If
    Else

'User is either doing a <Page Down>, <Page Up>, or Dynamic
scrolling
        Select Case x
            Case Is = PAGEDOWN
                Fetch_Next
            Case Is = PAGEUP
                Fetch_Previous
            Case Is > PAGEDOWN
                If ScrollOpt% = CURKEYSET% Then
                    Fetch_Random Int(x)
                Else
                    Fetch_Relative Int(x)
                End If
            Case Is < PAGEUP
                If ScrollOpt% = CURKEYSET% Then
```

```
                        Fetch_Random Int(x)
                Else
                        Fetch_Relative Int(x)
                End If
        End Select
    End If
End If


'Save the current scroll value for next time
CursorSliderValue = x
End Sub
```

Figure 10-4: *Microsoft's CURSORS project lets you experiment with different combinations and permutations of kinds of cursors and locking.*

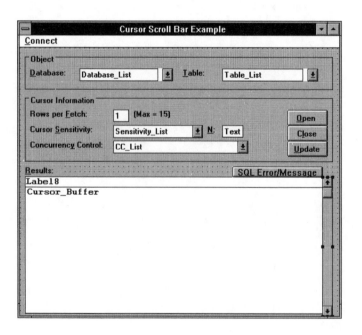

Summary

You don't have to use the Microsoft Programmer's Toolkit for SQL Server to write VB applications that access SQL Server. However, for optimal control and performance, you'll want to. Fortunately, Microsoft has given us a special VB version of the SQL Server DBLIB API.

References

A Hitchhiker's Guide to VBSQL by William R. Vaughn. Subtitled "The Developer's Roadmap to the Visual Basic Library for SQL Server," this 200+-page book is available directly from the author for $45 and contains invaluable hints and tips. Highly recommended. Beta V Systems Software, 2109 Sahalee Drive West, Redmond, WA 98053-6313.

11

Wrapping Your Application

You probably write VB applications for a purpose, not just for your own edification, and that means eventually installing then on alien machines. This chapter deals with distribution issues, creating your own custom help, and using both VB's SetupWizard and SETUP1 programs effectively. Of course, you don't need reminding, but it's easy to slide over the testing phase in your eagerness to deliver your application. Don't neglect testing, and test your program on as many different system configurations as possible. It's often some weird combination of hardware and software that comes back to bite you.

Test rigorously before you even *think* about setting up the distribution disks.

Planning for Distribution

VB developers face several potential problem areas. One is the problem of graphics resolutions ranging from EGA to Super VGA and beyond. The challenge of writing device-independent applications is one all Windows developers face. Another problem is the familiar one of file locations. You don't want to hard-code your program for a specific PATH that will be unacceptable for your end user's environment.

Finally, it pays to plan for program updates and changes. In other words, you'll probably want to declare certain variables as global because they're likely to be changed in subsequent versions or program updates.

Developing a Device-Independent Application

VB does a good job of displaying most controls, irrespective of screen resolution, but there are two types of controls you need to think about: controls that display bitmaps or support the Autosize property—picture box, image, and label controls—and combo boxes. Windows doesn't automatically display images consistently for different resolutions. For example, a bitmap (.BMP) on a Super VGA monitor looks smaller that the same bitmap on a VGA monitor. The same applies to the other graphics file formats supported by VB: .ICO, .RLE, and .WMF.

The easiest solution is to use an Image control and set the `Stretch` property to true. This results in some distortion on monitors of different resolutions. A circle bitmap created in VGA will look oval on an EGA display. Nevertheless, if that's acceptable for your application, `Stretch` is the easiest solution to implement. The other solution is to use the Picture Box control's `Autosize` property. The problem with this approach is that the image will occupy different amounts of screen real estate. Your image will display properly, but it may overlap other controls in the lower resolutions. Remember that with `Autosize` set to true, the top and left coordinates stay the same.

Varying screen resolutions can play havoc with your application. Plan for device independence by using either `Autosize` or `Stretch` properties for your graphics files.

Metafiles might seem like the perfect solution, since they automatically redraw themselves based on the size of the container and the screen resolution. However, as you know, .WMF aren't nearly as popular as .BMP files. There simply aren't as many tools for creating and editing metafiles.

Toolbars   Toolbars represent another common problem you need to anticipate, since toolbar bitmaps need to be aligned for every resolution. The best general strategy is probably to position each toolbar button in the Form_Load event. However, you may prefer to use multiple graphics files—one for each resolution as illustrated in the following code fragment:

```
Form_Load()
    'SCR_RES is global variable
    Dim YPix
    YPix = Screen.Height/'Screen.TwipsPerPixelY
    Select Case YPix
        Case 350    ' EGA
            SCR_RES = 0
        Case 480    'VGA
            SCR_RES = 1
        Case 600    'SVGA
            SCR_RES = 2
```

```
    Case 768    '8514
        SCR_RES = 3
    End Select


'Load appropriate graphic file
    LoadBitmap (SCR_RES)
'

End Sub
```

Combo Boxes   Simple combo boxes (style = 0) or drop-down combo boxes (style = 2) display a list box that grows to display all the items in a list, up to a certain point. When the maximum length—or height, if you prefer— is reached, a vertical scrollbar is automatically added.

The problem is that under differing resolutions, the maximum length of the list box varies. This will pose the biggest problem with EGA displays, since, again, the list box may overlap other controls if you aren't careful.

Data File Location

Unfortunately, there's no easy solution to the data file location problem. Your best bet is usually to set the data file location at runtime. Remember that for Access and Btrieve databases, the `DatabaseName` setting is simply the path and name of the database file (.MDB or .DBF). For dBASE III, dBASE IV, Paradox, and FoxPro databases, however, the DatabaseName property setting has to be the path to the *subdirectory* of the database file (.DBF, .DB). You may be able to use fully qualified network path names like \\MYSERVER\APPS\DATABASE.MDB or SYS:SYSTEM\APPS\DBAPPS\DATABASE.MDB.

Also remember that Access uses the SYSTEM.MDB database to store information about a system's Access databases and that it maintains information about index files for attached XBase databases, as for example, in an .INF file. Your application may need to be able to locate these files.

For ODBC database access, this property can be left blank if the control's `Connect` property identifies a data source name (DSN) registered in the ODBC.INI file. Controlling the end user's ODBC files—both location and contents—may be problematic. Remember from Chapter 5 that your application can either display the ODBC login box or not.

VB provides a `SetDataAccessOption` statement that you may have to use. `SetDataAccessOption` takes two parameters: a *numeric option* and a *variant value*. When *option* is set to 1, you provide the name and path of your application's initialization file (.INI) as the *value*. You *must* use this if your application's .INI file either isn't in the Windows subdirectory or isn't the same name as your application's .EXE. Note that this statement only takes effect when `SetDataAccessOption` is used before the data access functionality is loaded and initialized. Once data access has been initialized, you can't change this setting without first exiting the application.

Custom Help

End users are beginning to expect context-sensitive custom help, and professional-looking help at that. What's a person to do? If you have studiously avoided the `HelpContextID` property, it's time to take a quick lesson in creating help files.

VB 3.0 Professional comes with the Windows 3.1 Help Compiler, HC31.EXE. If you chose to install it, it should be in the \VB\HC subdirectory. To create your own context-sensitive help, you need an .RTF (Rich Text Format) editor like Word for Windows. In fact, using the Help Compiler is just the final step in creating a help file. The bulk of work consists of creating and coding RTF (rich text format) files. If you're familiar with applying tags and inserting formatting codes into desktop publishing documents, you know how painstaking that can be. Preparing a Windows Help file is a much worse. You spend a lot of time annotating Word for Windows documents to produce output like that shown in Figure 11-1. The ICONWRKS.RTF file illustrated in Figure 11-1, by the way, is provided as a sample in your HC subdirectory.

Figure 11-1: *Without third-party help file programs, creating help files means you have to prepare documents like this manually, adding codes and footnotes to identify hypertext jumps, popup definitions, browse sequences, and lots more.*

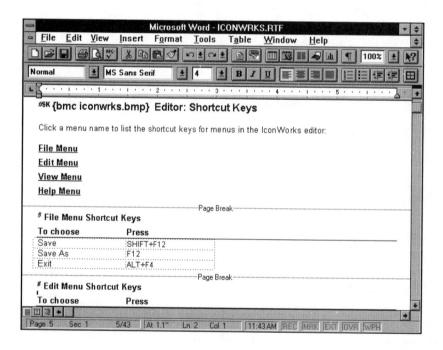

Third-Party Help Tools

Because of the tedious nature of hand-coding all the tags and formatting codes, third-party tools like RoboHelp 2.0 ($495, Blue Sky Software, 800-677-4946 or 619-459-6365; fax 619-459-6366) and Doc-to-Help 1.5 ($295, WexTech, 212-949-9595; fax 212-949-4007) have emerged as general-purpose Help tools. VB-specific help utilities are also becoming available. You'll find a shareware version of Visual Help 2.0e from WinWare on your disk. You can use it to create three help topics, but will have to register ($49) to get the "full blown" version.

RoboHelp 2.0 (see Figure 11-2) creates a visual authoring environment with point-and-click access to all Windows Help features and excellent debugging support, including an Error Wizard and link logic tester. While RoboHelp is generally considered best for creating new help files, Doc-to-Help seems to be best for converting existing documentation into on-line help. Third-party tools don't preclude your using the help compiler. They just help create the .RTF and .HPJ source files.

Figure 11-2: *RoboHelp is a popular third-party help utility.*

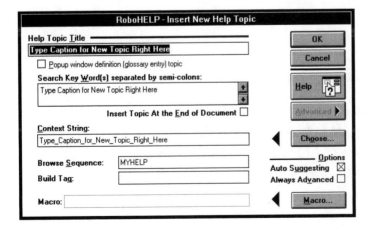

Third-party help tools will save you time by relegating most tagging to menu picks. The good ones also make debugging and testing easier.

Adding Help to your VB Application

When you assign a `HelpContextID` to VB controls in your application, VB automatically invokes WINHELP.EXE, the Windows Help engine, when users press F1. WINHELP requests the topic specified by the context number from your help file. One crucial step in creating your help file is mapping context IDs to context strings that identify help topics in your Help source file.

You assign these values to string in the [MAP] section of the help project file. The .HPJ file is an ASCII file that's used when you compile your Help file. It includes up to nine sections like [MAP] and [FILES]. Here's a fragment of code from the ICONWRKS.HPJ file:

```
[MAP]
CONTENTS 1
EDITOR_KEYBOARD 2
EDITOR_COMMANDS 3
VIEWER_KEYBOARD 5
VIEWER_COMMANDS 6
DEFINING_COLORS 1000
EDITOR_FILE_MENU 1100
```

Topics must be separated from the context IDs with spaces or tabs. Another way of coding the [MAP] section is to use the #include directive pointing to a header (.h) file. For example, you could create a MYHELP.H file with entries like

```
#define    contents        1
#define    Editor_Keyboard 2
#define    Editor_Commands 3
...
```

and use this entry in your MYHELP.HPJ file:

```
[MAP]
#include   myhelp.h
```

Help source files usually have lots of help topics, separated by hard carriage returns. Features are added to help topics in the footnote section of the help file. Footnote codes include # (the mandatory context string which must be unique), $ (an optional help topic title), K (an optional keyword that acts like a table of contents), + (an optional code which defines the browse order), and * (an optional build tag).

You can also create jumps and popups, by coding them as double-underlined / strike-through or single-underlined text respectively, in your source help file. You enter the context string of the destination topic, formatted as hidden text, immediately following—no spaces— the jump text. When editing the source file, be sure to set your word processor's Display Hidden Text option on. When you do, you'll see the underlined string "Defining_Colors" after the double-underlined jump topic in the following ICONWRKS.RTF file:

$ K + {bmc iconwrks.bmp} Editor: Color Menu

EDITOR_COLOR_MENU

$ Editor: Color Menu

K Color Menu; Save Colors; INI; ICONWRKS.INI; Mouse Colors; Left Button; Right Button; Default Colors; Solid Colors; Palette; Menu

+ Editor_Commands:035

Colors   This command opens the Custom Color Palette Window, DEFINING_COLORS, where you can define custom colors and assign them to the current color palette. You can use the Custom Color Palette window to select colors in the same way you select colors with the Color Palette displayed in the Editor. You can display your Custom Color Palette as a floating palette instead of the Color Palette in the Editor.

Adding Graphics   You can also include four kinds of graphics files in your context-sensitive help: bitmaps (.BMP), metafiles (.WMF), hypergraphics (.SHG), and multiple resolution bitmaps (.MRB). You create hypergraphics files with the hotspot editor, SHED.EXE (see Figure 11-3), and use MRBC.EXE to create multiple resolution bitmaps. When you use graphics files, you have to list them in the [FILES] section of the .HPJ file.

Figure 11-3: *Use the Hotspot Editor, SHED.EXE, to create hypergraphics files.*

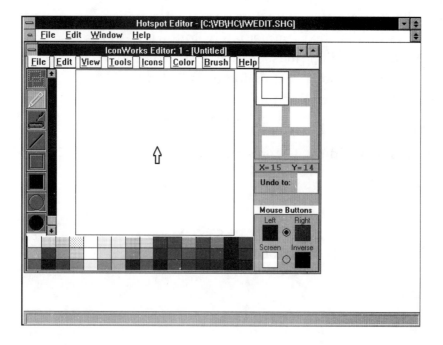

Compiling Your Help File   Once you've created the .RTF and .HPJ files, it's easy enough to compile them by typing `HC31 projectfile`. You can use the [OPTIONS] section of your .HPJ file to specify a compiler errorlog. Whether or not you generate errors, though, you need to test your topics, jumps, and popups. It's in the testing and debugging area where the third-party tools make life much easier. No one likes jumping between editing and compiling.

It's as easy to sound preachy about help files as it is about program documentation. We all know the benefit of each. Enough said. Let's move on to that final step—creating the distribution disks.

Creating Distribution Disks

Although there were some annoying bugs in the Visual Basic SetupWizard originally distributed with VB 3.0, (like giving you an error message about OLE2UI.DLL not found), we definitely recommend the SetupWizard for creating distribution disks for many VB applications. (By the way, your disk has both an updated version of SETUPWIZ.EXE 1.00.547 from Microsoft and an alternate freeware Setup program written by Mike Chapman.)

SetupWizard can save you time and package your product with Microsoft's "standard" installation routine. If you want to use a different compression utility, let the user have control over destination file location, or have better control over file versions, however, you'll have to write your own setup routine. You'll probably want to use Microsoft's Setup Toolkit and customize the VB sample SETUP1 program files. But before you do that, consider what SetupWizard has to offer.

SetupWizard

SetupWizard walks you through a six-step process:

1. Supply initial information, such as the location of your
    .MAK file. Based on the contents of your .MAK file, the
    SetupWizard tries to determine all files needed for distribu-
    tion. Saving all your .FRM and .BAS files as ASCII makes
    this easier for SetupWizard.

2. Check the check boxes corresponding to additional files
    used by your application, such as data access, OLE, DDE,
    Crystal Reports, and/or financial functions (see Figure 11-4).

Figure 11-4: *SetupWizard lets you select groups of files as menu picks.*

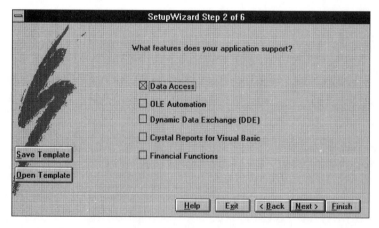

3. Supply data access information, if you indicated it was
    needed in Step 2.

4. Provide the SetupWizard with floppy disk information
    about the disk drive and disk type you want to use.

5. Add and remove files before building disks. Click on Setup-
    Wizard's "File Details" button to view information about
    versions (see Figure 11-5).

Figure 11-5: *SetupWizard provides an easy way to track file versions.*

6. Let the SetupWizard compress the files and create disk layouts. This can take some time. SetupWizard will also create the special SETUP.LST and SETUP1.EXE files and notify you of the number of *blank formatted* disks needed.

SetupWizard works fine for small applications.

A Few Caveats

If you use SetupWizard, make sure any required DLLs are all in the \WINDOWS\SYSTEM subdirectory or the Setup Wizard won't find them.

It's not uncommon to get a puzzling "Sharing Violation on CMDIALOG.VBX" error message, either. The trick is to have two copies of CMDIALOG.VBX—one in \WINDOWS\SYSTEM and one in \VB\SETUPKIT\KITFILES. There reason you need this is there's a problem with SetupWizard using the CMDIALOG.VBX and trying to compress it at the same time. If there are two copies, it will use one copy while compressing the other.

Determining the Files You Need to Distribute

Before running either the SetupWizard or SETUP1, it's a good idea to list all the files that will be included on the distribution disks. In addition to your application's .EXE, it may also require data files, custom controls (.VBX), or other files such as DLLs. The application-related files can generally be categorized as follows:

- YOURAPP.EXE

- YOURAPP.DAT (optional)

- YOURAPP.TXT (optional)

- YOURAPP.INI (optional)

- OTHER.DAT (optional data file)

- OTHER.MDB. OTHER.DBF, OTHER.DB (optional database files)

- OTHER.TXT (optional)

- OTHER.INI (optional)

- YOURCC.VBX (optional custom control)

- OTHERCC.VBX (option commercial VBX)

- YOURDLL.DLL (optional)

- OTHERDLL.DLL (optional)

Remember that VB doesn't compile custom controls or DLLs as part of your application's .EXE file. If your application uses any custom controls or DLLs, you have to include the appropriate .VBX and .DLL files on the distribution disks.

If your application uses OLE, you will probably need all these files:

- COMPOBJ.DLL

- MSOLE2.VBX

- MSOLEVBX.DLL

- OLE2.DLL

- OLE2.REG

- OLE2CONV.DLL

- OLE2DISP.DLL

- OLE2NLS.DLL

- OLE2PROX.DLL

- STORAGE.DLL

- VBOA300.DLL

Most applications will need some of the following custom controls and DLL files:

- GRID.VBX (Grid custom control)

- DDEML.DLL (Required for DDE)

- CMDIALOG.VBX (Common dialog custom control)

- COMMDLG.DLL (Required by the common dialog custom control)

- MSAFINX.DLL (Required if your app calls any of the VBasic financial functions)

- VBDB300.DLL (Required for data access)

- MSAES110.DLL (Required for data access)

- MSAJT110.DLL (Required for data access)

- BTRV110.DLL (Required for ODBC data access with Btrieve)

- PDX110.DLL (Required for ODBC data access with Paradox 3.5)

- XBS110.DLL (Required for ODBC data access to any XBase files)

The following are general ODBC files:

- COMMDLG.DLL

- CTL3D.DLL

- DBNMP3.DLL (if your network uses named pipes)

- ODBC.DLL

- ODBCADM.EXE

- ODBCINST.DLL

- ODBCINST.HLP

These ODBC files are associated with VB's Microsoft SQL Server support:

- SQLSRVR.DLL

- DBNMP3.DLL (if your network uses named pipes)

- INSTCAT.SQL

- INSTCAT.48

- DRVSSRVR.HLP

Files similar to these will represent Oracle ODBC support:

- SQORA.DLL

- ORASETUP.DLL

- ORA6WIN.DLL or ORA7WIN.DLL

- DRVORACL.HLP

- ORACLE.TXT

Crystal Reports Release 2.0 needs these files:

- CRYSTAL.VBX

- CRPE.DLL

- CRXLATE.DLL

- COMMDLG.DLL

Using the Setup Kit

If SetupWizard doesn't provide the flexibility you need, you'll have to create your own setup program. Fortunately, that isn't as bad as it used to be, thanks to the Setup Toolkit files, generally located in the \VB\SETUPKIT subdirectory. The Setup Toolkit consists of utilities, DLL, and a sample setup program written in VB.

With the Setup Toolkit, you can pre-install files required by your setup program on the end user's system, install files into the correct subdirectories, even if they don't have standard, such as \WINDOWS\SYSTEM names, use the version-stamping utility to prevent overwriting of more recent files, and create Windows groups and icons for your application. The setup program will need the following files: SETUP.EXE, SETUP1.EXE (or whatever you've named your setup program), SETUP.LST, SETUPKIT.DLL, VER.DLL, and VBRUN300.DLL. These files, along with any other files in SETUP.LST that need to be pre-installed will have to be on the first distribution disk. The Setup program doesn't allow you to split a file between disks.

Determining Where to Install Files on the User's Machine

Every VB application requires at least two files—your application's .EXE file and the VBRUN300.DLL runtime file. Before writing your setup program, you should decide where to install each of these files on the user's disk. The files required by your application can be divided into four classes:

- Program files

- Initialization files

- Operating system components

- Shared application resources

Typically, you'll want the program files to be installed together in the application directory, the directory specified by the user during setup. The sample code in SETUP1.BAS shows how to implement the interactive routine.

Additionally, your application's .INI file should be in the main Microsoft Windows directory on the user's disk. This is the directory in which the WIN.INI file is located (usually in the \WINDOWS subdirectory). You determine the name of this directory on the user's disk by calling the GetWindowsDirectory() Windows API function. The sample code in SETUP1.BAS shows how to call this function:

```
'----------------------------------------------------
' Calls the windows API to get the windows directory
'----------------------------------------------------
Function GetWindowsDir () As String
    temp$ = String$(145, 0)                 ' Size Buffer
    x = GetWindowsDirectory(temp$, 145)     ' Make API Call
    temp$ = Left$(temp$, x)                 ' Trim Buffer

    If Right$(temp$, 1) <> "\" Then         ' Add \ if
    ...necessary
      GetWindowsDir$ = temp$ + "\"
    Else
      GetWindowsDir$ = temp$
    End If
End Function
```

If you choose to distribute operating system files, files that are normally included with Microsoft Windows, be sure to install them in the correct directory. Call the GetSystemDirectory() Windows API function as illustrated in SETUP1.BAS:

```
'------------------------------------------------------------
' Calls the windows API to get the windows\SYSTEM directory
'------------------------------------------------------------
Function GetWindowsSysDir () As String
    temp$ = String$(145, 0)                      ' Size Buffer
    x = GetSystemDirectory(temp$, 145)           ' Make API Call
    temp$ = Left$(temp$, x)                       ' Trim Buffer

    If Right$(temp$, 1) <> "\" Then              ' Add \ if
    ...necessary
      GetWindowsSysDir$ = temp$ + "\"
    Else
      GetWindowsSysDir$ = temp$
    End If
End Function
```

Finally, a very important caveat—don't overwrite newer files with older versions. The CopyFile function in SETUP1.BAS uses the VerInstall API to copy files to the user's machine. If a file already exists on the user's machine, the CopyFile function displays a dialog that prompts the user to rename the older file.

Writing A Setup Program

The quickest way to write a setup program is to modify the source code of the sample included with the Setup Toolkit, SETUP1.MAK. This sample setup program is located in the \SETUPKIT\SETUP1 subdirectory of the main Visual Basic directory. SETUP1.MAK installs the sample application LOAN.EXE, which should be located in the \SAMPLES\GRID subdirectory of the main Visual Basic directory. LOAN.EXE is a small sample application that uses the grid custom control. In order to run correctly, LOAN.EXE requires that GRID.VBX be properly installed on the user's system. This is a good model to use, since almost all applications use special VBXes.

To customize the source code of SETUP1.MAK so that it installs your application instead of LOAN.EXE, you need to make a few changes. First, modify the appropriate constants in the declarations section of SETUP1.FRM. These include APPNAME, APPDIR, WINSYSNEEDED, and OTHERNEEDED. Then, in the Form_Load procedure of SETUP1.FRM, modify the arguments to the PromptForNextDisk function call. When the user enters the correct disk, the function returns True. Call the CopyFile function for each file on the current distribution disk. You must call CopyFile once for each file on the disk. After copying all the files on a disk, you call PromptForNextDisk again, to prompt the user to insert the next disk.

Repeat these steps for each of the distribution disks, creating a new block of PromptForNextDisk and CopyFile calls for each disk. Finally, modify the arguments to the CreateProgManGroup and CreateProgManItem procedure calls if you want to create your own group or icon.

To physically create your own distribution disks, follow these four steps:

1. Rename VER.DLL to VER.DL_ by typing

    ```
    rename a:ver.dll a:ver.dl_
    ```

2. Copy these files onto the first disk:

    - SETUP.EXE

    - SETUP.LST

- SETUP1.EXE (or whatever you have named your setup program)

- SETUPKIT.DLL

- VBRUN300.DLL

- VER.DL_

If you have compressed any of these files with Microsoft's MS-DOS COMPRESS.EXE program, the last character will be an underscore character. If you use another compression program, remember to include it in your distribution disks, along with any needed licensing information.

3. Copy the remaining files as specified by your disk layout.

4. Test your setup routine.

Summary

In this chapter, you've seen how to "wrap your app" by creating custom help files and distribution disks. Consider yourself a graduate of VB Database Programming!

Disk Files

The following files are in the \SETUPWIZ subdirectory:

SETUPW.EXE	Microsoft's SetupWizard 1.00.547
SETUP1.EXE	Microsft's updated SETUP files
SETUP.EXE	Microsoft's updated SETUP files
SETUP3.ZIP	Freeware alternative to SetupWizard provided by Mike Chapman
VH.ZIP	Shareware Visual Help 2.0e utility by Firas Bushnaq

Glossary

ACID (Atomic/Consistent/Isolated/Durable). An acronym referring to the notion that transactions need to be atomic, consistent, isolated, and durable.

Aggregate functions. Refers to SQL functions like SUM, AVG, MIX, MAX.

ANSI (American National Standards Institute). One of several standards-setting bodies. ANSI-SQL is its most important database-related standard.

API (Application Programming Interface). Specification or actual function library, typically in C, that programmers "write to." There are lots of APIs, but only some are made public and become industry standards.

APPC (Advanced Program to Program Communications). IBM's half-duplex, conversation-type method for interprocess communication specified in SNA. The APPC API is an interprogram protocol boundary between a TP (transaction program) and the Presentation Services (Layer 6) of SNA's architecture.

Asymmetrical multiprocessing.   The easiest kind of multiprocessor support that's essentially a master/slave setup. Typically, the OS runs on one processor and applications run on others. NetWare 3.x and 4.0 support asymmetrical multiprocessing, but not symmetrical multiprocessing.

Attribute.   Basically the same as field or column.

Back-end.   In client/server systems, same as server, host, database engine.

BCNF (Boyce-Codd Normal Form).   A subtle variation of third normal form (3NF) level of normalization.

Benchmarks.   Any of a variety of widely accepted standard tests you can run to try to compare the performance of hardware or software transaction performance. In the database world, the most common benchmarks are the Transaction Processing Council TPC-A, TPC-B, and TPC-C benchmarks. The TPC-A and TCP-B benchmarks model insert-intensive debit-credit transactions for a banking environment. TPC-C is a basket of transactions that models a mixed transaction and decision support environment. TPC-D is designed to measure the performance of decision support systems, and a new TPC-E benchmark is being created for enterprise computing. Most experts agree that the only way to predict performance is to create your own application- and environment-specific benchmark.

BIBLIO.   The widely-referenced sample database BIBLIO.MDB that ships with VB3.

BLOB (Binary Large Object).   Sometimes used to describe multimedia files, but can also refer to program or any other binary file. Often stored in long binary fields in databases.

Bound control.   Control that is "bound" to the data. Same as data-aware. In VB3, text boxes, images, picture boxes, labels, check boxes, the masked edit control, and the 3-D panel and 3-D checkbox can be bound controls.

Bridge.   Internetworking device related to routers gateways that works at the Media Access Control (MAC) sublayer of the Data Link Layer. Its purpose is to connect similar network segments into a single logical network so that either segment can forward network traffic to the segment on the other side of the bridge.

CASE (Computer-Aided Software Engineering). Wide range of tools that may help you design a database, reengineer an existing one, or even generate application source code. May refer to popular diagramming tools that can document graphical table relationships, e.g., print ER (entity-relationship) diagrams.

Catalog. Usually, same as database schema. Contains a description of the database tables, fields, and so on.

CICS (Customer Information Control System). Pronounced "kicks." One of IBM mainframes' four transaction teleprocessing environments (TSO, CICS/VS, Call Attach Facility/CAF, and IMS/DC). Widely used to write applications that control remote terminals.

Client. In client/server systems, same as front end. Typically the PC or workstation where applications are run and where all GUI processing is done.

Client/server. An architecture based on splitting processing between the host/server and client/PC. Usually refers to database client/server systems, but many systems are actually architected as client/server. The client PC requests services from the server, which provides them.

Clustered index. A kind of index, used by SQL Server and other back ends, where the logical order of the key values is the same as the physical order of the records. Clustered indexes have high overhead associated with inserts, but result in fast retrieval. Excellent for stable data.

Codd, E. F. A mathematician known as the "father" of relational databases. Codd formed a San Jose-based consultancy called Codd & Date with Chris Date, another relational database guru.

Column. Same as field. Columns have names, data types, and should represent the smallest meaningful unit of information in a database system.

COMMIT. Write the records to storage. COMMITs can happen both under programmer control through transaction processing commands or at the behest of the operating system, e.g., when the buffer is flushed to disk.

Concurrency.   A measure of the number of users with concurrent access to a database. Concurrency and locking to ensure consistency are usually inversely related.

Correlated subquery.   A special kind of SQL subquery with an EXISTS or NOT EXISTS. A subquery is a SQL SELECT within another SELECT.

Crystal.   Refers to the Crystal Services report writer and print engine program. VB3 includes a Crystal VBX.

Cursor.   Pointer to a record in a SQL result set. Concept invented to make SQL work more like record-oriented access methods.

Cursor stability.   An intermediate isolation level where only the current row pointed at by the cursor is locked. The lock is released on non-updated rows as the cursor scrolls forward or backward.

Data-aware controls.   Same as bound controls (i.e., text boxes, and list boxes). VB's grid is not data-aware; hence the burgeoning market of third-party data-aware grid controls.

Data dictionary.   Location of metadata which is data about the data. May be maintained on a database-by-database level, at the server level, or on an organization-wide level. Related to catalog, schema, and repository.

Database.   An organized collection of data.

Database server.   Same as DBMS, back end, or database engine. The software that handles storage, access, and security issues.

DB.   Filename extension for Borland's Paradox data files.

DBA (DataBase Administrator).   Usually the individual responsible for installing the DBMS, setting up database access and security, and monitoring database performance.

DBF.   Filename extension associated with popular file format used by dBASE DBMSs. Includes a header with field information.

DBLIB.   SQL Server's client API.

DBMS (Database Management System).   Database software packages ranging from Paradox and Access to Oracle and DB2. All let you create and maintain databases and manipulate the data stored in them.

DDL (Database Definition Language).   The subset of SQL statements used to define databases, e.g., CREATE TABLE, CREATE VIEW.

Deadlock.   A situation that sometimes occurs when two users want to read the records "locked" by the other. Sometimes referred to as a deadly embrace. Ultimately, the DBMS or operating system has to break the deadlock by picking a winner and a loser.

Decision support.   *See* DSS. A mode of using data that typically doesn't require on-line access to data.

Delta.   Microsoft's version control program.

Denormalization.   The process of combining small tables into larger ones for the sake of performance. Can lead to any of the problems associated with "bad" database design, e.g., inconsistent data.

Directory Services.   A "white pages" for WANs. X.500 is the OSI standard for directory services.

Distributed database.   A database that is spread out over more that one back end.

Distributed JOINs.   A JOIN across more than one server. May be heterogeneous or homogeneous.

Dirty read.   Allows other transactions to read changes to the database as they're made, i.e., even before they're committed or rolled back.

DML (Database Manipulation Language).   The subset of the SQL statements used to retrieve and manipulate data. The major DML statement is SELECT.

DROP.   A SQL statement that is used to drop entities like tables, columns, views, and indexes.

DSS.   Decision Support System. Used to describe systems where end users manipulate a subset of data off-line. Often used in contrast to OLTP to describe data that does not need to be absolutely up-to-date. Sometimes referred to as EIS, Executive Information Systems.

Downsizing.   Moving database applications off mainframe or minicomputers onto smaller, less expensive platforms.

Dynaset.   The Microsoft Access term for a kind of recordset that is similar to a SQL VIEW. Dynasets do not represent a live link to actual table data, but changes made to dynasets are written back to the original database, typically as the user moves from record to record.

Dynamic SQL.   A special form of SQL that uses either host language data structures or a DBMS-maintained SQL descriptor area to accommodate data whose values are not known at compile time.

EDA/SQL.   An ODBC-compliant middleware product sold by Information Builders Inc. (IBI). Requires a mainframe.

Edit mask.   A series of codes that represent allowable entries or display formats. For example ###-##-#### could be an edit mask for social security numbers.

EHLLAPI.   IBM's enhanced Emulator High Level Language Application Programming Interface (API) is the API PC programs need to write to for SNA-compliant access to mainframe programs. Provides read/write access from within an application to 3270 or 5250 sessions active on the system. This lets programmers retrieve all or portions of the screen either as a flat string or on a field-by-field basis. Actually EHLLAPI is a subset of HLLAPI. A Windows-specific version, WIN-EHLLAPI is becoming popular.

Embedded SQL.   SQL statements that are inside a "normal" high-level procedural language program. Embedded SQL must be preprocessed and mapped to host language statements.

Encapsulate.   Used both to describe one aspect of object-oriented technology and a data communications method for including one protocol "within" another one. For example, AppleTalk protocols can be "wrapped" in TCP/IP packets in a process called tunneling, which is one way to let Mac users access TCP/IP services.

Engine.   Same as server or back end. Same as table.

Entity.   Typically used to mean the same thing as table.

ER (Entity-Relationship).   Refers to the methodology and charting technique for designing and illustrating a relational database's design.

Exclusive lock.   Just like it sounds. Permits exclusive access to data, locking out others.

Executive Information System (EIS).   Similar to DSS, but often a custom, point-and-click application for individual executives.

Field.   Part of a table (or a screen representing a table). Basically the same as column or attribute.

Front end.   Same as a client in client/server parlance. Where the GUI and local data manipulation occurs.

Gateway.   A device, often a dedicated PC, that connects two dissimilar networks or network devices. Gateways may operate at OSI Reference Model layers 4 through 7 depending on the level of incompatibility between the networks. Micro Decisionware's MDI Gateway to DB2 is a popular gateway, as is Sybase's OminServer.

Hierarchical database.   One of the four major models (the others are network, relational, and object). Based on fast, pointer-based access.

HLLAPI.   *See* EHLLAPI. An IBM API, High Level Language API, used in writing applications that access mainframe data.

IDAPI.   Borland's Independent Database API. A multi-platform alternative to ODBC spearheaded by Borland, Novell, Lotus, and WordPerfect.

IDMS.   DBMS based on the CODASYL DBTG model. Originally developed by Cullinet, IDMS has been extended as IDMS/R to include relational properties and is now available from Computer Associates (CA).

IMS (Information Management System).   Transaction processing DBMS developed by IBM. Uses DL/1 as the database access language.

Index.   A file maintained by the DBMS to provide faster access to records than a sequential full-table scan would. Indexes are basically look-up tables with pointers to individual records. Indexes slow things down during data entry and updates, but speed up queries.

INSERT.   The SQL statement for adding data to tables.

IP (Internet Protocol).   Standard internetwork routing protocol in the TCP/IP stack.

IPC (InterProcess Communications).   Methods like Named Pipes, IBM's APPC, Windows' DDE and OLE, remote procedure calls (RPCs), and AT&T's Streams and Sockets are IPCs that support communications between two processes or applications.

IPX (Internet Exchange Protocol).   Novell's packet assembly and routing protocol, corresponding more or less to the data link and network layers of the 7-layer OSI Reference Model. Part of Novell's proprietary IPX/SPX network protocol.

ISAM (Indexed Sequential Access Method).   A popular file format dating from tape storage where records are typically stored in ascending or descending index (or primary key) order. In an ISAM disk file, special index tracks are usually maintained. ODBC drivers for XBase and Paradox data are called ISAM drivers.

Isolation level.   Refers to level of locking. The SQL-92 standard prescribes four levels in order from least locked to most locked: read uncommitted, read committed, repeatable read, and serializable.

Key field.   A field that is either a primary or foreign key field. Primary key fields should contain only unique, non-null data in order to provide unambiguous access to any single record. Primary keys are usually indexed, but don't have to be. Foreign keys are link fields. They are primary keys from one table in a related table.

JAD (Joint Application Development).   Refers to application development where MIS works closely with end users.

Jet.   A Microsoft term for the Access database engine.

JOIN.   Combining data from one or more tables. Varieties include inner joins, outer joins, self-joins, and theta joins.

Journal.   Related to a log file or transaction log file. Used to document transactions so the DBMS can perform ROLLBACKs and RESTOREs if necessary.

LAT (Local Area Transport).   A terminal-to-host protocol developed by DEC in the 80s. Lacks a routing layer but can be bridged. One of its strengths is its ability to multiplex multiple sessions onto a single virtual circuit. Most other protocols require the creation of new virtual circuits for every terminal session.

Legacy data.   Usually refers to non-SQL data on Mainframe systems.

Locking.   In multiuser environments, the technique that denies other users access to files, pages, or individual records while some activity is being performed. Locking and concurrency and mutually exclusive.

Log.   A file, separate from the actual database data file(s) where transactions are temporarily stored until committed.

LU (Logical Unit).   IBM terminology for abstract devices (hardware or software) that provide end users access to network resources and manages transfer of information between two users. LU2 (for the IBM 3270 terminal family) and LU6.2 (for APPC-style communications) are the most common LUs. LU6.2 is sometimes called the "independent" LU since either device can initiate communications.

MAPI.   Microsoft's original Messaging API for Windows. Sometimes referred to as SMAPI, the subset of the "real" MAPI, known as Simple MAPI. The "real" MAPI is now known as EMAPI, for Extended MAPI. Competes with the Lotus and cc:Mail VIM (Vendor Independent Messaging) API, and the compromise CMC.

MDB.   The Microsoft DataBase file format, used by Microsoft Access and its Jet Engine. Unlike XBase or Paradox files, for example, Access MDB files are monolithic, containing data, reports, queries, and macros.

Metadata.   Data about data. Used to describe repositories, data dictionaries, or system catalogs that contain such information.

Middleware.   Any of a variety of API and protocols that work as go-betweens between clients and servers.

Multiprocessor, multiprocessing.   Refers to a computer with more than one CPU and its operations. PC LAN superservers often have dual processors, but high end systems supporting parallel computing can have many. Multiprocessing can be asymmetrical (simple) or symmetrical. The latter supports features like load balancing.

Named Pipes.   One type of interprocess communication (IPC) where a named two-way connection (the "pipe") between a client process and a server process is established. Used in OS/2 and NT LANs, but also available for DOS clients running NetWare via the NetWare Requester for OS/2.

NDIS (Network Driver Interface Specification).   Microsoft's protocol-multiplexing scheme, analogous to Novell's ODI and a Packet Driver Specification (PDS) from the UNIX community. These protocols all define an interface between LAN adapter device drivers and higher-level network software.

Nested query.   A query within a query. Same as nested SELECT, subquery.

NetBIOS (Network Basic Input/Output System).   A session level interface for peer-to-peer communications introduced by IBM in 1984. Implemented as a protocol, NetBIOS Protocol (NBP) has become a *de facto* standard for MS-DOS and OS/2 LANs. NetBIOS provides name, datagram, and session support, along with some additional application services general commands but is itself relatively protocol independent.

NFS (Network File System).   A protocol for sharing files developed by Sun Microsystems in 1984, but licensed by Sun to other vendors for use on over 110 platforms. NFS is popular enough that NFS support is now routinely added to many TCP/IP protocol stacks. Widely associated with the UNIX world, but not limited to it, although its fairly high memory requirements have limited its use in MS-DOS systems. Remote File System (RFS) and Andrew File System are competing filing standards used in the UNIX world. NFS is library of remote procedures that can be implemented as an RPC for operating system independence.

Network database.   One of four major database models (the others are relational, hierarchical, and object). Associated with fast, pointer-based data access.

NLM (NetWare Loadable Module).   An application that runs under NetWare 3.XX or higher. Many database engines are available as NLMs.

Normalization.   Act of converting an arbitrary database design into a "good" one according to precise steps (1NF, 2NF, 3NF, 4NF, 5NF). Third normal form (3NF) is typically considered "good enough."

Notes, Lotus Notes.   A popular groupware product that works like a document-centered database system.

Null.   Missing entry. Null fields are not the same as zero or a space character, and should be avoided in primary key fields.

ODBC.   Open DataBase Connectivity, a popular Windows API based on C-language SQL call-level interface. Many vendors are providing ODBC-compliant front ends and back ends, bringing us closer to "plug 'n play" interoperability.

ODI (Open Datalink Interface).   Novell's protocol multiplexing scheme (see NDIS).

OLE (Object Linking and Embedding).   A technique, introduced by Microsoft in 1989 where graphics and other OLE-compliant objects could be added to a document either by reference (linked) or as part of the document (embedded).

OLE Automation.   The ability to program other applications' objects which have been "exposed" and registered as OLE 2.0 objects.

OLE container.   An OLE "client" that contains OLE objects.

OLE object.   An Excel chart, macro, spreadsheet, or range of cells, for example, or a sound or video clip. A discrete entity that has been "exposed" by the OLE "server" program and registered as an OLE object.

OLTP (On-Line Transaction Processing).   A system where end-users are connected to host data real-time. Contrasted with decision support systems (DSS) where end users access replicas, copies, snapshots, or extracts of the original ("real") data.

Optimizer.   In the database world, usually refers to the portion of a database engine's code that optimizes SQL queries. DBMSs provide varying levels of programmer override.

OSI (Open Systems Interconnection).   Protocols developed by the ISO. Based on the 7-layer Reference Model.

Page lock.   A common locking method that affects all the records in a page of memory.

Pipe (noun or verb).   Using the output from one process as the input for another, or the channel through which the data moves.

Portability.   The desirable feature of code that can be run with little or no change in several operating environments.

Precompiler.   A tool that prepares SQL commands as embedded SQL in a host language.

Primary key.   A field or group of fields chosen to uniquely identify every row in table.

Protocol.   Generic term that is often used as a synonym for "standard." Network protocols are the rules for establishing communications between network devices. Leading network protocols include TCP/IP, DECnet, and IPX/SPX (see chart). We often use the 7-layer ISO/OSI Reference Model as a tool for comparing different protocol suites. Protocol stacks are combinations of protocols and typically reside in RAM. It is increasingly important to have both hardware and network software that support multiple protocol stacks.

PU (Physical Unit).   IBM terminology for a hardware node. Intelligent workstations or minicomputers capable of handling peer-to-peer communications are PU2.1 devices.

PVCS.   Popular version control program sold by Intersolv.

QBE (Query By Example).   An intuitive, visual method for asking questions about information stored in databases. Used in Access and Paradox and many other products.

Query.   Typically an "ad hoc" request for data from a database. Often equated to SQL SELECT statements or referenced in terms of the user interface, as in QBE or QBF (Query By Form).

RAD (Rapid Application Development).   Using object-oriented tools to develop applications quickly.

Referential integrity.   Data that *reference* data in another table must remain consistent. If a master client record is deleted, all records in other tables related to that master record should also be deleted. It is generally accepted that RI should be maintained by the server, not the application.

Repeatable read.   A fairly high level of locking that guarantees that if you're scrolling through records on the screen, you'll see the same data when you "revisit" the records.

Replicate.   Same as copy. Used to provide off-line access to production data.

RISC (Reduced Instruction Set Computing).   Refers to either underlying architecture or actual high performance processors based on RISC technology.

Repeater.   A device that amplifies signal at Physical Layer. Concentrators (Ethernet) and active hubs (ARCNet) are basically repeaters.

ROLLBACK.   A SQL transaction processing command that backs out incomplete transactions.

Router.   A device that routes traffic between similar networks. *See also* Bridge, Gateway.

RPC (Remote Procedure Call).   A mechanism whereby a specific function (a mini program written in a procedural language) is executed on a different computer than the one which is running the calling program. Can be used by VB, for example, to access IBM mainframe files other than DB2, for which many gateways are available.

SAA (Systems Application Architecture).   IBM's proprietary specification for network architecture and protocols. It includes APIs, protocols, and user interface conventions and consists of four elements: the Common Programming Interface (CPI), Common Communications Support (CCS), the Common User Interface (CUA), and Common Applications.

Schema.   "Recipe" for a database. Generally refers to a series of SQL statements including CREATE TABLE, CREATE INDEX, and so on.

SCO (Santa Cruz Operation).   Pronounced "skoh." Refers either to the firm or the UNIX operating systems software it sells.

SELECT.   The main SQL statement for retrieving data. Basic syntax: SELECT * FROM tablename WHERE conditionlist ORDER BY columnname.

Self-join.   A special form of correlated subquery that allows records to be retrieved based on comparisons with other records in the same table.

Serializable.   The strictest isolation level, which gives the illusion that all transactions are executed in a serial fashion. *See also* dirty read, cursor stability.

Set.   Mathematical term referring to the fundamental design of relational databases. Results from queries typically contain more than one record; they are result sets.

SMTP (Simple Mail Transfer Protocol).   A session and application layer protocol in the TCP/IP stack.

SNA (System Network Architecture).   IBM's architecture describing all aspects of distributed enterprise-wide computing and networking, from communication protocols to network management, to software design.

Snapshot.   A read-only recordset that provides good performance for small datasets. A special kind of dynaset.

Socket.   The specific address of a process running on a port (terminal or workstation) connected to a TCP/IP LAN. WinSock refers to the Windows version of the sockets API.

SQL (Structured Query Language).   A *de facto* standard query language for today's relational databases. Because SQL was designed to be a query language, not a complete database language, most database vendors have added their own extensions.

SQL Server.   The popular "high end" DBMS engine created by Sybase and licensed by Microsoft. Microsoft's current version runs under NT.

Stored Procedure.   Named, precompiled sequence of code stored and executed on the server. Offers performance and security benefits relative to running the same code on the client.

Structured Query Language.   *See* SQL.

Table.   A subset of a database containing information about a single topic, e.g., Authors, Titles, or Publishers. Tables are two-dimensional structures.

TCP/IP (Transmission Control Protocol/Internet Protocol).   A   packet-oriented family of network and application protocols originally developed by the DOD. Now a *de facto* industry standard, pervasive in the UNIX world.

TELNET.   Popular remote terminal login program for TCP/IP networks.

Token ring.   LAN protocol widely used in IBM networks. The token ring protocol uses source routing which is incompatible with Ethernet's transport layer routing.

Transaction.   A unit of work. Typically "bracketed" by BEGIN TRANSACTION and END TRANSACTION statements. In OLTP systems, incomplete transactions can be "rolled back" to their original state.

Transaction log.   A "all or nothing" file maintained by high end database engines to provide a record of transactions. The transaction log is used by the DBMS during ROLLBACKs and RESTOREs.

Trigger.   A method of enforcing referential integrity developed by Sybase and used by SQL Server.

T-SQL.   Transact-SQL, the version of SQL used by SQL Server.

UNION.   Combining two tables that have the same structure. An append process.

UPDATE.   The SQL statement for submitting edited data to the server.

Variant data type.   A flexible data type that can take any kind of data. Obviously not associated with strong data typing or optimal performance.

VBA.   Microsoft's Visual Basic for Applications. Appears to be an emerging standard Macro and scripting language.

VBSQL.   Refers to the Visual Basic Programmer's Toolkit for SQL Server. Provides VB programmers with access to SQL Server's DB-LIB API.

VBX.   A special kind of DLL used by Visual Basic and Visual C++.

View.   Virtual tables that provide a "personal" view of data from one or more tables. Can be a row or column subset and can contain other selection criteria. Similar to Access recordsets.

Visio.   An OLE 2.0 complaint drawing package sold by ShapeWare (Seattle, WA).

VSAM (Virtual Sequential Access Method).   Variation on basic ISAM file access method used by some non-relational DBMSs.

Vim.   Lotus' Vendor Independent-Messaging protocol that competes with MAPI.

X.25.   Standard for wide-area public packet switched networks.

X.400 Message Handling System.   OSI protocol for E-mail systems.

X.500 Directory Services.   OSI standard for naming services that will liberate applications from having to "hard code" destination systems' addresses. Required if distributed systems are to achieve "location transparency."

XNS (Xerox Network System).   A 5-level protocol developed by Xerox in the 60s. Novell's IPX/SPX is based on XNS.

Appendix A

This appendix gives you a quick and comprehensive comparison of Microsoft's four major dialects of Basic. Although we have done our best to be complete and accurate, the entries for both VBA and WordBasic were based on beta versions of the software.

Access Basic	Visual Basic	VBA	Word Basic
Abs Function	Abs Function	Abs Function	Abs Function
		Accelerator Property	
	Action Property		
	Activate Event	Activate Method	Activate Statement
		ActivateMicrosoftApp Method	
		ActivateNext Method	
			ActivateObject
		ActivatePrevious Method	
		ActiveCell Property	
		ActiveChart Property	

Access Basic	Visual Basic	VBA	Word Basic
ActiveControl Property	ActiveControl Property		
		ActiveDialog Property	
ActiveForm Property	ActiveForm Property		
		ActiveMenuBar Property	
		ActivePane Property	
		ActivePrinter Property	
ActiveReport Property			
		ActiveSheet Property	
		ActiveWindow Property	
		ActiveWorkbook Property	
		Add Method	
			AddAddIn Statement & Function
			AddButton Statement
		AddChartAutoFormat Method	
AddColon Property			
		AddCustomList Method	
			AddDropDownItem Statement
		AddFields Method	
		"AddInAddIns Objects"	
			AddInState Statement and Function
		AddIndent Property	
		AddIns Method	
	AddItem Method	AddItem Method	
AddMenu Action		AddMenu Method	
AddNew Method	AddNew Method		
		"AddressAddressLocal Methods"	
AfterUpdate Property		AddVertex Method	
		AdvancedFilter Method	
		AlertBeforeOverwriting Property	
	Align Property		
	Alignment Property		
			AllCaps Statement and Function
AllowEditing Property			
AllowFilters Property			
AllowUpdating Property			
		AltStartupPath Property	
			AnnotationRefFromSel$ Function
	App Object		
AppActivate Statement	AppActivate Statement	AppActivate Statement	AppActivate Statement

Access Basic	Visual Basic	VBA	Word Basic
			AppClose Statement
			AppCount Function
	Append Method	Append Statment	
AppendChunk Method	AppendChunk Method		
			AppGetNames Statement and Function
			AppHide
			AppInfo$ Function
	AppIsRunning Property		AppIsRunning Function
		"Application ObjectProperty"	
		ApplyDataLabels Method	
ApplyFilter ActionAs			
		ApplyNames Method	
		ApplyOutlineSytles Method	
			AppMaximize Statement and Function
			AppMinimize Statement and Function
			AppMove Statement
			AppRestore Statement and Function
			AppSendMessage Statement
			AppShow Statement
			AppSize Statement
			AppWindowHeight Statement and Function
			AppWindowPosLeft Statement and Function
			AppWindowPosTop Statement and Function
			AppWindowWidth Statement and Function
		"ArcArcs Objects"	
		Arcs Method	
		Archive Property	
		"Areas ObjectMethod"	
		Areas3DGroup Property	
		AreaGroup Method	

Access Basic	Visual Basic	VBA	Word Basic
	Arrange Method	Arrange Method	
		Array Function	
		ArrowHeadLength Property	
		ArrowHeadStyle Property	
		ArrowHeadWidth Property	
Asc Function	Asc Function	Asc Function	Asc Function
		AskToUpdateLinks Property	
			AtEndOfDocument Function
Atn Function	Atn Function	Atn Function	
			AtStartOfDocument Function
	Attributes Property		
		Author Property	
	AutoActivate Property		
		AutoFill Method	
		AutoFiler Method	
		AutoFilterMode Property	
		AutoFit Method	
		AutoFormat Method	
AutoLabel Property			
		AutomaticStyles Property	
			AutoMarkIndexEntries Statement
		AutoOutline Method	
	AutoRedraw Property		
AutoRepeat Property			
AutoResize Property			
		Autoscaling Property	
	AutoRedraw Property	AutoSize Property	AutoSize Property
		AutoText Property	AutoText Statement
			AutoTextName$ Function
		AutoUpdate Property	
	AutoVerbMenu Property		
Avg Function	Avg Function		
		Axes Object and Method	
		Axis Object	
		AxisBetweenCategories Property	
		AxisGroup Property	

Access Basic	Visual Basic	VBA	Word Basic
		"AxisTitle ObjectProperty"	
BackColor Property	BackColor Property		
		Backgroup Property	
BackStyle Property	BackStyle Property		
		Backward Property	
		Bar3dGroup Property	
		BarGroups Method	
		BaseField Property	
		BaseItem Property	
Beep Action		BCCRecipients Property	
Beep Statement	Beep Statement	Beep Statement	Beep Statement
BeforeUpdate Property			
	BeginTrans Method		
BeginTrans Statement	BeginTrans Statement		
			BeginDialog...EndDialog
		BlackAndWhite Property	
BOF Property	BOF Property		
		Bold Property	Bold Function
Bookmark Property	Bookmark Property		
Bookmarkable Property	Bookmarkable Property		
			BookmarkName$ Function
		"Border ObjectProperty"	
		BorderAround Method	
			BorderBottom Statement and Function
BorderColor Property	BorderColor Property		
			BorderInside Statement and Function
			BorderLeft Statement and Function
			BorderLineStyle Statement and Function
			BorderNone Statement and Function
			BorderOutside Statement and Function
			BorderRight Statement and Function
		"Borders ObjectMethod"	

Access Basic	Visual Basic	VBA	Word Basic
BorderStyle Property	BorderStyle Property		
			BorderTop Statement and Function
BorderWidth Property	BorderWidth Property		
		BottomMargin Property	
		BottomRightCell Property	
BoundColumn Property			
		BringToFront Method	
		BuiltIn Property	
		Button Object	
		"Buttons ObjectMethod"	
		Calculate Method	
		CalculateBeforeSave Property	
		Calculation Property	
Call Statement	Call Statement	Call Statement	Call Statement
		Cakller Property	
Cancel Property	Cancel Property		Cancel Property
			Cancel Statement
		CancelButton Property	CancelButton Statement
	CancelError Property		
CancelEvent Action			
CanGrow Property			
		CanPlaySounds Property	
		CanRecordSounds Property	
CanShrink Property			
Caption Property	Caption Property		Caption Property
			Cancel Statement
		CancelButton Property	CancelButton Statement
	CancelError Property		
CancelEvent Action			
CanGrow Property			
		CanPlaySounds Property	
		CanRecordSounds Property	
CanShrink Property			
Caption Property	Caption Property		Caption Property
		Category Property	
		CategoryLocal Property	
		CategoryNames Property	
		CBool Function	

Access Basic	Visual Basic	VBA	Word Basic
CCur Function	CCur Function	Ccur Function	
		CCurRecipients Property	
		CDate Function	
CDbl Function	CDbl Function	CDbl Function	
		CellDragAndDrop Property	
		Cells Method	
	CellSelected Property		
		CenterFooter Property	
		CenterHeader Property	
		CenterHorizontally Property	
			CenterPara Statement and Function
		CenterVertically Property	
		CentimetersToPoints Method	
			ChangeCase Statement and Function
	ChangeEvent		
		ChangeFileAccess Method	
		ChangeLink Method	
		ChangeScenario Method	
		ChangingCells Property	
		Characters Object and Method	
			CharColor Statement and Function
			CharLeft Statement and Function
			CharRight Statement and Function
		Chart Object and Property	
		ChartArea Object and Property	
		ChartGroup Object and Method	
		ChartGroups Object and Method	
		ChartObject Object	
		ChartObjects Object and Method	

Access Basic	Visual Basic	VBA	Word Basic
		Charts Object and Method	
		ChartSize Property	
		ChartTitle Object and Property	
		ChartWizard Method	
			ChDefaultDir Statement
ChDir Statement	ChDir Statement	ChDir Statement	ChDir Statement
ChDrive Statement	ChDrive Statement	ChDrive Statement	
	Check Box Control	CheckBox Object	CheckBox Statement
		CheckBoxes Object and Method	
			CheckBoxFormField Statement
	Checked Property	Checked Property	
		CheckSpelling Method	
		ChildField Property	
		ChildItems Method	
Choose Function	Choose Function		
			ChooseButtonImage Statement
"Chr	Chr$ Functions"	"ChrChr$ Functions"	
			Chr$ Function
CInt Function	CInt Function	CInt Function	
Circle Method	Circle Method		
	Class Property		
			CleanString$ Function
	Clear Method	Clear Method	
			ClearAddIns Statement
		ClearArrows Method	
		ClearContents Method	
		ClearFormats Method	
			ClearFormField Statement
		ClearNotes Method	
		ClearOutline Method	
	Click Event		
	Clip Property		
	Clipboard Object		
		ClipboardFormats Property	
	ClipControls Property		
CLng Function	CLng Function	CLng Function	
Clone Method	Clone Method		
Close Action			
Close Method	Close Method	Close Method	
Close Statement	Close Statement	Close Statement	Close
			ClosePane

Access Basic	Visual Basic	VBA	Word Basic
			ClosePreview Statement
			CloseUpPara Statement
			CloseViewHeader Footer Statement
	Cls Method		
	"ColCols Properties"		
	ColAlignment Property		CmpBookmarks Function
	CollatingOrder Property		
	Color Property	Color Property	
		ColorButtons Property	
		ColorIndex Property	
		Colors Property	
Column Property		Column Property	
		Column3DGroup Property	
ColumnCount Property			
		ColumnDifferences Method	
		ColumnFields Method	
		ColumnGrand Property	
		ColumnGroups Method	
ColumnHeads Property			
		ColumnRange Property	
	Columns Property	Columns Method	
			ColumnSelect Statement
ColumnWidths Property		ColumnWidth Property	
	ColWidth Property		ComboBox Statement
	Combo Box Control		
	Command Button Control		
"Command, Command$ Functions"	"Command, Command$ Function"	Command Function	
		CommandUnderlines Property	
			CommandValid Function
		"Comment, Comments Properties"	
CommitTrans Statement	CommitTrans Statement and Method		
	Common Dialog Control		
	CompactDatabase Statement		

Access Basic	Visual Basic	VBA	Word Basic
		Compare Keyword	
	Connect Property		Connect Statement
		Consolidate Method	
		ConsolidationFunction Property	
		ConsolidationOptions Property	
		ConsolidationSources Property	
Const Statement	Const Statement	Const Statement	
		ConstrainNumeric Property	
ConstantsControl Properties			ControlRun Statement
	ControlBox Property		
ControlName Property			
	Controls Collection		
ControlSource Property			
			Converter$ Function
			ConverterLookup Function
		ConvertFormula Method	
			ConvertObject Statement
	Copies Property		
		Copy Method	
			CopyBookmark Statement
			CopyButtonImage Statement
		CopyFace Method	
			CopyFile Statement
			CopyFormat Statement
CopyObject Action		CopyObjecsWithCells Property	
		CopyPicture Method	
			CopyText Statement
		Corners Object and Property	
Cos Function	Cos Function	Cos Function	
Count Function	Count Function		
Count Property	Count Property	Count Property	
			CountAddIns Function
			CountAutoTextEntiries Function
			CountBookmarks Function
			CountDirectories Function

Access Basic	Visual Basic	VBA	Word Basic
			CountDocumentVars Function
			CountFiles Function
			CountFonts Function
			CountFoundFiles Function
			CountKeys Function
			CountLanguages Function
			CountMacros Function
			CountMenuItems Function
			CountMenus Function
			CountMergeFields Function
			CountStyles Function
			CountToolbarButtons Function
			CountToolbars Function
			CountToolsGrammarStatistics Function
			CountWindows Function
		CreateBackup Property	
	CreateDatabase Function		
CreateDynaset Method	CreateDynaset Method		
		CreateNames Method	
	CreateObject Function	CreateObject Function	
		CreatePublisher Method	
CreateQueryDef Method	CreateQueryDef Method		
CreateSnapshot Method	CreateSnapshot Method		
			CreateSubdocument Statement
		CreateSummary Method	
		Creator Property	
		Crosses Property	
		CrossesAt Property	
CSng Function	CSng Function	CSng Function	
CStr Function	CStr Function	CStr Function	
"CurDir, CurDir$ Functions"	"CurDir, CurDir$ Functions"	"CurDir, CurDir$ Functions"	
		CurrentArray Property	
CurrentDB Function			
		CurrentPage Property	

Access Basic	Visual Basic	VBA	Word Basic
		CurrentRegion Property	
"CurrentX, CurrentY Properties"	"CurrentX, CurrentY Properties"		
		CustomListCount Property	
		Cut Method	
		CutCopyMode Property	
CVar Function	CVar Function	CVar Function	
CVDate Function	CVDate Function	CVDate Function	
		CVErr Function	
	Data Control		
DataType Property	Data Property		
	"Database Object, Databases Collection"		
	Database Property		
	DatabaseName Property		
		DataBodyRange Property	
	DataChanged Property		
		DataEntryMode Property	
	DataField Property	DataFields Method	
		DataLabel Object and Property	
		DataLabels Object and Method	
		DataRange Property	
		DataSeries Method	
	DataSource Property		
	DataText Property		
		DataType Property	
"Date, Date$ Functions"	"Date, Date$ Functions"	"Date, Date$ Functions"	Date$ Function
"Date, Date$ Statements"	"Date, Date$ Statements"	Date Statement	
		Date1904 Property	
DateAdd Function	DateAdd Function		
DateCreated Property	DateCreated Property		
DateDiff Function	DateDiff Function		
DatePart Function	DatePart Function		
DateSerial Function	DateSerial Function	DateSerial Function	DateSerial Function
DateValue Function	DateValue Function	DateValue Function	DateValue Function
DAvg Function	DAvg Function		
Day Function	Day Function	Day Function	Day Function
			Days360 Function
	DblClick Event		
DCount Function	DCount Function		
DDB Function	DDB Function		

Access Basic	Visual Basic	VBA	Word Basic
DDE Function		DDEAppReturnCode Property	
DDEExecute Statement		DDEExecute Method	DDEExecute Statement
DDEInitiate Function		DDEInitiate Method	DDEInitiate Function
DDEPoke Statement		DDEPoke Method	DDEPoke Statement
DDERequest Function		DDERequest Method	DDERequest$ Function
DDESend Function			
DDETerminate Statement		DDETerminate Statement	DDETerminate Statement
DDETerminateAll Statement			DDETerminateAll Statement
	Deactivate Event		
Debug Object	Debug Object	Debug Object	
DecimalPlaces			
Declare Statement	Declare Statement	Declare Statement	Declare Statement
Default Property	Default Property		
		DefaultButton Property	
DefaultEditing Property			
	DefaultExt Property		
		DefaultFilePath Property	
DefaultValue Property			
DefaultView Property			
		DefBool Statement	
		DefCur Statement	
		DefDate Statement	
		DefDbl Statement	
		DefInt Statement	
		DefLng Statement	
		DefObj Statement	
		DefSng Statement	
		DefStr Statement	
Def type Statements	Def type Statements		
		DefVar Statement	
Delete Method	Delete Method	Delete Method	
			DeleteAddIn Statement
			DeleteBackWord Statement
			DeleteButton Statement
		DeleteChartAutoFormat Method	
		DeleteCustomList Method	
		DeleteNumberFormat Method	
DeleteQueryDef Method	DeleteQueryDef Method		
			DeleteWord Statement
		Delivery Property	

Access Basic	Visual Basic	VBA	Word Basic
			DemoteList Statement
			DemoteToBodyText Statement
		Dependents Property	
		DepthPercent Property	
Description Property			
		Deselect Method	
DFirst Function	DFirst Function		
		Dialog Object	Dialog Statement and Function
		DialogBox Method	
			DialogEditor Statement
		DialogFrame Object and Property	
		Dialogs Object and method	
		DialogSheet Object	
		DialogSheets Object and Method	
	DialogTitle Property		
Dim Statement	Dim Statement	Dim Statement	Dim Statement
"Dir, Dir$ Functions"	"Dir, Dir$ Functions"	"Dir, Dir$ Functions"	
		DirectDependents Property	
	Directory List Box Control		
		DirectPrecedents Property	
			DisableAutoMacros Statement
			DisableInput Statement
		DismissButton Property	
		Display3DShading Property	
		DisplayAlerts Property	
		DisplayAutomaticPage-Breaks Property	
		DisplayBlankAs Property	
		DisplayClipboard-Window Proeprty	
		DisplayDrawingObjects Property	
		DisplayEquation Property	
		DisplayExcel4Menus Property	
		DisplayFormulaBar Property	

Access Basic	Visual Basic	VBA	Word Basic
		DisplayFormulas Property	
		DisplayFullScreen Property	
		DisplayGridlines Property	
		DisplayHeadings Property	
		DisplayHorizontalScrollBar Property	
		DisplayInfoWindow Property	
		DisplayNotesIndicator Property	
		DisplayOutline Property	
		DisplayRecentFiles Property	
		DisplayRightToLeft Property	
		DisplayRSquared Property	
		DisplayStatusBar Property	
	DisplayType Property		
		DisplayVerticalScrollBar Property	
DisplayWhen Property			
		DisplayWordkbookTabs Property	
		DisplayZeros Property	
DLast Function	DLast Function		
			DlgControlId Function
			DlgEnable Statement and Function
			"DlgFilePreview Statement, DlgFilePreview$ Function"
			"DlgFocus Statement, DlgFocus$ Function"
			DlgListBoxArray Statement and Function
			DlgSetPicture Statement
			"DlgText Statement, DlgText$ Function"
			DlgUpdateFilePreview Statement

Access Basic	Visual Basic	VBA	Word Basic
			"DlgValue Statement
			DlgVisible Statement and Function
DLookUp Function	DLookup Function		
"DMax, DMin Func-tions"	"DMin, DMax Functions "		
			DocClose Statement
			DocMaximize Statement and Function
			DocMove Statement
			DocRestore Statement
			DocSize Statement
			DocSplit Statement and Function
			DocumentStatistics
			DocWindowHeight Statement and Function
			DocWindowPosLeft Statement and Function
			DocWindowPosTop Statement and Function
			DocWindowWidth Statement and Function
Do...Loop Statement	Do...Loop Statement	Do...Loop Statement	
DoCmd Statement			
"DoEvents Function, Stmt"	DoEvents Statement and Function	DoEvents Statement	
			DoFieldClick Statement
DoMenuItem Action			
			DOSToWin$ Function
			DottedUnderline Statement and Function
		DoubleClick Method	
			DoubleUnderline Statement and Function
		DoughnutGroups Method	
		DoughnutHoleSize Property	
		DownBars Property	
		Draft Property	
	Drag Method		
	DragDrop Event		

Access Basic	Visual Basic	VBA	Word Basic
	DragIcon Property		
	DragMode Property		
	DragOver Event		
			DrawAlign Statement
			DrawArc Statement
			DrawBringForward Statement
			DrawBringInFrontOfText Statement
			DrawBringToFront Statement
			DrawCallout Statement
			DrawClearRange Statement
			DrawCount Function
			DrawCountPolyPoints Function
			DrawDisassemblePicture Statement
			DrawEllipse Statement
			DrawExtendSelect Statement
			DrawFlipHorizontal Statement
			DrawFlipVertical Statement
			DrawFreeformPolygon Statement
			DrawGetCalloutTextbox Statement
			DrawGetPolyPoints Statement
			DrawGetType Function
		Drawing Object	
		DrawingObjects Object and Method	
		Drawings Object and Method	
			DrawInsertWordPicture Statement
			DrawLine Statement
DrawMode Property	DrawMode Property		
			DrawNudgeDown Statement
			DrawNudgeDown Pixel Statement
			DrawNudgeLeft Statement
			DrawNudgeLeftPixel Statement

Access Basic	Visual Basic	VBA	Word Basic
			DrawNudgeRight Statement
			DrawNudgeRightPixel Statement
			DrawNudgeUp Statement
			DrawNudgeUpPixel Statement
			DrawRectangle Statement
			DrawResetWordPicture Statement
			DrawReshape Statement
			DrawRotateLeft Statement
			DrawRoundRectangle Statement
			DrawSelect Statement and Function
			DrawSelectNext Statement
			DrawSelectPrevious Statement
			DrawSendBackward Statement'
			DrawSendBehindText Statement
			DrawSendToBack Statement
			DrawSetCalloutTextbox Statement
			DrawSetInsertToAnchor Statement
			DrawSetInsertToTextbox Statement
			DrawSetPolyPoints
			DrawSetRange Statement and Function
			DrawSnapToGrid Statement
DrawStyle Property	DrawStyle Property		
			DrawTextBox Statement
			DrawUngroup Statement
			DrawUnselect Statement
DrawWidth Property	DrawWidth Property		

Access Basic	Visual Basic	VBA	Word Basic
	Drive List Box Control		
	Drive Property		
	DropDown Event	DropDown Object	
			DropDownFormField Statement
		DropDownLines Property	
		DropDowns Object and Method	
		DropLines Ojbect and Property	
			DropListBox Statement
"DStDev, DStDevP Functions"	"DStDev, DStDevP Functions"		
DSum Function	DSum Function		
		Duplicate Method	
"DVar, DVarP Func-tions"	"DVar, DVarP Functions "		
Dynaset Object	Dynaset Object		
Echo Action			
Edit Method	Edit Method	Edit Method	
			EditAutoText Statement
			EditBookmark Statement
		EditBox Object	
		EditBoxes Object and Method	
			EditButtonImage Statement
			EditClear
			EditConvertAllEndNotes Statement
			EditConvertNotes Statement
			EditCopy Statement
			EditCut Statement
		EditDirectlyInCell Property	
			EditFind Statement
			EditFindChar Statement
			EditFindClearFormatting Statement
			EditFindFont Statement
			EditFindFound Function
			EditFindLang Statement

Access Basic	Visual Basic	VBA	Word Basic
			EditFindPara Statement
			EditFindStyle Statement
			EditGoTo Statement
		EditingInPlace Property	
		EditionOptions Method	
			EditLinks Statement
	EditMode Property		
			EditObject Statement
			EditPaste Statement
			EditPasteSpecial Statement
			EditPicture Statement
			EditRedo Statement
			EditRepeat Statement
			EditReplace Statement
			EditReplaceChar
			EditReplaceClearForma tting Statement
			EditReplaceFont Statement
			EditReplaceLang Statement
			EditReplacePara Statement
			EditReplaceStyle Statement
			EditSelectAll Statement
			EditSwapAllNotes Statement
			EditToACategory Statement'
			EditUndo Statement
		Elevation Property	
			EmptyBookmark Function
Enabled Property	Enabled Property		
			EnableFormField Statement
		EnableTipWizard Property	
		Enclosures Property	
End Statement	End Statement	"End Statement, Method"	
	EndDoc Method		

Access Basic	Visual Basic	VBA	Word Basic
			EndOfColumn Statement and Function
			EndOfDocument Statement and Function
			EndOfLine Statement and Function
			EndOfRow Statement and Function
			EndOfWindow Statement and Function
		EndStyle Property	
		EntireColumn Property	
		EntireRow Property	
"Environ, Environ$ Functions"	"Environ, Environ$ Function"		Environ$ Function
EOF Function	EOF Function	EOF Function	Eof Function
EOF Property	EOF Property		
Eqv Operator			
Erase Statement	Erase Statement	Erase Statement	
Erl Function	Erl Function	Erl Function	
Err Function	Err Function	Err Function	
Err Statement	Err Statement	Err Statement	Err Statement
	Errl Function		
	Error Event	Error, Error$ Function	******************
Error Statement	Error Statement	Error Statement	Error Statement
		ErrorBar Method	
		ErrorBars Object and Property	
Eval Function		Evaluate Method	
		Excel4MacroSheets Method	
	Exclusive Property		
Execute Method	Execute Method		
		ExecuteExcel4Macro Method	
	ExecuteSQL Method		
	EXEName Property		
			ExistingBookmark Function
Exit Statement	Exit Statement	Exit Statement	
			ExitWindows Statement
Exp Function	Exp Function	Exp Function	
		Explosion Property	
		Extend Method	
			ExtendMode Function

Access Basic	Visual Basic	VBA	Word Basic
			ExtendSelection Statement
	Field Object		
	Fields Collection		
	Fields Property		
FieldName Property			
			FieldSeparator Statement and Function
FieldSize Method	FieldSize Method		
FieldSize Property			
	File List Box Control		
FileAttr Function	FileAttr Function	FileAttr Function	
			FileClose Statement
			FileCloseAll Statement
			FileClosePicture Statement
			FileConfirmConversions Statement and Function
		FileConverters Property	
	FileCopy Statement	FileCopy Statement	
	FileDateTime Function	FileDateTime Function	
			FileExit Statement
			FileFind Statement
		FileFormat Property	
	FileLen Function	FileLen Function	
			FileList Statement
	FileName Property		FileName$ Function
			FileNameFromWindows$ Function
			FileNameInfo$ Function
			FileNew Statement
			FileNewDefault Statement
	FileNumber Property		
			"FileNumber
			FileOpen Statement
			FilePageSetup Statement
			FilePreview Statement
			FilePrint Statement
			FilePrintDefault Statement
			FilePrintPreview Statement and Function

Access Basic	Visual Basic	VBA	Word Basic
			FilePrintPreviewFullScreen Statment
			FilePrintPreviewPages Statement and Function
			FilePrintSetup Statement
			FileRoutingSlip Statement
			Files$ Function
			FileSave Statement
			FileSaveAll Statement
			FileSaveAs Statement
			FileSendMail Statement
			FileSummaryInfo Statement
			FileTemplates Statement
	FileTitle Property		
		FillAcrossSheets Method	
FillColor Property	FillColor Property		
		FillDown Method	
		FillLeft Method	
		FillRight Method	
FillStyle Property	FillStyle Property		
		FillUp Method	
Filter Property	Filter Property		
	FilterIndex Property		
		FilterMode Property	
		Find Method	
		FindFile Method	
FindFirst Method	FindFirst Method		
FindLast Method	FindLast Method		
FindNext Action	FindNext Method	FindNext Method	
FindNext Method			
FindPrevious Method	FindPrevious Method	FindPrevious Method	
FindRecord Action			
First Function	First Function		
		FirstPageNumber Property	
		FirstSliceAngle Property	
		FitToPagesTall Property	
		FitToPagesWide Property	
Fix Function	Fix Function	Fix Function	

Access Basic	Visual Basic	VBA	Word Basic
	FixedAlignment Property		
	"FixedCols, FixedRows Properties"		
		FixedDecimal Property	
		FixedDecimalPlaces Property	
	Flags Property (several)		
		Floor Object and Property	
		Focus Property	
		Font Object and Property	"Font Statement, Font$ Function"
FontBold Property	FontBold Property		
	FontCount Property		
FontItalic Property	FontItalic Property		
FontName Property	FontName Property		
	Fonts Property		
FontSize Property	FontSize Property		FontSize Statement and Function
			FontSizeSelect Statement
	FontStrikethru Property		
		FontStyle Property	
			FontSubstitution Statement
	FontTransparent Property		
FontUnderline Property	FontUnderline Property		
FontWeight Property			
		FooterMargin Property	
		For Each...Next Statement	
For...Next Statement	For...Next Statement	For...Next Statement	For...Next Statement
ForceNewPage Property			
ForeColor Property	ForeColor Property		
	Form Object		
Format Property	Format Property		
"Format, Format$ Functions"	"Format, Format$ Functions"	"Format, Format$ Functions"	
			FormatAddrFonts Statement
			FormatAutoFormat Statement
			FormatBordersand-Shading Statement
			FormatBullet Statement

Access Basic	Visual Basic	VBA	Word Basic
			FormatBulletDefault Statement and Function
			FormatBulletsAnd-Numbering Statement
			FormatCallout Statement
			FormatChangeCase Statement
			FormatColumns Statement
FormatCount Property			
			FormatDefineStyle-Borders Statement
			FormatDefineStyleFont Statement
			FormatDefineStyle-Frame Statement
			FormatDefineStyle-Lang Statement
			FormatDefineStyle-Numbers Statement
			FormatDefineStylePara Statement
			FormatDefineStyleTabs Statement
			FormatDrawingObject Statement
			FormatDropCap Statement
			FormatFont Statement
			FormatFrame Statement
			FormatHeaderFooter-Link Statement
			FormatHeadingNumber Statement
			FormatHeadingNumbering Statement
			FomatMultiLevel Statement
			FormatNumber Statement
			FormatNumberDefault Statement and Function
			FormatPageNumber Statement
			FormatParagraph Statement

Access Basic	Visual Basic	VBA	Word Basic
			FormatPicture Statement
			FormatRetAddrFonts Statement
			FormatSectionLayout Statement
			FormatStyle Statement
			FormatStyleGallery Statement
			FormatTabs Statement
			For...Next
			FormFieldOptions Statement
FormName Property			
			FormShading Statement and Function
Forms Object	Forms Collection		
		Formula Property	
		FormulaArray Property	
		FormulaHidden Property	
		FormulaLocal Property	
		FormulaR1C1 Property	
		FormulaR1C1Local Property	
		Forward Property	
		ForwardMailer Method	
			FoundFileName$ Function
	Frame Control		
FreeFile Function	FreeFile Function	FreeFile Function	
	FreeLocks Statement		
		FreezePanes Property	
	FromPage Property		
		FullName Property	
Function Statement	Function Statement	Function Statement and Property	Function Statement
		FunctionWizard Method	
FV Function	FV Function		
		GapDepth Property	
		GapWidth Property	
Get Statement	Get Statement	Get Statement	
			GetAddInID Function
			GetAddInNames$ Function
	GetAttr Function	GetAttr Function	GetAttr Function
			GetAutoCorrect$ Function

Access Basic	Visual Basic	VBA	Word Basic
			GetAutoText$ Function
			GetBookmark$ Function
GetChunk Method	GetChunk Method		
			GetCurValues Statement
		GetCustomListContents Method	
		GetCustomListNum Method	
	GetData Method		
			GetDirectory$ Function
			GetDocumentVar$ Function
			GetDocumentVarName$ Function
			GetFieldData$ Function
	GetFormat Method		
			"GetFormResult
			GetMergeField$ Function
	GetObject Function	GetObject Function	
		GetOpenFilename Method	
			GetPrivateProfileString$ Function
			GetProfileString$ Function
		GetSaveAsFilename Method	
			GetSelEndPos Function
			GetSelStartPos Function
			"GetSystemInfo Statement
	GetText Method		GetText$ Function
Global Statement	Global Statement	Global Keyword	
		Go Keyword	
		GoalSeek Method	
			GoBack Statement
GoSub...Return State-ments	GoSub...Return Statement	GoSub...Return Statement	
	GotFocus Event		
GoTo Statement	GoTo Statement	GoTo Statement and Method	Goto Statement
			GoToAnnotationScope Statement
GoToControl Action			

Access Basic	Visual Basic	VBA	Word Basic
			GoToHeaderFooter Statement
			GotoNextitem
GoToPage Action			
			GotoPreviousitem
GoToRecord Action			
	Grid Control		
		GridLineColor Property	
		GridLineColorIndex Property	
	GridLines Property	Gridlines Object	
	GridLineWidth Property		
"GridX, GridY Properties"			
		Group Method	
		Groupbox Object	GroupBox Statement
		Groupboxes Object and Method	
		GroupLevel Property	
		GroupObject Object	
		GroupObjects Object and Method	
			GrowFont Statement
			GrowFontOnePoint Statement
			HangingIndent Statement
		HasArray Property	
		HasAutoFormat Property	
		HasAxis Property	
		HasDataLabel Property	
		HastDropLines Property	
		HasErrorBars Property	
		HasFormula Property	
		HasHiLoLines Property	
		HasLegend Property	
		HasMailer Property	
		HasMajorGridlines Property	
		HasMinorGridlines Property	
		HasPassword Property	
		HasRadarAxisLabels Property	
		HasRoutingSlip Property	
		HasSeriesLines Property	

Access Basic	Visual Basic	VBA	Word Basic
		HasTitle Property	
		HasUpDownBars Property	
	hDC Property		
		HeaderMargin Property	
Height Property	Height Property	Height Property	
		HeightPercent Property	
		Help Method	Help Statement
			HelpAbout Statement
			HelpActiveWindow Statement
		HelpButton Property	
	HelpCommandProperty		
			HelpContents Statement
	HelpContext Property		
HelpContextID Property	HelpContextID Property		
			HelpExamplesAnd-Demos Statement
HelpFile Property	HelpFile Property		
			HelpIndex
	HelpKey Property		
			HelpKeyboard
			HelpPSSHelp
			HelpQuickPreview Statement
			HelpSearch Statement
			HelpTipOfTheDay Statement
			HelpTool Statement
			HelpUsingHelp Statement
			HelpWPHelpOpt Statement
"Hex, Hex$ Functions"	"Hex, Hex$ Functions"	"Hex, Hex$ Functions"	
	Hidden Property	Hidden Property	Hidden Statement and Function
		HiddenFields Method	
		HiddenItems Method	
	Hide Method	Hide Method	
HideDuplicates Property			
	HideSelection Property		
	HighLight Property		
		HiLoLines Object and Property	
			HLine Statement
		HorizontalAlignment Property	

Access Basic	Visual Basic	VBA	Word Basic
	Horizontal Scroll Bar		
	HostName Property		
Hour Function	Hour Function	Hour Function	Hour Function
Hourglass Action			
			HPage Statement
			HScroll Statement and Function
hWnd Property	hWnd Property		
	Icon Property		
		Id Property	
If...Then...Else Statement	If...Then...Else Statement	If...Then...Else Statement	If...ElseIf...Else...End If
	If TypeOf Statement		
		IgnorRemoteRequests Property	
IIf Function	IIf Function		
	Image Control		
	Image Property		
		IMEStatus Function	
			Indent Statement
	Index Object		
Index Property	Index Property		
Index1...Index5 Properties			
Indexed Property			
	Indexes Collection		
	InitDir Property		
		Import Method	
		InchesToPoints Method	
		IncludeAlignment Property	
		IncludeBorder Property	
		IncludeFont Property	
		IncludeNumber Property	
		IncludePatterns Property	
		IncludeProtection Property	
		Index Property	
		InnerDetail Property	
	Inner Join Operation		
Input # Statement	Input # Statement	Input # Statement	
"Input, Input$ Functions"	"Input, Input$ Functions"	"Input, Input$ Functions"	"Input Statement, Input$ Function"
		"InputB, InputB$ Functions"	
"InputBox, InputBox$ Functions"	"InputBox, InputBox$ Functions"	InputBox Function and Method	InputBox$ Function
		InputType Property	

Access Basic	Visual Basic	VBA	Word Basic
		Insert Method	Insert Statement
	Insert Into Statement		
			InsertAddCaption Statement
			InsertAnnotation Statement
			InsertAutoCaption Statement
			InsertAutoText Statement
			InsertBreak Statement
			InsertCaption Statement
			InsertCaptionNumbering Statement
			InsertChart Statement
			InsertColumnBreak Statement
			InsertCrossReference Statement
			InsertDatabase Statement
			InsertDateField Statement
			InsertDateTime Statement
			InsertDrawing Statement
			InsertEquation Statement
			InsertExcelTable Statement
			InsertField Statement
			InsertFieldChars Statement
		InsertFile Method	InsertFile Statement
			InsertFootnote Statement
			InsertFormField Statement
			InsertFrame Statement
			InsertIndex Statement
			InsertMergeField Statement
			InsertObject Statement
			InsertPageBreak Statement
			InsertPageField Statement

Access Basic	Visual Basic	VBA	Word Basic
			InsertPageNumbers Statement
			InsertPara Statement
			InsertPicture Statement
			InsertSectionBreak Statement
			InsertSound Statement
			InsertSpike Statement
			InsertSubDocument Statement
			InsertSymbol Statement
			InsertTableOfAuthorities Statement
			InsertTableOfContents Statement
			InsertTableOfFigures Statement
			InsertTimeField Statement
			InsertWordArt Statement
		Installed Property	
InStr Function	InStr Function	InStr Function	InStr Function
		InStrB Function	
Int Function	Int Function	Int Function	Int Function
		Interactive Property	
		Intercept Property	
		InterceptIsAuto Property	
		Interior Object and Property	
		International Property	
		Intersect Method	
	Interval Property		
		InvertIfNegative Property	
IPmt Function	IPmt Function		
IRR Function	IRR Function		
		IsArray Function	
IsDate Function	IsDate Function	IsDate Function	
			IsDocumentDirty Function
IsEmpty Function	IsEmpty Function	IsEmpty Function	
		IsError Function	
			IsExecuteOnly Function
		IsGap Property	
			IsMacro Function

Access Basic	Visual Basic	VBA	Word Basic
		IsMissing Function	
IsNull Function	IsNull Function	IsNull Function	
IsNumeric Function	IsNumeric Function	IsNumeric Function	
		IsObject Function	
			IsTemplateDirty Function
		Italic Property	Italic Statement and Function
Item Property		Item Method	
	ItemData Property		
		Iteration Property	
		Justify Method	
			JustifyPara Statement and Function
KeepTogether Property			
			KeyCode Function
	"KeyDown, KeyUp Events"		
			KeyMacro$ Function
	KeyPress Event		
	KeyPreview Property		
		Keywords Property	
Kill Statement	Kill Statement	Kill Statement	Kill Statement
	Label Control	Label Object	
		LabelRange Property	
		Labels Object and Method	
LabelAlign Property			
"LabelX, LabelY Properties"			
			"Language Statement, Language$ Function"
		LargeButtons Property	
	LargeChange Property	LargeChange Property	
		LargeScroll Method	
Last Function	Last Function		
	LastModified Property		
LastUpdated Property	LastUpdated Property		
LayoutForPrint Property			
LBound Function	LBound Function	LBound Function	
"LCase, LCase$ Functions"	"LCase, LCase$ Functions"	"LCase, LCase$ Functions"	LCase$ Function
Left Property	Left Property		
	Left Join Operation		
"Left, Left$ Functions"	"Left, Left$ Functions"	"Left, Left$ Functions"	Left$ Function
		"LeftB	LeftB$ Functions"
	LeftCol Property		
		LeftFooter Property	
		LeftHeader Property	

Access Basic	Visual Basic	VBA	Word Basic
		LeftMargin Property	
			LeftPara Statement and Function
		Legend Object and Property	
		LegendEngtries Object and Method	
		LegendEntry Object	
		LegendKey Object and Property	
Len Function	Len Function	Len Function	Len Function
		LenB Function	
Let Statement	Let Statement	Let Statement	Let Statement
		LibraryPath Property	
LimitToList Property			
	Line Control	Line Object	
Line Input # Statement	Line Input # Statement	Line Input # Statement	Line Input Statement
Line Method	Line Method		
			LineDown Statement and Function
		Lines Object and Method	
LineSlant Property			
		LineStyle Property	
			LineUp Statement and Function
LinkChildFields Property			
	LinkClose Event		
		LinkCombo Method	
		LinkedCell Property	
		LinkedObject Property	
	LinkError Event		
	LinkExecute Event and Method		
		LinkInfo Method	
	LinkItem Property		
LinkMasterFields Property			
	LinkMode Property		
	LinkNotify Event		
	LinkOpen Event		
	LinkPoke Method		
	LinkRequest Method		
	LinkSend Method		
		LinkSources Method	
	LinkTimeout Property		
	LinkTopic Property		
	List Box Contro		
	List Property	List Property	

Access Basic	Visual Basic	VBA	Word Basic
		ListBox Obje	ListBox Statement
		ListBoxes Object and Method	
	ListCount Property	ListCount Property	
ListFields Method	ListFields Method		
		ListFillRange Property	
	ListIndex Property	ListIndex Property	
ListIndexes Method	ListIndexes Method		
ListParameters Method	ListParameters Method		
ListRows Property			
ListTables Method	ListTables Method		
ListWidth Property			
Load Event			
	Load Statement	Load Statement	
	LoadPicture Function	LoadPicture Statement	
Loc Function	Loc Function	Loc Function	
		LocationInTable Property	
Lock Statement	Lock Statement	Lock Statement	
Locked Property		Locked Property	
			LockDocument Statement and Function
LockEdits Property	LockEdits Property		
		LockedText Property	
			LockFields Statement
LOF Function	LOF Function	LOF Function	Lof Function
Log Function	Log Function	Log Function	
	LostFocus Event		
	LpOleObject Property		
LSet Statement	LSet Statement	LSet Statement	
"LTrim, LTrim$ Functions"	"LTrim, LTrim$ Functions"	"LTrim, LTrim$ Functions"	LTrim$ Function
		MacID Function	
			MacroCopy Statement
			MacroDesc$ Function
			MacroName$ Function
			MacroNameFromWindows$ Function
		MacroType Property	
		MacScript Statement	
			Magnifier Statement and Function
		Mailer Object and Property	
		MailLogoff Method	
		MailLogon method	
		MailSession Property	
		MailSystem Property	
			MailMerge Statement

Access Basic	Visual Basic	VBA	Word Basic
			MailMergeAskToConvertChevrons Statement and Function
			MailMergeCheck Statement
			MailMergeConvert-Chevrons Statement and Function
			MailMergeCreateData-Source Statement
			MailMergeCreate-HeaderSource Statement
			MailMergeDataForm Statement
			MailMergeDataSource$ Function
			MailMergeEditData-Source Statement
			MailMergeEditHeader-Source Statement
			MailMergeEditMainDocument Statement
			MailMergeFindRecord Statement
			MailMergeFirstRecord Statement
			MailMergeFoundRecord Function
			MailMergeGotoRecord Statement and Function
			MailMergeHelper Statement
			MailMergeInsertAsk Statement
			MailMergeInsertFillin Statement
			MailMergeInsertIf Statement
			MailMergeInsertMerge-Rec Statement
			MailMergeInsertMerge-Seq Statement
			MailMergeInsertNext Statement
			MailMergeInsertNextIf Statement
			MailMergeInsertSet Statement

Access Basic	Visual Basic	VBA	Word Basic
			MailMergeInsertSkipIf Statement
			MailMergeLastRecord Statement
			MailMergeMainDocumentType Statement and Function
			MailMergeNextRecord Statement
			MailMergeOpenData-Source Statement
			MailMergeOpen-Header-Source Statement
			MailMergePrevRecord Statement
			MailMergeQueryOptions Statement
			MailMergeReset Statement
			MailMergeState Function
			MailMergeToDoc Statement
			MailMergeToPrinter Statement
			MailMergeViewData Statement and Function
		MajorGridlines Property	
		MajorUnit Property	
		MajorUnitIsAuto Property	
			MarkCitation Statement
		MarkerBackgroundColor Property	
		MarkerBackgroundColor Index Property	
		MarkerForegroundColor Property	
		MarkerForegroundColor Index Property	
		MarkerStyle Property	
			MarkIndexEntry Statement
			MarkTableOfCont4ents-Entry Statement
		MathCoprocessorAvailable Property	

Access Basic	Visual Basic	VBA	Word Basic
Max Function	Max Property	Max Property	
	MaxButton Property		
		MaxChange Property	
	MaxFileSize Property		
Maximize Action			
MaxLength Property			
		MaxScale Property	
		MaxScaleIsAuto Property	
		MaxIterations Property	
	MDI Form		
	MDIChild Property		
		MemoryFree Property	
		MemoryTotal Property	
		MemoryUsed Property	
	Menu Control	Menu Object	
		MenuBar Object	
		MenuBars Object and method	
		MenuItem Object	
			MenuItemMacro$ Function
		MenuItems Object and Method	
			MenuItemText$ Function
			MenuMode Statement
		Menus Object and method	
			MenuText$ Function
		Merge Method	
			MergeFieldName$ Function
			MergeSubdocument Statement
		Message Property	
			MicrosoftAccess
			MicrosoftExcel
			MicrosoftFox
			MicrosoftMail
			MicorosoftPowerPoint
			MicrosoftProject
			MicrosoftPublisher
			MicrosoftSchedule
			MicrosoftSystemInfo Statement
"Mid, Mid$ Functions"	"Mid, Mid$ Functions"	"Mid, Mid$ Functions"	Mid$ Function
"Mid, Mid$ Statements"	"Mid, Mid$ Statement"	Mid Statement	
		"MidB, MidB$ Functions"	

Access Basic	Visual Basic	VBA	Word Basic
Min Function	Min Function and Property	Min Property	
	MinButton Property		
Minimize Action			
		MinimumScale Property	
		MinimumScaIIsAuto Property	
		MinorGridlines Property	
		MinorTickMark Property	
		MinorUnit Property	
Minute Function	Minute Function	Minute Function	Minute Function
MIRR Function	MIRR Function		
	MiscFlags Property		
MkDir Statement	MkDir Statement	MkDir Statement	MkDir Statement
Modal Property			
		Module Object	
		Modules Method	
Month Function	Month Function	Month Function	Month Function
		MouseAvailable Property	
	"MouseDown, MouseUp Events"		
	MouseMove Event		
	MousePointer Propert		
	Move Method	Move Method	
		MoveAfterReturn Property	
			MoveButton Statement
MoveFirst Method	MoveFirst Method		
MoveLast Method	MoveLast Method		
MoveLayout Property			
MoveNext Method	MoveNext Method		
MovePrevious Method	MovePrevious Method		
MoveSize Action			
			MoveText Statement
			MoveToolBar Statement
MsgBox Action			
MsgBox Statement	MsgBox Statement		MsgBoxStatement
MsgBox Function	MsgBox Function	MsgBox Function	MsgBox Function
	MultiLine Property	MultiLine Property	
	MultiSelect Property	MultiSelect Property	
	Name Property	"Name Property, Object"	
Name Statement	Name Statement	Name Statement	Name Statement
		NameIsAuto Property	
		NameLocal Property	

Access Basic	Visual Basic	VBA	Word Basic
		Names Object and Method	
		NavigateArrow Method	
	NewIndex Property		
	NewPage Method		
NewRowOrCol Property			
			NewToolbar Statement
		NewWindow Method	
		Next Property	
			NextCell Statement and Function
			NextField Statement and Function
		NextLetter Method	
			NextObject Statement
			NextPage Statement and Function
NextRecord Property			
			NextTab Function
			NextWindow Statement
NoMatch Property	NoMatch Property		
	Normal Property		
			NormalFontPosition Statement
			NormalFontSpacing Statement
			NormalStyle Statement]
			NormalViewHeaderArea Statement
			NoteOptions Statement
		NoteText Method	
Now Function	Now Function	Now Function	Now Function
NPer Function	NPer Function		
NPV Function	NPV Function		
		NumberFormat Property	
		NumberFormatLinked Property	
		NumberFormatLocal Property	
	Object Property	Object Property	
	ObjectAcceptFormats Property		
	ObjectAcceptFormatsCount		
	ObjectGetFormats Property		

Access Basic	Visual Basic	VBA	Word Basic
	ObjectGetFormat-sCount Property		
	ObjectVerbFlags Property		
	ObjectVerbs Property		OK Statement
	ObjectVerbsCount Property		OKButton Statement
"Oct, Oct$ Functions"	"Oct, Oct$ Functions"	"Oct, Oct$ Functions"	
		Offset Method	
OldValue Property			
OLEClass Property			
	OLE Control		
		OLEObject Object	
		OLEObjects Object and Method	
	OLEType Property	OLEType Property	
	OLETypeAllowed Property		
On Error Statement	On Error Statement	On Error Statement	On Error Statement
On...GoSub Statement	On...GoSub Statement	On...GoSub Statement	
On...GoTo Statement	On...GoTo Statement	On...GoTo Statement	
		OnAction Property	
		OnCalculate	
OnClose Property			
OnCurrent Property			
		OnData Property	
OnDblClick Property		OnDoubleClick Property	
OnDelete Property			
OnEnter Property		OnEntry Property	
OnExit Property			
OnFormat Property			
OnInsert Property			
		OnKey Method	
OnMenu Property			
OnOpen Property			
OnPrint Property			
OnPush Property			
		OnRepeat Method	
		OnSheetActivate	
		OnSheetDeactivate	
		OnTime Method	OnTime Statement
Open Statement	Open Statement	Open Statement	
OpenDatabase Function	OpenDatabase Function		
			Open...For...As Statement
OpenForm Action			
		OpenLinks Method	
OpenQuery Action			

Access Basic	Visual Basic	VBA	Word Basic
OpenQueryDef Method	OpenQueryDef Method		
OpenReport Action			
			OpenSubdocument Statement
OpenTable Action and Method	OpenTable Method		
		OpenText Method	
			OpenUpPara Statement
		OperatingSystem Property	
Option Base Statement	Option Base Statement	Option Base Statement	
	Option Button Control	OptionButton Object	OptionButton Statement
		OptionButtons Object and Method	
Option Compare State-ment	Option Compare Statement	Option Compare Statement	
Option Explicit State-ment	Option Explicit Statement	Option Explicit Statement	
			OptionGroup Statement
		Option Private Statement	
	Options Property		
		Order Property	
OptionValue Property			
	OrdinalPosition Property		
		OrganizationName Property	
			Organizer Statement
		Orientation Property	
			OtherPane Statement
		Outline Object and Property	
			OutlineCollapse Statement
			OutlineDemote Statement
			OutlineExpand Statement
		OutlineFont Property	
		OutlineLevel Property	OutlineLevel Function
			OutlineMoveDown Statement
			OutlineMoveUp Statement

Access Basic	Visual Basic	VBA	Word Basic
			OutlinePromote Statement
			OutlineShowFirstLine Statement and Function
			OutlineShowFormat Statement
		Output Keyword	
		Oval Object	
		Ovals Object and method	
		Overlap Property	
			Overtype Statement and Function
Page Property	Page Property		
		PageBreak Property	
			PageDown Statement and Function
		PageFields Method	
PageFooter Property			
PageHeader Property			
		PageRange Property	
		PageSetup Object and Property	
			PageUp Statement and Function
	Paint Event		
		Pane Object	
		Panes Object and Method	
		PaperSize Property	
			ParaDown Statement and Function
			ParaKeepLinesTogether Statement and Function
			ParaKeepWithNext Statement and Function
			ParaPageBreakBefore Statement and Function
			ParaUp Statement and Function
			ParaWidowOrphanContr ol Statement and Function
Parent Property	Parent Property	Parent Property	
		ParentField Property	
		ParentItem Property	

Access Basic	Visual Basic	VBA	Word Basic
		ParentItems Method	
		ParentShowDetail Property	
		Parse Method	
Partition Function	Partition Function		
	PasswordChar Property		
		Paste Method	PasteButtonImage Statement
		PasteFace Method	
			PasteFormat Statement
	PasteOK Property		
		PasteSpecial Method	
	Path Property	Path Property	
	PathChange Event		
			PathFromMacPath$ Function
		PathSeparator Property	
	Pattern Property	Pattern Property	
	PatternChange Event		
		PatternColor Property	
		PatternColorIndex Property	
			PauseRecorder Statement
		Period Property	
		Perspective Property	
		PhoneticAccelerator Property	
Picture Property	Picture Property	Picture Object	Picture Statement
	Picture Box Control		
		Pictures Object and Method	
		PictureType Property	
		PictureUnit Property	
		Pie3DGroup Property	
		PieGroups Method	
		PivotField Object and Property	
		PivotFields Object and Method	
		PivotItem Object and Property	
		PivotItems Object and Method	
		PivotTable Ojbect and Property	

Access Basic	Visual Basic	VBA	Word Basic
		PivotTabls Object and Method	
		PivotTableWizard Method	
		Placement Property	
		Play Method	
		PlotArea Object and Property	
		PlotOrder Property	
		PlotVisibleOnly Property	
Pmt Function	Pmt Function		
	Point Method	Point Object	
		Points Object and Method	
PopUp Property			
	PopupMenu Method		
		Position Property	
PPmt Function	PPmt Function		
		Precedents Property	
		PrecisionAsDisplayed Property	
		PrefixCharacter Property	
			PrevCell Statement and Function
			PrevField Statement and Function
	PrevInstance Property		
		Previous Property	
		Previous Selections Property	
			PrevObject Statement
			PrevPage Statement and Function
			PrevTab Function
			PrevWindow Statement
Primary Property			
PrimaryKey Property			
Print Action			Print Statement
Print Method	Print Method	Print Method	
Print # Statement	Print # Statement	Print # Statement	
		PrintArea Property	
PrintCount Property			
Printer Object			
	PrinterDefault Property		
	PrintForm Method		
		PrintGridlines Property	
		PrintHeadings Property	
		PrintNotes Property	

Access Basic	Visual Basic	VBA	Word Basic
		PrintObject Property	
		PrintOut Method	
		PrintPreview Method	
		PrintQuality Property	
PrintSection Property			
		PrintTitleColumns Property	
		PrintTitleRows Property	
		Private Statement	
			PromoteList Statement
		PromptForSummaryInfo Property	
		Property Get Statement	
		Property Let Statement	
		Property Set Statement	
		Protect Method	
		ProtectContents Property	
		ProtectDrawingObjects Property	
		ProtectScenarios Property	
		ProtectStructure Property	
		ProtectWindows Property	
PSet Method	PSet Method		
		Public Statement	
			PushButton Statement
		Pushed Property	
Put Statement	Put Statement	Put Statement	
			PutFieldData Statement
PV Function	PV Function		
QBColor Function	QBColor Function		
QueryDef Object	QueryDef Object		
	QueryUnload Event		
Quit Action		Quit Method	
		RadarAxisLabels Property	
		RadarGroups Method	
Randomize Stateme	Randomize Statement	Randomize Statement	
		Range Object and Method	
Rate Function	Rate Function		
			Read Statement
	ReadOnly Property	ReadOnly Property	

Access Basic	Visual Basic	VBA	Word Basic
		ReadOnlyRecommended Property	
		Received Property	
		Recipients Property	
		Record Method	
RecordCount Property	RecordCount Property		
RecordLocks Property			
		RecordMacro Method	
			RecordNextCommand Statement
		RecordRelative Property	
	Recordset Property		
RecordSelectors Property			
RecordSource Property	RecordSource Property		
		Rectangle Object	
		Rectangles Object and Method	
ReDim Statement	ReDim Statement	ReDim Statement	ReDim Statement
		ReferenceStyle Property	
		RefersTo Property	
		RefersToLocal Property	
		RefersToR1C1 Property	
		RefersToR1C1Local Property	
	Refresh Method		
		RefreshDate Property	
		RefreshName Property	
		RefreshTable Method	
	RegisterDatabase Statement		
		RegisteredFunctions Property	
		RegisterXLL Method	
Rem Statement	Rem Statement	Rem Statement	Rem Statement
			RemoveAllDropDownItems Statement
		RemoveAllItems Method	
			RemoveBulletsNumbers Statement
			RemoveDropDownItem Statement
			RemoveFrames Statement
	RemoveItem Method	RemoveItem Method	

Access Basic	Visual Basic	VBA	Word Basic
			RemoveSubdocument Statement
		RemoveSubtotal Method	
Rename Action			
			RenameMenu Statement
RepaintObject Action			
	RepairDatabase Statement		
		Repeat Method	
			RepeatFind Statement
		Replace Method	
		Reply Method	
		ReplyAll Method	
Reports Object			
Requery Action	Reposition Event		
Reset Statement	Reset Statement	Reset Statement and Method	
			ResetButtonImage Statement
			ResetChar Statement and Function
			ResetNoteSepOrNotice Statement
			ResetPara Statement and Function
		ResetTipWizard Method	
		Reshape Method	
	Resize Event	Resize Method	
Restore Action			
Resume Statement	Resume Statement	Resume Statement	
RGB Function	RGB Function	RGB Function	
"Right, Right$ Functions"	"Right, Right$ Functions"	"Right, Right$ Functions"	Right$ Function
	Right Join Operation		
		"RightB, Right$ Functions"	
		RightAngleAxes Property	
		RightHeader Property	
		RightMargin Property	
			RightPara Statement and Function
RmDir Statement	RmDir Statement	RmDir Statement	RmDir Statement
Rnd Function	Rnd Function	Rnd Function	Rnd Function
Rollback Statement	RollBack Statement and Method		

Access Basic	Visual Basic	VBA	Word Basic
		RoundedCorners Property	
		Route Method	
		Routed Property	
		RoutingSlip Object and Property	
	"Row, Rows Properties"	Row Property	
RowColChange Event			
		RowDifferences Method	
		RowFields Method	
		RowGrand Property	
	RowHeight Property	RowHeight Property	
		RowRange Property	
		Rows Method	
RowSource Property			
RowSourceType Property			
RSet Statement	RSet Statement	RSet Statement	
"RTrim, RTrim$ Functions"	"RTrim, RTrim$ Functions"	"RTrim, RTrim$ Functions"	RTrim$ Function
		Run Method	
RunApp Action			
		RunAutoMacros Method	
RunCode Action			
RunMacro Action			
RunningSum Property			
			RunPrintManager Statement
RunSQL Action			
		Save Method	
		SaveAs method	
		SaveCopyAs Method	
		Saved Property	
		SaveData Property	
		SaveLinkValues Property	
	SavePicture Statement	SavePicture Statement	
			SaveTemplate Statement
		SaveType Property	
Scale Method	Scale Method		
ScaleHeight Property	ScaleHeight Property		
ScaleLeft Property	ScaleLeft Property		
ScaleMode Property	ScaleMode Property		
ScaleTop Property	ScaleTop Property		
		ScaleType Property	
ScaleWidth Property	ScaleWidth Property		

Access Basic	Visual Basic	VBA	Word Basic
Scaling Property			
		Scenario Object	
		Scenarios Object and Method,	
Screen Object	Screen Object		
			ScreeRefresh Statement
		ScreenUpdating Property	ScreenUpdating Statement and Function
	Scroll Event		
		ScrollBar Object	
ScrollBars Property	ScrollBars Property	ScrollBars Object and Method	
		ScrollColumn Property	
		ScrollRow Property	
		ScrollWorkbookTabs Method	
Second Function	Second Function	Second Function	Second Function
Section Property			
Seek Function	Seek Function	"Seek, Seek$ Functions"	
Seek Method	Seek Method		
Seek Statement	Seek Statement	Seek Statement	Seek Statement and Function
	SelChange Event		
	SelCount Property		
		Select Method	
Select Case Statement	Select Case Statement	Select Case Statement	Select Case Statement
			SelectCurAlignment Statement
			SelectCurColor Statement
			SelectCurFont Statement
			SelectCurIndent Statement
			SelectCurSentence Statement
			SelectCurSpacing Statement
			SelectCurTabs Statement
			SelectCurWord Statement
			SelectDrawingObjects Statement
	Selected Property	Selected Property	
		SelectedSheets Method	

Access Basic	Visual Basic	VBA	Word Basic
		Selection Property	Selection$ Function
			SelectionFileName$ Function
	"SelEndCol, SelStartCol Properties"		
	"SelEndRow, SelStartRow Properties"		
	"SelLength, SelStart	SelText Properties"	
SelectObject Action			
			SelInfo Function
			SelType Statement and Function
		SendDateTime Property	
		Sender Property	
SendKeys Statement and Action	SendKeys Statement	SendKeys Statement and Method	SendKeys Statement
		SendMail Method	
		SendMailer Method	
		SendToBack Method	
			SentLeft Statement and Function
			SentRight Statement and Function
		Series Object	
		SeriesCollection Object and Method	
		SeriesLines Object and Property	
Set Statement	Set Statement	Set Statement	
	SetAttr Statement	SetAttr Statement	SetAttr Statement
			SetAutoText Statement
SetData Method			
	SetDataAccessOption Statement		
		SetDefaultChart Method	
	SetDefaultWorkspace Statement		
			SetDocumentDirty Statement
			SetDocumentVar Statement and Function
			SetEndOfBookmark Statement
			SetFormResult Statement
	SetFocus Method		

Access Basic	Visual Basic	VBA	Word Basic
		SetInfoDisplay Method	
		SetLinkOnData Method	
			SetPrivateProfileString Statement and Function
			SetProfileString Statement and Function
			SetSelRange Statement
			SetStartOfBookmark Statement
			SetTemplateDirty Statement
	SetText Method		
SetValue Action			
SetWarnings Action			
Sgn Function	Sgn Function	Sgn Function	Sgn Function
			ShadingPattern Statement and Function
		Shadow Property	
	Shape Control		
	Shape Property		
		Sheets Object and Method	
		SheetsInNewWorkbook Property	
Shell Function	Shell Function	Shell Function	Shell Statement
	Shortcut Property		
		ShortcutKey Property	
		ShortCutMenus Method	
	Show Method	Show Method	
		ShowAllData Method	
			ShowAll Statement and Function
			ShowAllHeadings Statement
ShowAllRecords Action			
			ShowAnnotationBy Statement
		ShowDataForm Method	
		ShowDependents Method	
		ShowDetail Property	
		ShowErrors Method	
ShowGrid Property			
			ShowHeadingnumber Statements

Access Basic	Visual Basic	VBA	Word Basic
		ShowLegendKey Property	
		ShowLevels Method	
			ShowNextHeaderFooter Statement
		ShowPages Method	
		ShowPrecedents Method	
			ShowPrevHeaderFooter Statement
		ShowToolTips Property	
			ShowVars Statement
			ShrinkFont Statement
			ShrinkFontOnePoint Statement
			ShrinkSelection Statement
Sin Function	Sin Function	Sin Function	
	Size Property	Size Property	
	SizeMode Property		
			SizeToolbar Statement
		SizeWithWindow Property	
			SkipNumbering Statement and Function
SLN Function	SLN Function		
			SmallCaps Statement and Function
	SmallChange Property	SmallChange Property	
		SmallScroll Method	
		Smooth Property	
Snapshot Object shot Object	Snap-		
Sort Property	Sort Property Sort Method		
			SortArray Statement
	Sorted Property		
		SoundNote Object and Property	
		SourceData Property	
	SourceDoc Property		
	SourceField Property		
	SourceItem Property		
		SourceName Property	
SourceObject Property			
	SourceTableName Property		
"Space, Space$ Func-tions"	"Space, Space$ Function"	"Space, Space$ Functions"	

Access Basic	Visual Basic	VBA	Word Basic
			SpacePara1 Statement and Function
			SpacePara2 Statement and Function
			SpacePara15 Statement and Function
Spc Function	Spc Function	Spc Function	
		SpecialCells Method	
SpecialEffect Property			
			Spike Statement
		Spinner Object	
		Spinners Object and Method	
		Split Property	
		SplitColumn Property	
		SplitHorizontal Property	
		SplitRow Property	
			SplitSubdocument Statement
		SplitVertical Property	
SQL Property	SQL Property		
		SQLBind Function	
		SQLClose Function	
		SQLError Function	
		SQLExecQuery Function	
		SQLGetSchema Function	
		SQLOpen Function	
		SQLRequest Function	
		SQLRetrieve Function	
		SQLRetrieveToFile Function	
Sqr Function	Sqr Function	Sqr Function	
		StandardFont Property	
		StandardFontSize Property	
		StandardHeight Property	
		StandardWdth Property	
			StartOfColumn Statement and Function
			StartOfDocument Statement and Function

Access Basic	Visual Basic	VBA	Word Basic
			StartOfLine Statement and Function
			StartOfRow Statement and Function
			StartOfWindow Statement and Function
		StarupPath Property	
Static Statement	Static Statement	Static Statement	
		Status Property	
StatusBarText Property		StatusBar Property	
"StDev, StDevP Functions"	"StDev, StDevP Functions "		
Step Statement			
Stop Statement	Stop Statement	Stop Statement	Stop Statement
StopAllMacros Action			
StopMacro Action			
"Str, Str$ Functions"	"Str, Str$ Functions"	"Str, Str$ Functions"	Str$ Function
StrComp Function	StrComp Function	StrComp Function	
		StrConv Function	
	Stretch Property		
		Strikethrough Property	Strikethrough Statement and Function
"String, String$ Functions"	"String, String$ Functions"	"String, String$ Functions"	String$ Function
	Style Property	Style Object and Property	Style Statement
			StyleDesc$ Function
			StyleName$ Function
		Styles Object and Method	
Sub Statement	Sub Statement	Sub Statement	Sub Statement
		Subject Property	
		SubscribeTo Method	
		Subscript Property	SubScript Statement and Function
		Subtotal Method	
		Subtotals Property	
		SubType Property	
Sum Function	Sum Function		
		Summary Property	
		SummaryColumn Property	
		SummaryRow Property	
		Superscript Property	Superscript Statement and Function
		SurfaceGroup Property	
			SymbolFont Statement
Switch Function	Switch Function		

Access Basic	Visual Basic	VBA	Word Basic
SYD Function	SYD Function		
	System Property		
Tab Function	Tab Function	Tab Function	
	TabIndex Property		
			TabLeader$ Function
Table Object	Table Object	Table method	
			TableAutoFormat Statement
			TableAutoSum Statement
			TableColumnWidth Statement
	TableDef Object		
	TableDefs Collection		
			TableDeleteCells Statement
			TableDeleteColumn Statement
			TableDeleteRow Statement
			TableFormula Statement
			TableGridlines Statement and Function
			TableHeadings Statement and Function
			TableInsertCells Statement
			TableInsertColumn Statement
			TableInsertRow Statement
			TableInsertTable Statement
			TableMergeCells Statement
		"TableRange1, TableRange2 Properties"	
			TableRowHeight Statement
			TableSelectColumn Statement
			TableSelectRow Statement
			TableSelectTable Statement
			TableSort Statement

Access Basic	Visual Basic	VBA	Word Basic
			TableSortAToZ Statement
			TableSortZToA- Statement
			TableSplit Statement
			TableSplitCells Statement
			TableToText Statement
			TableUpdateAuto-Format Statement
		TabRatio Property	
	TabStop Property		
			TabType Function
	Tag Property		
Tan Function	Tan Function	Tan Function	
	Text Property	Text Property	Text Statement
TextAlign Property			
	TextBox Control	TextBox Object	TextBox Statement
		TextBoxes Object and Method	
			TextFormField Statement
TextHeight Method	TextHeight Method		
		TextToColumns Method	
			TextToTable Statement
TextWidth Method	TextWidth Method		
		ThisWorkbook Property	
		TickLabelPosition Property	
		TickLabels Object and Property	
		TickLabelsSpacing Property	
		TickMarkSpacing Property	
"Time, Time$ Functions"	"Time, Time$ Functions"	"Time, Time$ Functions"	Time$ Function
"Time, Time$ Statements"	"Time, Time$ Statements"	Time Statement	
	Timer Control		
	Timer Event		
Timer Function	Timer Function	Timer Function	
TimeSerial Function	TimeSerial Function	TimeSerial Function	TimeSerial Function
TimeValue Function TimeValue Function	TimeValue Function	TimeValue Function	
	Title Property		Title Property
			Today Function
			ToggleFieldDisplay Statement

Access Basic	Visual Basic	VBA	Word Basic
			ToggleFull Statement
			ToggleHeaderFooterLink Statement
			ToggleMainTextLayer Statement
			TogglePortrait Statement
			ToggleScribbleMode Statement
		"ToolbarToolbars Objects"	
		ToolbarButton Object	ToolbarButtonMacro$ Function
		ToolbarButtons Object and Method	
			ToolbarName$ Function
			ToolbarState Function
			ToolsAddRecordDefault Statement
			ToolsAdvancedSettings Statement
			ToolsAutoCorrect Statement
			ToolsAutoCorrectDays Statement and Function
			ToolsAutoCorrectInitialCaps Statement and Function
			ToolsAutoCorrectReplaceText Statement and Function
			ToolsAutoCorrectSentenceCaps Statement and Function
			ToolsAutoCorrect-SmartQuotes Statement and Function
			ToolsBulletListDefault Statement
			ToolsBulletsNumbers Statement
			ToolsCalculate Statement and Function
			ToolsCompareVersions Statement

Access Basic	Visual Basic	VBA	Word Basic
			ToolsCreateEnvelope Statement
			ToolsCreateLabels Statement
			ToolsCustomize Statement
			ToolsCustomizeKeyboard Statement
			ToolsCustomizeMenu-Bar Statement
			ToolsCustomizeMenus Statement
			ToolsGetSpelling Statement and Function
			ToolsGetSynonyms Statement and Function
			ToolsGrammar Statement
			ToolsGrammarStatistics Array Statement
			ToolsHyphenation Statement
			ToolsHyphenation-Manual Statement
			ToolsLanguage Statement
			ToolsMacro Statement
			ToolsManageFields Statement
			ToolsMergeRevisions Statement
			ToolsNumberListDefault Statement
			ToolsOptions Statement
			ToolsOptionsAuto-Format Statement
			ToolsOptionsCompatibility Statement
			ToolsOptionsEdit Statement
			ToolsOptinsFileLocations Statement
			ToolsOptionsGeneral Statement
			ToolsOptionsGrammar Statement

Access Basic	Visual Basic	VBA	Word Basic
			ToolsOptionsPrint Statement
			ToolsOptionsRevisions Statement
			ToolsOptionsSave Statement
			ToolsOptionsSpelling Statement
			ToolsOptionsUserInfo Statement
			ToolsOptionsView Statement
			ToolsProtectDocument Statement
			ToolsProtectSection Statement
			ToolsRemoveRecordDefault Statement
			ToolsRepaginate Statement
			ToolsReviewRevisions Statement
			ToolsRevisionAuthor$ Function
			ToolsRevisionDate$ Statement and Function
			ToolsRevisions Statement
			ToolsRevisionType Function
			ToolsShrinkToFit Statement
			ToolsSpelling Statement
			ToolsSpellSelection Statement
			ToolsThesaurus Statement
			ToolsUnprotectDocument Statement
			ToolsWordCount Statement
Top Property	Top Property	Top Property	
	ToPage Property		
	TopIndex Property		
		TopLeftCell Property	
		TopMargin Property	
	TopRow Property		
		ToRecipients Property	

Access Basic	Visual Basic	VBA	Word Basic
		TotalLevels Property	
		TrackStatus Property	
Transactions Property	Transactions Property		
TransferDatabase Action			
TransferSpreadsheet Action			
TransferText Action			
	Transform Statement		
		TransitionExpEval Property	
		TransitionFormEntry Property	
		TransitionMenuKey Property	
		TransitionMenuKeyActio n Property	
		TransitionNavigKeys Property	
Transparent Property			
		Trendline Object	
		Trendlines Object and Method	
"Trim, Trim$ Functions"	"Trim, Trim$ Functions"	"Trim	
	"TwipsPerPixelX, TwipsPerPixelY Properties"		
	Type Property	Type Property	
Type Statement	Type Statement	Type Statement	
		TypeName Function	
UBound Function	UBound Function	UBound Function	
"UCase, UCase$ Functions" "UCase, UCase$ Functions"	"UCase, UCase$ Functions"	UCase$ Function	
		Underline Property	Underline Statement and Function
		Undo Method	
			UnHang Statement
		Ungroup Method	
			UnIndent Statement
		Union Method	
	Unique Property		
		Unjoin Method	
			UnLinkFields Statement
	Unload Event		
	Unload Statement	Unload Statement	
Unlock Statement	Unlock Statement	Unlock Statement	
			UnLockFields Statement

Access Basic	Visual Basic	VBA	Word Basic
		Unprotect Method	
		UpBars Object and Property	
Updatable Property	Updatable Property		
Update Method Update Method	Update Method		
	UpdateControls Method		
	Updated Event		
UpdateMethod Property			UpdateFields Statement
		UpdateFromFile Method	
		UpdateLink Method	
	UpdateOptions Property		
	UpdateRecord Method		
		UpdateRemoteReferences Property	
			UpdateSource Statement
		UsableHeight Property	
		UsableWidth Property	
		UsedRange Property	
	User-Defined Data Type	User-Defined Data Type	
User Function			
		UserName Property	
		UseStandardHeight Property	
		UseStandardWidth Property	
Val Function	Val Function	Val Function	Val Function
	Validate Event		
ValidationRule Property			
ValidationText Property			
	Value Property	"Value, Values Properties"	
"Var, VarP Functions"	"Var, VarP Functions "		
VarType Function	VarType Function	VarType Function	
		VaryByCategories Property	
	Verb Property	Verb Method	
		Version Property	
		VerticalAlignment Property	
	VerticalScrollbar Control		
		Vertices Property	

Access Basic	Visual Basic	VBA	Word Basic
			ViewAnnotations Statement and Function
			ViewBorderToolbar Statement
			ViewDraft Statement and Function
			ViewDrawingToolbar Statement
			ViewEndnoteArea Statement and Function
			ViewEndnoteContNotice Statement
			ViewEndnoteContSeparator Statement
			ViewEndnoteSeparator Statement
			ViewFieldCodes Statement and Function
			ViewFooter Statement and Function
			ViewFootnoteArea Statement and Function
			ViewFootnoteContNotice Statement
			ViewFootnoteContSeparator Statement
			ViewFootnotes Statement and Function
			ViewFootnoteSeparator Statement
			ViewHeader Statement and Function
			ViewMasterDocument Statement and Function
			ViewMenus Function
			ViewNormal Statement and Function
			ViewOutline Statement and Function
			ViewPage Statement and Function
			ViewRibbon Statement and Function

Access Basic	Visual Basic	VBA	Word Basic
			ViewRuler Statement and Function
ViewsAllowed Property			
			ViewStatusBar Statement and Function
			ViewToggleMasterDocument Statement
			ViewToolbars Statement
			ViewZoom Statement
			"ViewZoom100
			ViewZoomPageWidth Statement
			ViewZoomWholePage Statement
Visible Property	Visible Property	Visble Property	
		VisibleFields Method	
		VisibleItems Method	
		VisibleRange Property	
			VLine Statement
		Volatile Method	
			VPageStatement
			VScroll Statement and Function
		Wait Method	
			WaitCursor Statement
		Walls Object and Property	
		WallsAndGridlines2D Property	
Weekday Function	Weekday Function	Weekday Function	Weekday Function
	Weight Property		
While...Wend Statement	While...Wend Statement	While...Wend Statement	While...Wend Statement
Width Property	Width Property		
Width # Statement	Width # Statement	Width # Statement	
	Window Object	Window Function	
			Windownumber Statement
			WindowArrangeAll Statement
	WindowList Property		WindowList Statement
			WindowName$ Function
			WindowNewWindow Statement
		WindowNumber Property	
			WindowPane Function

Access Basic	Visual Basic	VBA	Word Basic
		Windows Object and Method	
		WindowsFroPens Property	
	WindowState Property	WindowState Property	
			WinToDOS$ Function
		With Statement	
	WITH OWNER-ACCESS OPTION		
			WordLeft Statement and Function
			WordRight Statement and Function
			WordUnderline Statement and Function
WordWrap Property			
		Workbook Object	
		Workbooks Object and Method	
		Worksheet Object and Property	
		Worksheets Object and Method	
		WrapText Property	
			Write Statement
Write # Statement	Write# Statement	Write # Statement	
		WriteReserved Property	
		WriteReservedBy Property	
	"X1, Y1, X2, Y2 Properties"		
		XValues Property	
		XYGroups Method	
Year Function	Year Function	Year Function	Year Function
		Zoom Property	
	ZOrder Method	ZOrder Property	

Index